# THE BUZZ ON™

# PROFESSIONAL WRESTLING

Scott Keith

**LF** LEBHAR-FRIEDMAN BOOKS

NEW YORK • CHICAGO • LOS ANGELES • LONDON • PARIS • TOKYO

*The Buzz On Professional Wrestling*

Lebhar-Friedman Books
425 Park Avenue
New York, NY 10022

Published by Lebhar-Friedman Books
Lebhar-Friedman Books is a company of Lebhar-Friedman, Inc.

Printed in the United States of America

Library of Congress Cataloging in Publication Data on file at the Library of Congress

ISBN: 0-86730-866-4

Produced by Progressive Publishing
Editor: John Craddock; Creative Director: Nancy Lycan; Art Director: Angela Connolly
Editorial Contributors: Michele Thomareas, Rusty Fischer, Paul Love, Peter Royland
Designers: David Womble, Linda Rodriguez, Rena Bracey, Marco Echevarria, Vivian Torres, Suzanne Miller, Lanette Fitzpatrick
Production Managers: John Craddock III, Mike Bilicki

Visit our Web site at lfbooks.com

Volume Discounts
This book makes a great gift and incentive. Call (212) 756-5248 for information on volume discounts

# THE BUZZ ON
## PROFESSIONAL WRESTLING

## ACKNOWLEDGMENTS

Thanks to Dave Meltzer of the *Wrestling Observer Newsletter*, Wade Keller of the *Pro Wrestling Torch Newsletter*, and Michael Samuda for all the info and great reading over the years.

Thanks to Jeff Amdur for the catchphrase, Sean Shannon for helping create the "Buzz On" me via the Web site, and Lindsay Grad for a bunch of stuff.

Finally, thanks to the various wrestlers in this book for doing what they do best and giving me the dirt to dish in the first place.

# THE BUZZ ON
## PROFESSIONAL WRESTLING

# CONTENTS

# FOREWORD

In wrestling, there is an old adage that allows its fans to keep track of the ever-changing history of their "sport" the only way they can, and it is the one thing that separates professional wrestling from all of the other forms of sports and entertainment. It goes like this: "If it didn't happen on TV, it didn't happen."

That phrase has been the backbone upon which 90% of arguments over championship titles, feuds, and matches can be settled in one fell swoop. Having an argument over whether someone won a World title or not? Well, most of the time, if you didn't see it happen on TV or Pay-Per-View—or hear an announcer mention it on TV!—then for all intents and purposes, it didn't happen. This is a truly unique attribute to wrestling.

For instance, you don't see baseball games where the final score has no effect on the standings simply because it wasn't televised. On TV shows, if there is a dispute over what happened in a past episode, it's very easy to go back and watch that episode to clear up the argument. In wrestling, history is dictated by those who collect the money, and if they say that something didn't happen, then it didn't happen, all evidence to the contrary be damned!

Listen to either Hulk Hogan or Vince McMahon give an interview to an unsuspecting media member some time—chances are good that at some point in the interview they will mention one of the following "facts":

1) In 1984, Vince McMahon and the World Wrestling Federation (WWF) went national and took wrestling out of smoky bars with 200 people in the stands and made it a multinational business.
2) In 1987, at *Wrestlemania III*, an event that drew 93,173 people to the Pontiac Silverdome, Hulk Hogan handed Andre the Giant his first pinfall loss in 20 years.

Both are commonly accepted as truth by casual fans and reporters who don't do very thorough research. Both are in fact bold-faced lies, easily disproven. Rarely is that done because it's akin to exposing Santa Claus as a made-up fairy tale, and instead, most wrestling fans simply choose to "play along" until they themselves believe whatever the major promotions choose to feed them as this week's version of The Truth.

So why then is wrestling populated by so many modern con men and liars? How come no one's ever done anything about it before? How much are wrestling fans prepared to swallow before they start rejecting one notion of the truth and demanding a better one?

The first two questions have been asked by outsiders to the business for many years, and probably will be for many years to come. The third question is one that has not only created empires in wrestling, but also destroyed other ones. It is the question that drives the entire business, as promoters constantly struggle to find the breaking point of fans' tolerance of ticket prices and story lines. Oddly enough, it's usually the story line that ends up wrecking things more often than the ticket prices.

Case in point:

In 1983, when wrestling was supposed to be playing in "smoky bars in front of 200 people," Verne Gagne's American Wrestling Association (AWA) was drawing about 30,000 people to a major show in Minneapolis called "Super Sunday." The main attraction? Gagne's version of the

World title was being defended by longtime villain ("heel") Nick Bockwinkel. His opponent? Up-and-coming superstar Hulk Hogan, who, according to revisionist history, was supposedly not a major star until he entered the rival WWF in 1984.

The match itself was a fairly routine matter in wrestling terms: Hogan, the massively popular hero ("babyface"), pinned Bockwinkel for the three-count. However, Hogan had used a foreign object to knock Bockwinkel out, and the decision was reversed when tape of the incident was reviewed. What no one expected, or could possibly have predicted, is that this one single match would end up altering the entire destiny of wrestling for years to come, both directly and indirectly, with effects that are still being felt strongly today.

That sort of thing actually happens all the time in wrestling—one event has a domino effect on many others, it's just that it takes a few years to truly sort itself out. And, as a fan, you have to be paying pretty close attention.

For instance, in 1988, a much more experienced and worldly Hulk Hogan lost his prized WWF World title to Andre the Giant after a four-year title reign in front of a prime time network audience. While this match was deemed historic, in fact, a far more important match happened on the same show but no one knew it at the time. You see, the Honky Tonk Man defended his Intercontinental title (the secondary title in the WWF) against constant rival Randy "Macho Man" Savage in a match where Savage's win should have been a mere formality.

However, for political reasons, Honky Tonk Man was allowed to keep his title on a last-minute decision by the bookers—the guys who "book" the show, the matches, and their outcomes. This decision would set off a chain of events that would lead to the demise of the WWF's golden age and send them spiraling into a slump that would take nearly 10 years to fully break out of.

So you see, wrestling isn't just scripts—it's a human drama the likes of which no soap opera junkie has ever seen. Sit back, relax, and enjoy.

A sk yourself this question: Do you believe in magic?

If so, then don't you know it's all fake?

Fans of pro wrestling have endured that second question for decades, while being asked the first one every time they watch. It's a complicated paradox, and who would think that a couple of sweaty guys in spandex rolling around on the mat would inspire such loyalty and passion from so many people, but it's done so for a hundred years and shows no signs of letting up.

HULK HOGAN AND
KARL MALONE

# FAN-ATICS!

and comparing how well they do it. He uses a ratings system to give himself a point of comparison if he wants to rate David Copperfield's act against some no-name street performer from Podunk, Iowa. He's still seeing the same tricks, but in his mind, he knows that what he's watching is "fake." But at the

Let's take the fans themselves. There are two kinds: The "marks" and the "smarts." You probably know a mark or two yourself: They think wrestling is "real," and they're generally entertained by the soap-opera story lines and the big moves performed. Thanks to the Internet, that breed of fan is slowly dying out, but they still exist and make lots of money for lots of people in the wrestling business.

To put it in magic terms, these are the people who go to see David Copperfield and leave wondering how the woman was able to survive being sawed in half. This is not meant to be an insulting thing by any means—a belief in magic is a great thing—but there is a difference between appreciating magic as a fun form of entertainment and actually believing that what you see is real.

The other type of fan is what becomes of a "mark" after a certain point. The transition is usually triggered by finding out some small bit of information that they weren't supposed to know, at which point the floodgates open. To carry on our magic analogy, pretend that the magic fan liked the first Copperfield show so much that he flew to the next city and saw it again. However, this time he had seats that were at a slightly different angle. He notices that Copperfield and his assistant do the exact same "spontaneous" conversation and banter as in the last city. He has already seen the trick done before, so this time, out of curiosity, he happens to watch the feet of the woman, and notices that the ones poking out of the box aren't the ones that she had before she went in.

"A-ha," he thinks, "so that's how it's done!" Now he starts to watch other magicians doing the same trick,

same time, he can appreciate it on a deeper level because he understands (or thinks he does) what's really going on behind the scenes.

*The Buzz On Professional Wrestling* is the story of what's really been going on in wrestling for the past hundred years, and why fans have followed, and will still follow it, even when they know how the rabbit gets in and out of the hat.

# 1
# WRESTLING
# HISTORY

**W**hile it can be argued that nearly everything in wrestling that has ever happened or ever will happen can be traced back to the sport's origins in the late 1800s (and even more primitive origins since the dawn of man), it's often hard to substantiate anything said from before 1960 or so due to the notoriously fluid state of the "truth" in wrestling and the general lack of records on the part of those involved.

ROAD
WARRIOR
HAWK

# WRESTLING'S WONDER YEARS

There are, however, a few things about wrestling's wonder years that we do know for certain:

1) There is no point in the history of wrestling where you can nostalgically look back and say that "it wasn't fake." It was always predetermined, but it used to be much more purely athletic and lacking in story lines, so the illusion of realism was easier to create. "Lou Thesz loses to Wilbur Snyder" was pretty straightforward, and all the motivations for the next show stemmed from the wrestling in the previous one. Thesz lost, so now he wants revenge. QED. If you really feel like going back far enough, you could say that the earliest professional matches with legitimate Olympic stars like George Hackenschmidt, at the turn of the century, were likely "real," but then they also lasted two or three hours and featured long stretches with both men lying on the mat in a headlock, so it's somewhat of a moot point to begin with. Suffice it to say that by 1925, when Stanislaus Zbyszko

"SUPERSTAR" BILLY GRAHAM

won the World title against the wishes of the promoter, the "fake" aspect of the sport was already ingrained enough that this burst of reality was, indeed, a rare occurrence.

2) The first time that there was a real and tangible World Heavyweight title in pro wrestling was 1948, with the formation of the National Wrestling Alliance (NWA), which had the support of dozens of local promoters around North America. Claims are frequently made by the remnants of this once-great organization today about that title dating back to 1904, but this is roughly on par with Hollywood claiming that *Braveheart* is legally binding proof of William Wallace's actions four centuries ago—merely a fanciful invention of the imagination of the creators, and nothing more.

3) Pro wrestling was absolutely not staged in the bingo halls and smoky bars that some would have you believe it was prior to the early '80s. In fact, the WWF themselves released tapes on their Coliseum Video label showing old matches held in the '60s or earlier,

featuring arenas holding upwards of 30,000 people without the benefit of "sports entertainment" to fill them. The "smoky bars" line (fed to the press on a seemingly daily basis) was an invention of the early '90s, when the WWF was going through a very rough financial period and was reduced to doing the wrestling equivalent of barnstorming—minor-league hockey arenas, convention centers, and other humble venues—and thus needed a convenient comparison point. And so the excuse of "Sure, it looks bad now, but even 10 years ago this company was doing bingo halls…" was born. Hulk Hogan, who is often heralded as the savior of wrestling from such small beginnings, was himself on the undercard of a show in 1982 that drew more than 50,000 people to New York's Shea Stadium to see Bruno Sammartino face rival Larry Zbyszko. And the "Hogan and the WWF saved wrestling" argument doesn't even take the influence of Japan into account, where tens of thousands of people flocking to see wrestling was a regular occurrence before any of them had even heard of Hogan.

With those notions out of the way, let's talk about the NWA. Pretty much everything that ever happened up until the 1990s can be related to that organization.

# WWF CHAMPIONS BEFORE HULK HOGAN

- Buddy Rogers, 1963
- Bruno Sammartino, 1963–1971, 1973–1977
- Ivan Koloff, 1971
- Pedro Morales, 1971–1973
- Stan Stasiak, 1973
- "Superstar" Billy Graham, 1977
- Bob Backlund, 1978–1983
- Antonio Inoki, 1979; title reign not acknowledged in U.S., and lasted only 6 days
- The Iron Sheik, 1983
- Hogan won the title for the first time from the Iron Sheik in January of 1984

No problem, more money for everyone, right? Right—up until a point. Today it's second nature in wrestling, or even boxing, for the focal point of a match to be the title at stake—the right to say that one man is better than the other and have the belt to back it up. It's a very manly thing. However, "Southeast Georgia mid-heavyweight champion" just didn't have that money-making ring to it, and further, it didn't have the kind of scope that the sheer bombast of wrestling pretty much demands by itself. So in the very early part of the century, a lot of promoters came to the exact same conclusion at the same time: We need a World champion. Trouble is, all of them started claiming that their champion was the one, leading to situations like a promoter in San Francisco claiming his guy was the World champion, despite that champion never having left San Francisco! This was fairly common, happening all over the country.

A note on World titles before we go any further: It is generally accepted that there are five titles in

In this age of having only two major promotions (World Championship Wrestling and the World Wrestling Federation), it's hard to fathom, but before 1948 there used to be dozens of different promotions, manned by an equal number of promoters, covering just about every square inch of America once wrestling got hot after the Great Depression.

wrestling as of the year 2000 that are true "World" titles: The WWF championship, the WCW World title, the ECW World title, All Japan's Triple Crown, and New Japan's IWGP title. Any other claims to a "World" title at this point are dubious at best. The WWF does not refer to theirs as a "World" title—the kayfabed reason is that "World Wrestling Federation World champion" is redundant. The true reason is that they just like to be pretentious and hold their title above the rest. Whatever the reason, wherever the WWF is concerned in this book the terms "WWF title" and "World title" are considered interchangeable.

Some of the individual promotions' titles were generally accepted as bigger than others, mainly because the people who held them had more drawing power. Former weightlifting champion George Hackenschmidt brought instant credibility to his claim as a champion, as did such major stars as Ed "Strangler" Lewis. The problem was not merely one of credibility, it was actual legitimacy of the title itself. It was fine for the fans to think that Lewis was the only true champion, but what if he lost the title? Would that title retain the same legitimacy just because someone beat him for it, or would the result be in doubt enough that people would

still consider Lewis to be the rightful champion, since it was a self-proclaimed title rather than a crowning by the promotion. This problem actually went on for a good forty years before legal reasons solved it.

In 1947, several Midwest promoters attempted to get around the extremely strict anti-trust laws of the time by forming an alliance (instead of merging into

SCOTT HALL

HULK HOGAN

KEVIN NASH

one monopoly) and recognizing a single World champion between the various promotions. This uber-promotion became known as the National Wrestling Alliance (or NWA for short) and would last for more than 50 years as a major force in wrestling. The first champion as named by the NWA was (not coincidentally) group member Orville Brown, and the most widely accepted of the "other" World champions left was National Wrestling Assocation champion Lou Thesz. A match was scheduled between Brown and Thesz to unify the titles, but a car accident ended Brown's career before that could happen and Thesz was awarded the NWA World title on November 25, 1949, his first of six.

Nearly every major happening that occurred between 1950 and the start of the "modern era" was because of something that the NWA did.

By the late 1950s, other promoters had aspirations

of covering the kind of area that the NWA did. The only major strongholds of wrestling not covered by the NWA at that point were the northern regions (which were in kind of a tenuous love-hate partnership with the NWA) and the Northeast (which were ruled unquestionably by Toots Mondt and Vince McMahon, Sr., who in turn could be called faithful NWA members in the same sense that Frank Gifford could be called a faithful husband). The fact that McMahon controlled the all-important New York market (and specifically Madison Square Garden) was a sore spot that haunted the NWA for years to come.

The first real sign of trouble with the NWA's "undisputed" World title came in 1957, as Eduardo Carpentier defeated Lou Thesz to win the belt in a best-of-three falls match (the standard for title matches at that time). However, one of the falls was decided on a DQ, so one group of NWA promoters chose not to recognize that title switch, while another group (led by Nebraska promoter Wally Karbo) chose not only to recognize Carpentier, but to continue recognizing that claim when Minnesota amateur wrestling legend Verne Gagne won the title from him in 1958. The situation worsened until finally Karbo's group (led, not coincidentally, by Gagne himself) split off in dramatic fashion to

VINCE McMAHON JR.

form the American Wrestling Association (or AWA for short), the first major challenger to the NWA's dominance of wrestling in America. Verne Gagne was given the first AWA World title, shocking no one. The AWA lasted some forty years before folding in 1991 for monetary reasons.

A more dramatic and earthshaking change came when the NWA in the early '60s put their title on Buddy Rogers, who until that point had been the exclusive property of Toots Mondt in the Northeast. Toots rarely let Rogers defend that title outside of his territory, and indeed, when the time came for Lou Thesz to win the NWA title back, Toots (and mastermind Vince McMahon) simply refused to recognize that switch, and (in wrestling terms) dared the NWA to do something about it. They didn't, and in April 1963, they split from the NWA and formed the third major promotion in the U.S.: The World Wide Wrestling Federation, which today is the worldwide juggernaut simply known as the WWF. Rogers "won" the first WWWF World title in Rio de Janeiro in a tournament of which no footage exists (wink, wink), but his reign was short-lived, as heart problems forced him to drop that title to rising star Bruno Sammartino later that year in a 43-second match. Bruno would hold that title for an amazing eight years, selling out arenas all over the eastern seaboard.

While the upstart WWWF and AWA each boasted their own version of the World title, it was agreed by everyone outside the business that the NWA was the true class of the wrestling promotions. While the WWWF had a tendancy to focus on showmanship and musclemen like Sammartino, and the AWA was essentially Verne Gagne's one-man show, the NWA featured the best wrestling action and biggest stars night after night. In fact, the WWWF actually rejoined the NWA in the early '70s during rough financial times and accepted a demotion of their World title to a lesser status. At the same time, however, something very big was happening that no one at the time really understood yet.

Vince McMahon's son, Vince Jr., had been a part of the WWWF promotion since he was a teenager. His main role was on-screen announcer and interviewer, but he did some work behind the scenes as well in preparation to inherit the family business when his father passed away. Up until that point, there was rivalry between the promotions and old grudges carried from years past, but everyone generally behaved themselves. Vince, however, had different ideas.

When he assumed control of his father's Capitol Sports Group in 1979, the first thing he did was buy out his father's share completely, along with those of longtime employees Robert Marella (better known as Gorilla Monsoon) and Pat Patterson, then dropped the "Wide" from the company name, officially renaming the promotion the World Wrestling Federation. He also dissolved the Capitol Sports Group and replaced it with Titan Sports Inc. By 1983, he found the laws and regulations of the NWA too restrictive, so he quit the group and started picking fights with NWA promoters over territorial rights. When he split from the NWA, he restored the WWF title to World title status, then took the title off six-year reigning champion Bob Backlund and put it on evil foreigner the Iron Sheik, in preparation for a change that would send shockwaves throughout the business and forever alter the public perception of wrestling, making him millions of dollars in the process.

You may have heard of the guy who he picked to lead the way—Hulk Hogan.

HULK HOGAN

# PROFESSIONAL WRESTLING TIMELINE

Take a trip through wrestling's past and peer into its future with our time capsule of heroic highlights.

• **1873:** The first masked wrestler appears, named The Masked Wrestler, setting a fashion trend for wrestling, which continues to this day.

• **February 6, 1877:** William Muldoon wins the Greco-Roman title by defeating the French champion, Christol.

• **July 20, 1877:** Wrestling's first real star, George Hackenschmidt, is born in Dorpat, Russia.

• **January 19, 1880:** More than 3,000 fans come out to Gilmore's Gardens (the site that would later become Madison Square Garden) to watch William Muldoon defend the Greco-Roman title. Muldoon beats Thebaud Bauer in a 2-of-3 falls contest.

• **March 14, 1887:** Evan "Strangler" Lewis defeats Joe Acton for the American Catch-as-Catch-Can championship in Chicago.

• **March 2, 1893:** "Strangler" Lewis unites the Catch-as-Catch-Can and Greco-Roman titles by defeating Ernest Roeber in a best of five falls match, with each fall alternating between Catch and Greco styles.

• **April 20, 1895:** "Strangler" Lewis loses the American Heavyweight title to Martin "Farmer" Burns in Chicago.

• **September 1896:** Eighteen-year-old George Hackenschmidt makes his wrestling debut.

• **October 26, 1897:** Dan McLeod beats Martin "Farmer" Burns, winning the American Heavyweight championship in Indianapolis.

• **1901:** San Francisco hosts wrestling's first tag team matches.

• **November 7, 1901:** Tom Jenkins wins the American Heavyweight title from Dan McLeod.

• **December 26, 1902:** In a best-of-three falls contest, Dan McLeod regains the title from Tom Jenkins.

• **February 22, 1903:** Tom Jenkins and Frank Gotch meet in the first match between the dominant wrestlers of the era. Jenkins wins.

- **April 3, 1903:** Tom Jenkins takes the American Heavyweight title back from Dan McLeod, winning two straight falls in a best-of-three falls match that lasts 91 minutes.

- **January 27, 1904:** Frank Gotch beats Jenkins for the American Heavyweight title, taking two straight falls.

- **March 15, 1905:** Tom Jenkins wins the American title for a record third time, beating Frank Gotch at Madison Square Garden.

- **May 5, 1905:** The first ever World Champion is crowned in North America as World Greco-Roman champion George Hackenschmidt defeats American champ Tom Jenkins. Hackenschmidt becomes the World Catch-as-Catch-Can champion, the title that later becomes the original NWA World title, now known as the WCW World title.

- **April 3, 1908:** In a match that is a prelude to modern day wrestling, Frank Gotch and George Hackenschmidt do battle at Chicago's Dexter Park. Gotch fouls Hackenschmidt repeatedly throughout the match, and even oils himself down to make it difficult for his opponent to get hold of him. A frustrated Hackenschmidt leaves the ring, leaving Gotch with the World title.

- **November 25, 1909:** Frank Gotch and Stanislaus Zbyszko wrestle in a non-title contest. Gotch wins, but the contest generates heat between the two, marking the beginning of modern-day wrestling rivalries.

- **September 4, 1911:** Three years after the famous Gotch-Hackenschmidt match in Chicago's Dexter Park, the two meet again. The match draws the largest ticket sales up to that point in wrestling history. Gotch wins due to a Hackenschmidt knee injury.

- **April 1, 1913:** Frank Gotch retires from wrestling.

- **July 4, 1915:** Joe Stecher defeats Charlie Cutler to become the World champ.

- **January 1916:** More preludes to modern wrestling. Alex Aberg beats Waldek Zbyszko in the final of a two month international tournament. Early in the tournament, a wrestler named The Masked Marvel emerges from the crowd, demanding to participate.

- **April 9, 1917:** Joe Stecher and Earl Caddock compete in a best-of-three falls title match. Stecher wins the first fall, but Caddock takes the second. Stecher claims not to have been pinned, and walks away in frustration, giving the title to Caddock.

- **December 13, 1920:** Ed "Strangler" Lewis, the second "Strangler" Lewis in wrestling, becomes World champion.

- **April 1963:** The WWWF (World Wide Wrestling Federation) is formed, with Buddy Rogers as its first champion.

- **May 17, 1963:** Bruno Sammartino becomes WWWF World champion.

- **1971:** Bob Backlund wins the NCAA Division II 190-pound amateur wrestling championship.

- **January 1971:** After holding the WWWF title for seven years, Bruno Sammartino loses it to Ivan Koloff.

IVAN KOLOFF

- **May 18, 1971:** Andre the Giant (much slimmer than in his WWF days) wins the annual IWA tournament.

- **March 1972:** New Japan Pro Wrestling is formed, with top stars Antonio Inoki, Osamu Kido, and Tatsumi Fujinami.

- **September 16, 1972:** Harley Race becomes the first NWA Missouri State champion.

- **October 1972:** All-Japan Pro Wrestling stages its first matches. The stars are Shohei "Giant" Baba, Motoshi Okuma, Akio Sato, and Mitsuo Momota.

- **December 19, 1972:** The Destroyer becomes the first American to compete in Japan on a regular basis after losing a match to "Giant" Baba. The match carried a stipulation, which caused Destroyer to wrestle full-time for All-Japan.

- **February 27, 1973:** Giant Baba completes a 10-match series of historic challenges. He goes 8-0-2 against Bruno Sammartino (a win and a draw), Terry Funk, Abdullah the Butcher, The Destroyer, Wilbur Snyder (a win and a draw), Don Leo Johnathan, Pat O'Connor, and Bobo Brazil.

- **May 18, 1973:** Bill Watts wins the NWA Georgia title from Mr. Wrestling II.

- **May 24, 1973:** Harley Race defeats Dory Funk, Jr. to win his first NWA World title.

- **May 9, 1975:** The first-ever WWWF title match held in Japan sees Bruno Sammartino put his title on the line against PWF champ Giant Baba in a champion against champion brawl. Fans are disappointed, however, as the match ends in no decision.

- **November 8, 1975:** Nick Bockwinkel ends Verne Gagne's AWA title reign of more than seven years. Bockwinkel would hold the title for nearly five years.

- **December 10, 1975:** Terry Funk wins the NWA World title from Jack Brisco, making Terry and his brother Dory the only siblings to hold the NWA belt.

- **April 26, 1976:** Stan Hansen becomes famous for the clothesline as promoters claim the move broke Bruno Sammartino's neck.

- **May 24, 1976:** Ric Flair beats Wahoo McDaniel for the Mid-Atlantic title.

- **December 25, 1976:** Ric Flair and Greg Valentine beat Gene and Ole Anderson for the NWA World tag titles.

- **February 6, 1977:** Harley Race defeats Terry Funk for the NWA World title in one of the best wrestling matches of the 1970s.

- **April 30, 1977:** "Superstar" Billy Graham defeats Bruno Sammartino for the WWWF World title in Baltimore. Graham held the belt for ten months. His flamboyant style influenced many up and coming wrestlers.

- **September 26, 1977:** Bob Backlund wrestles his first match in Madison Square Garden.

- **July 1979:** The first edition of *Pro Wrestling Illustrated* hits the newsstands. It is still considered one of the best publications about professional wrestling.

- **April 1979:** The World Wide Wrestling Federation drops the "Wide," and becomes the World Wrestling Federation.

MADISON SQUARE GARDEN

- **July 8, 1979:** Ric Flair defeats Buddy Rogers. Flair later uses aspects of Rogers' persona, including his nickname (The Nature Boy) and his finishing move (the figure-four leglock).

- **August 1979:** Jack Tunney demonstrates his power as a promoter, getting AWA World champion Nick Bockwinkel to face WWF champ Bob Backlund in a cross-promotion battle. The match ends in a double countout.

- **November 30, 1979:** Antonio Inoki beats Bob Backlund for the WWF title in Japan.

- **December 6, 1979:** Backlund regains the WWF title from Inoki. The WWF never told the U.S. audience that Backlund lost the belt while out of the country.

- **June 1982:** Vince McMahon, Jr., buys out his father's share in the WWF, setting off the modern era of sports entertainment.

- **September 1983:** The WWF begins broadcasting its matches on the USA Network.

- **November 1983:** The WWF signs top stars such as Hulk Hogan, Bobby Heenan, Gene Okerlund, and Roddy Piper.

- **January 1984:** The reign of Hulkamania begins as Hulk Hogan defeats The Iron Sheik for the WWF World title.

- **March 31, 1985:** The WWF holds its first *Wrestlemania* event.

- **May 10, 1985:** The first *Saturday Night's Main Event* airs.

- **September 1985:** Saturday morning cartoon Rock 'N' Wrestling appears and runs for almost two years.

RIC FLAIR

STEVE AUSTIN

- **November 26, 1987:** The first *Survior Series* airs on PPV.

- **January 24, 1988:** WWF airs its first *Royal Rumble*.

- **February 1988:** Andre the Giant ends Hulk Hogan's first title reign of four years.

- **October 1988:** According to *Forbes* magazine, the WWF is listed as being worth $100 million.

- **November 22, 1990:** The Undertaker debuts at *Survivor Series*.

- **June 1991:** A drug policy is quickly formed in the WWF as ringside doctor George Zahorian is accused of selling steroids to wrestlers.

- **July 1992:** "Macho Man" Randy Savage admits to taking steroids in the past in a live interview.

- **January 1993:** The debut of *Monday Night Raw*.

- **January 27, 1993:** Superstar wrestler Andre the Giant dies of a heart attack.

- **November 1993:** Vince McMahon, Jr., is charged with steroid possession.

- **June 1994:** Hulk Hogan leaves WWF to go to WCW.

- **1995:** "Stone Cold" Steve Austin signs with the WWF.

- **November 1985:** WWF airs its first pay-per-view event, *The Wrestling Classic*.

- **March 29, 1987:** At *Wrestlemania III*, Hulk Hogan becomes one of few wrestlers to ever bodyslam Andre the Giant.

JESSE VENTURA

- **November 1997:** DX officially forms with Chyna, Shawn Michaels, and HHH as the first members.

- **November 1997:** Bret Hart makes his final appearance in the WWF as Shawn Michaels and Vince McMahon, Jr., break from the script and cheat him out of the World title.

- **November 1998:** Former wrestler Jesse Ventura is elected governor of Minnesota.

- **May 23, 1999:** Owen Hart dies after falling from the ceiling during his entrance into the ring.

- **June 1999:** Sable quits the WWF and sues for $110 million.

- **August 1999:** Gov. Jesse Ventura makes a guest referee appearance at *Summerslam*.

- **November 1999:** Stephanie McMahon is duped into marrying HHH. The saga continues . . .

- **April 1996:** Mick Foley debuts on *Raw*.

- **June 1996:** "Stone Cold" begins his "Austin 3:16" gimmick after defeating Jake "The Snake" Roberts at *King of the Ring*.

- **July 7, 1996:** Hulk Hogan turns heel to join Kevin Nash and Scott Hall to form the nWo, declaring war on WCW.

- **November 17, 1996:** The Rock debuts at *Survivor Series*.

- **November 1996:** WWF receives negative publicity after Brian Pillman pulls a gun on "Stone Cold" Steve Austin.

- **October 1997:** Kane makes his debut during a "Hell in a Cell" match with Undertaker and Shawn Michaels.

OWEN HART

# 2
# WRESTLING
# 101

**P**retend for the sake of argument that you're going to be a wrestler. What do you have to know? Well, how to wrestle, obviously, but that'll only get you so far. If you truly want to succeed, you need to know how to do all the other silly things that accompany the athletic side of wrestling, and really impress a promoter with them.

LEX LUGER

# THE PROMO

First of all, the interview, or "promo," as it's known within the business, is of ultra-importance. Promos are a vital part of wrestling because that's where the money is made. You have to tell the people where the matches are before they'll go see them, and if they're not watching TV then, you need another method. "Cutting promos" is a method of advertising that pre-dates even TV wrestling, and there's one definite way to go about it.

Every promo should have three elements: Motivation, intent, and hype (or, why, what, and where). All should be included for maximum effect, and all are equally important.

Motivation is the reason why you want to wrestle someone. Another guy kidnapped your dog and stole your wife, and now you want revenge! Tell that to the audience, in one or two sentences at most. Here's an example, using some hypothetical names: "Masked Avenger, last week in the main event, you jumped me from behind with a steel chair and left me for dead! That pissed me off."

See, right to the point. Wrestling is a very to-the-point business, as it has to be to maintain the short attention spans of the fans. The above conveys what happened (he was attacked with a steel chair), what the result was (he was left for dead) and

## BEST WRESTLER GIMMICKS

- Undertaker – A stoic undead creature, his slow, deliberate walk to the ring was unbeatable.
- "Million Dollar Man" Ted Dibiase – A personification of Vince McMahon: a super-wealthy, arrogant heel who went so far as to create his own championship belt, the "Million Dollar Belt."
- nWo – A group of wrestlers who joined together and plotted to take over the WCW, both in the story line and behind the scenes.
- Mankind – One of Mick Foley's multiple personalities—complete with a Hannibal Lecter-like mask and a sock puppet, this complete wacko is one of wrestling's most recognizable and memorable characters.
- The Rock – Simplicity at its best, he's just plain cocky and the fans eat it up.

his feelings on the issue (he's pissed off). The viewer now has the basic information as to why these guys are fighting.

The next element is intent. What does the wronged wrestler want to do about it? Again, tell it to the audience so they know what to expect in the big match, and in this case embellishment is a good thing.

"I'm gonna beat you to within an inch of your life, and then hit my finisher on that same steel chair you attacked me with and take your title!"

Okay, not exactly Shakespeare, but it does the job. It's even got a bit of poetic justice for anyone who cares

to remember it when the PPV comes, and it also sets up what the fans will expect to be the big spot in the match: The irate wrestler bringing in that same steel chair and hitting his finisher on it. Using a title for motivation is also a good way to draw money, because properly built-up titles make the fans care about a match all that much more.

Finally, the hype: All the above is meaningless without the final flourish to let the paying customer know where to pay, so we add:

## WORST WRESTLER GIMMICKS

- Oz – Kevin Nash with green tights and silver hair. Accompanied to the ring by Dorothy, Toto, the Tin Man and others, thankfully, this act only lasted a few months.
- I.R.S. – The evil accountant, Irwin R. Shyster, was a complete bore. Although it was fun to see him getting dragged around by his tie, anyone with a finishing move called the "Write-Off" is doomed from the beginning.
- Doink the Clown – An evil clown, now that's original!
- Brutus "The Barber" Beefcake – He strutted around like a ridiculous playboy in pink tights and a bowtie, giving free haircuts.
- The Giant – He was supposed to be playing the son of legend Andre The Giant, but it was an exercise in bad taste, since Andre had died of a heart attack the previous year.

"So, if you've got the guts, bring your belt to the WrestleDeath 2000 PPV next Sunday night and I'll leave with it!"

You have to always include a plug for the big show or PPV to give the fans something to want to buy. Otherwise the promo is pointless character development. That's great if you're doing a play, but it doesn't draw money.

Many wrestlers can master two of the three (usually intent and hype), but motivation is what separates the truly great characters of the business from the one-dimensional caricatures who burn out after a year or so of overexposure. As a general rule these days, the standard "yelling and screaming" interview that is stereotypical of wrestling is very much out, and a more realistic style is in.

# THE MOVES

by Terry Gordy in the '80s, a bomb is the generic name for any slam where the impact is on the shoulders rather than the back.

**4) Driver** – Based on the standard piledriver invented by Lou Thesz in the '40s, a driver is the generic name for any of the above moves where the impact is on the head.

Okay, onto your moves in the ring. In case you want to impress your friends the next time you're watching a wrestling show, here's a rundown of all the basic—and not-so-basic—moves you're likely to see and hear about on those shows.

First of all, when you're talking about naming a move, you can essentially divide everything into four categories right off the bat: Slams, suplexes, bombs, and drivers. Just about every "technical" move name that you'll use or hear is some variation of one of these. They are as follows:

**1) Suplex** – Taken from the move of the same name in amateur wrestling, a suplex in professional wrestling is the generic name for any throw in which a wrestler is taken into the air and over the other wrestler's head and shoulder, usually landing on his back.

**2) Slam** – Based on the standard bodyslam, a slam is the generic name for any move in which a wrestler is picked off the mat and dropped back down without going over the shoulder. The impact will be on the back.

**3) Bomb** – Based on the standard powerbomb invented

KEVIN NASH AND
DIAMOND DALLAS PAGE

So, knowing that much, let's start slow and work from there. Take two wrestlers: Masked Avenger #1 and Masked Avenger #2. Avenger #1 is doing the moves, Avenger #2 is taking them.

The first two things you need to know are "reverse" and "inverted." This is the most often confused pair of words in wrestling lingo, so we'll go over them here. "Reverse" refers to the motion of a move, like putting a car in reverse. "Inverted" refers to the position of the people doing the move.

Avenger #1 does a suplex on Avenger #2. The basic way to do a suplex is for Avenger #1 and Avenger #2 to be standing face to face. #1 puts his arm over #2's neck, grabs a hold of #2's tights, and lifts him vertically into the air, and brings him back down to the mat, landing on his back and dropping #2 on his. In theory the suplex hurts #2 more than #1 because the arc is bigger for #2. Wrestling and physics don't mix, so don't bother thinking too hard about it.

Okay, that's a basic suplex. Now, from that same

position we can proceed in a whole bunch of different ways:

Instead of dropping #2 behind him, #1 falls forward and makes #2 hit the mat face-first. That's a front suplex—last seen years back when Arn Anderson used it as a finisher and called it the "Gourdbuster."

Instead of dropping #2 behind him, #1 drops #2 on his head. That's called a brainbuster, and Eddy Guerrero uses it from time to time. It's not generally done because of the obvious danger. It's really an illusion—the head is protected by the attacker's arm—but if it goes wrong, look out.

If #1 hooks #2's leg before suplexing him and holds onto it, that's a fisherman's suplex. Bonus combo alert: If you do a fisherman's suplex and then finish by dropping the guy on his head like a brainbuster, that's a fisherman's buster.

Instead of dropping #2 behind him, #1 drops #2 on his back without falling down with him. That's called a drop suplex and was done by Kevin Nash for a long time because he got lazy and didn't want to have to get up after doing a move.

Instead of dropping #2 behind him, #1 drops #2 in front of him, sitting down at the same

time. That's called a Falcon Arrow in Japan; in the States, Bob Holly uses it as his finisher, calling it the "Hollycaust."

Instead of dropping #2 behind him, #1 catches #2 in a piledriver position and tombstones him in one motion. That's called a Screwdriver and the only person who can pull it off without killing his opponent is Scott Steiner, although he rarely uses it.

Instead of dropping #2 behind him, #1 falls forward and lands on #2's chest as they hit the mat. That's a jackhammer and it's used by Goldberg as his finisher.

Big finish: Instead of dropping #2 behind him, #1 brings #2 down in front of him on the back of his head, using his own momentum to increase the power of the move. This is called the Orange Crush and is used by Kenta Kobashi in Japan. No one in the U.S. uses it, mainly because Japanese wrestlers tend to drop each other on their heads all the time with no ill effects and no one can figure out how.

That's just scratching the surface. If you switch positions around you get another dozen suplex combos…

Instead of being thrown by the shoulder, #1 puts his arms around #2 and throws him using his entire upper body. This is called a belly-to-belly suplex, and is a standard move in amateur wrestling that carried over to pro wrestling.

If #1 is behind #2 and puts his arms around him, then suplexes him over his head, that's called a German suplex. If #1 puts an arm under #2's leg and uses that leverage to help him with the suplex, that's a belly-to-back or backdrop suplex.

If #1 puts his head under #2's arm and puts his arms around #2's waist before suplexing him, that's a Northern Lights suplex. Most of these are named in Japan where they have much more imagination about move names, so don't ask why they're called what they are.

If #1 puts #2 on the top rope before doing any of these, then that's a "superplex."

On to the slam: Pick the guy up, slam him down. Everyone knows this one. Modifying it is pretty easy,

BRYAN ADAMS AND KURT HENNING

too: Pick him up by the side and slam him that way, and that's a side slam. Pick him up or catch him on the run and slam him powerfully, and that's a powerslam. Kids stuff.

Bombs and drivers are a little more convoluted and often mixed up by overworked wrestling announcers. Both generally start with Masked Avenger

## WORST FINISHING MOVES

- Hulk Hogan's leg drop
- British Bulldog's running powerslam
- Ric Flair's figure-four leglock
- Undertaker's Tombstone Piledriver
- Mankind's Mandible Claw

#2's head between Masked Avenger #1's legs. I'm sure many will immediately have a dirty joke in mind from that description, but considering that the entirety of wrestling is based on two half-naked sweaty guys rolling around on the mat in their underwear, it's a mere drop in the ocean, so save it. At any rate, you've probably seen a piledriver: #1 picks up #2 by the waist, then sits down, driving his head into the mat. If you do this move in Memphis, it's considered a disqualification and a serious injury for the victim, thanks to years of conditioning of the fans.

The powerbomb was invented by Lou Thesz accidentally years ago, when he tried a piledriver but ended falling forward and putting his opponent down on his shoulders instead of his head. The move was popularized by Sid Vicious in the late '80s, as he was one of the few people strong enough to hold the victim in mid-air before dropping them back down on their shoulders. This slight innovation made the move into an effective finisher for him and allowed others to copy the same style, most notably Vader.

From there there are literally hundreds of possible ways to drop a guy on his head or back, so it's impossible to list all the variations of each move. Here's a quick sampling of powerbomb variations to start you with. Assume that each one starts in the basic position, with #2's head between #1's legs…

#1 starts a powerbomb, but as he sits down with the move he hooks his legs over #2's arms so that he's in position to pin #2 when they hit the mat. This is a Tiger Bomb.

Before #1 starts the powerbomb, he hooks both of #2's arms, then finishes the move like that. This is a Tiger Driver, although really the name should be "Tiger Bomb" because it's a form of powerbomb. But that name's allready taken.

If #1 starts the move, then spins around a few times before powerbombing #2, that's a Rotation Powerbomb.

If you want to be vicious, #1 can do the move facing a turnbuckle and simply drop #2 on the back of his head on the top turnbuckle. That's a corner powerbomb.

Now let's hit some piledriver variations. Normally, the victim is facing away from the attacker as he's being piledriven. If #2 (our victim) is facing toward #1 as the move is being done, that's an inverted piledriver (because #2's body position is inverted)—or as it's more popularly known, a Tombstone piledriver. The move name actually pre-dates the Undertaker's use of it—it was just a handy coincidence that it was named as such.

Remember the Tiger Driver from the last bit? Well, imagine that instead of powerbombing poor #2, #1 brings him down on his head instead. Ouch. That's a Tiger Driver '91, and the only person in the world who can do it without causing serious injury is the inventor, Mitsuhara Misawa. If you start from the basic position, hook both arms, but simply drop down and drive #2's head into the mat, then you've done HHH's Pedigree. Lift the guy in the air before dropping down and it's Stevie Ray's Slapjack.

# MOVES & MORE

Consider this as a rough guide to naming the thousands of moves in wrestling. Even the best announcers are generally overworked and stressed, and often make stuff up to get by, as long as it sounds good. Here are a few other terms to help you get by…

You'll probably run across the terms "tope" (pronounced Toe-Pay), "plancha," or "pescado" in your travels. These names are all from Mexican wrestling (or "lucha libre") and all refer to a dive from inside the ring to a guy outside the ring. It's a little hard to keep track, but the official definitions are as follows:

A tope is a running dive over the top rope, where you land in a vertical position on your victim.

A plancha is a dive through the ropes where you land in a horizonal position on your victim.

A pescado is a standing dive, where you use the ropes to slingshot yourself over and out of the ring, and onto your victim.

But wait, there's more! A tope suicida ("suicide dive") sees the attacker running and diving through the ropes head first, plowing into the poor guy on the floor.

A tope con hilo ("dive on a thread") sees the attacker diving over the top rope, without touching it, and landing on his victim.

Another one you'll hear a lot is "hurricanrana." This actually isn't the proper name for it, but it's too late to change now. The move is done by jumping in the air, wrapping your legs around your victim's neck, and backflipping while holding on, thus sending your opponent to the mat headfirst. Generally done as a counter to a powerbomb rather than a move on its own, the move is called a "rana" in Mexico, or a hurricanrana if done by a relative of the legendary Hurricane Ramirez. It was the second term that got imported to the U.S., however, and the name stuck.

No young wrestler these days is complete without some kind of insane top-rope move to wow the crowd, and here's a quick guide to the big winners in the jaw dropping department.

If you're on the top rope and you do a backflip off there and onto your opponent, that's a moonsault, invented by the Great Muta in the late '80s.

If you're up there and you dropkick your opponent, that's a missile dropkick.

If you jump off and splash your opponent, that's either a Superfly splash or a Money Shot depending on your tastes.

If you spin around about a million times before you do that splash, that's a Sky Twister Press. If you somersault like a diver three times before that splash, that's a 450 or Firebird splash. The "450" refers to 450 degrees of rotation, of course.

If you turn yourself the other way (rotate clockwise instead of counter-clockwise), then that's a Shooting Star Press. That one's pretty tricky to pull off.

If you do only one somersault and land backfirst on the guy, that's a senton bomb (or Swanton bomb if you're Jeff Hardy).

If you jackknife your body, again like a diver does, before that splash, it's a frog splash. Because you're "hopping" like a frog, see?

If you come off the top and do a legdrop, then it's a "_____ Jam", and you fill in that blank with whatever state you're from. It's a wrestling thing, don't ask. For pretty much anything else you choose to do off the top (clothesline, elbow, kneedrop, whatever), just a "flying" at the beginning (flying clothesline, flying elbow, flying kneedrop) will do.

The general rule overall is that if you're not sure, make up something that sounds impressive and stick with it. That usually works for the pros.

## BEST WRESTLER MANAGERS

"Captain" Lou Albano
Jimmy "Mouth of the South" Hart
Bobby "The Brain" Heenan
Mr. Fuji
Paul Bearer
Jim Cornette
Sunny
Slick
"Classy" Feddie Blassie

# THE WEAPONS

But enough talking about talking and moving—let's get to the good stuff: Weapons!

## THE STEEL CHAIR

Long a favorite of the business, the folding steel chair is the preferred vehicle of destruction for most wrestlers throughout history because of the wonderful properties it displays. First of all, it has give, which is extremely important in avoiding serious injury. Many people ponder how chairs can be used without it hurting, and the answer to that is simple: They can't. Make no mistake, it hurts to be hit with a steel chair.

However, it would hurt much more to experience the alternative, which is being hit with an unfolded chair or a wooden chair. The design of the chair is such that it absorbs most of the impact itself when used as a weapon, leaving less to be taken up by the wrestler's body. And generally speaking, a wrestler will take the shot on the back, which is capable of withstanding more punishment than the other parts of the body. So it hurts, but it's not doing any serious or permanent damage unless done horribly wrong by the person swinging the chair.

## TABLES

Another recent favorite of fans and wrestlers alike is the breaking table. This one is a little more recent, having been added on a regular basis beginning in ECW's early years (1994) and spreading to the other two major promotions from there. The solution to this one is really quite simple: Physics, and when that fails, cheating. Physics says that if you hit a standard table right in the center at a decent velocity, the legs will not be able to absorb the force and the table will then break, and a crowd will generally cheer.

If you're worried about all those detailed calculations, then just do what the major promotions do, and run a saw in a straight line about halfway through the thickness of the table, right down the center—from the bottom, of course, to make it less obvious that the table is pre-cut. This is generally the preferred method, because there's much less chance of harmful table shards injuring the person going through it. Why, you may ask, are tables such a popular prop? Well, mostly they look cool. But more important for the wrestler, a table will absorb the impact of being put through it, giving the wrestler a shorter distance to hit the ground.

# BLOOD

A great tradition in wrestling, dating back to before the days of TV. For some reason, maybe having something to do with some study of primitive man and pagan rituals that you can probably read elsewhere, wrestling fans like blood. And lots of it. One notable instance saw Terry Funk bleeding all over an ECW arena, and some enterprising fans dipping their tickets into the rapidly growing pool of blood that he was leaving. Now that's dedication. But if you want to bleed, there are three basic ways:

1) Take a really hard shot to the nose or mouth. Blood will usually flow. Oh, sorry, you were under the impression that it was all Hollywood stage blood? Hate to disappoint you, but accidents do happen quite often and it's very easy to rupture something enough to draw a good flow of blood. As a hint, if you're bleeding from the mouth, mix it with copious amounts of saliva to make it look worse than it actually is. Great for scaring little old ladies at ringside. Advantages: Looks real, because it is. Disadvantages: Limited control of placement and flow; hurts like hell.

2) Use a blade. This is the standard method. Wrestlers used to wear athletic tape on their wrists to provide better grip in wrestling holds, but since actual wrestling is hardly a consideration anymore, the tape is more often than not used to conceal a piece of razor blade. Take the blade out of the tape at an opportune moment, go into "the blading position" (laying on the ground covering your face with your arms) and cut a straight line across your forehead with the edge of the blade until blood flows. Kids, don't try this at home. Generally considered disgusting and barbaric by opponents of the sport, it's just the way things have always been done in wrestling and will continue to do so. The AIDS scares of the early '90s nearly called a halt to the venerated blade, but when they proved to be unfounded in regards to blood and wrestling, it made a big comeback. Advantages: Easy to control where and how much blood; convenient to hide blade again after use. Disadvantages: Unrealistic! Have you ever seen someone bleed from the forehead in real life? Messy if done wrong. The scar tissue will no longer heal after a certain point, leaving your forehead a disgusting mess of blade marks until you're forced to put Vaseline on your forehead to keep from bleeding in public. True story, Abdullah the Butcher has to do that all the time.

RIC FLAIR AND KURT HENNING

3) Blood capsules. This one was merely an urban legend for the longest time—until the WWF actually started using them on a regular basis in 1999. There are actually two different kinds that can be used. First of all, this only applies to "internal bleeding" in wrestling story lines, where the story calls for a wrestler to be "bleeding from the mouth." All external bleeding is either blading or real ("hardway"). The hygenic and socially acceptable method of bleeding from the mouth is the actual Hollywood blood capsule, a small disc that contains a red, blood-like liquid, which can be conveniently slipped into the mouth and bitten down on to produce a somewhat convincing flow of blood. The other, and more traditional, method of producing blood this way is to take that fake blood and put some into a condom, which is then slipped to the wrestler at the appropriate time and bitten down on. This one tends to be shunned, because frankly it's pretty gross.

# ASIAN MIST

Wrestlers such as the Great Muta and his story line father the Great Kabuki made their name by blowing a deadly green mist into the eyes of their opponents to "blind" them when they needed an advantage. Most fans will probably be disappointed to learn that the method of doing so is roughly similar to the more disgusting method of mouth-bleeding: Water with green food-coloring is put into a condom or small balloon, which is then slipped to the wrestler by the referee at the right time. The wrestler bites down to release the liquid, and spits it out in a mist.

Now, actually producing that mist effect is a tricky thing in itself. If you just spit out the water, you'll make a mess of yourself and look like an idiot. The trick is apparently using the tongue and teeth to regulate the water as it leaves your mouth, although it seems to be a difficult thing to pull off in practice. Wrestlers like HHH and the Rock do it with plain water all the time as part of their shtick, as does Gangrel with a goblet of "blood."

## POPULAR FOREIGN OBJECTS USED BY WRESTLERS

Folding chairs
Tables
Crutches
Garbage cans
Title belts
Canes
Flagpoles
Forks
Megaphones
Barbed Wire
PVC pipe
Bats
Ladders
Metal railings
2x4s
Bamboo canes
Various powders
Fire extinguishers
Metal rods
Guitars
Nightsticks

STING AND BRET HART

# FIREBALLS

Sadly missing from U.S. wrestling these days is one of the great heel-heat getters of the '70s and '80s—the dreaded fireball. An effective visual and a credible threat, it was actually fairly safe and easy to pull off. Any magician can tell you how: Flash paper. A substance called nitrocellulose is put onto a piece of tissue paper. When lit, it burns extremely quickly and brightly, so much so that throwing it at someone's face will give the illusion of tossing fire at them. In fact, the "fire" burns out long before it reaches their face, and the heat produced is minimal. Injuries resulting from this sort of thing are rare, which is why people like Jerry Lawler used it so freely in the '70s.

If you're really in a sadistic mood, you can blow fire the same way they do in the "hardcore" Japanese promotions: Take a big swig of kerosene in your mouth, light a torch, and then spit it out through the flame to produce a dramatic fireball in the direction of your opponent. Of course, woe is the poor guy who happens to be standing too close to the intensely hot and very real flame, but that's showbiz.

# POWDER

Another classic. Still going strong after 70+ years of service to the industry, vile heels have been tossing all sorts of eye-stinging powders and salts into the faces of babyfaces since nearly when wrestling began. That's the nice thing about television: The home audience can't smell the distinctive talcum powder scent that it leaves as it harmlessly hits the face of the victim. And you thought talc was just for diapering babies.

HULK HOGAN

# THE NAME GAME

## TYPES OF WRESTLING MATCHES

- **Ladder match** - A ladder is set up in the entryway. A belt is hung above ring on a rope. First to get the belt, wins. No rules, goes until someone grabs the belt.
- **Cage match** - Cage surrounds ring. Only way to win is to get out of the cage.
- **Barbwire match** - Barbwire replaces the ropes.
- **2 out of 3 falls** - First person to score 2 pins or submissions wins.

- **Royal rumble** - 30 man battle. 2 start out in the ring, 1 comes in every minute. No pinfall or submission, wrestler is out when he's thrown over the top rope.
- **Street Fight** - Fight in a back alley.
- **Buried Alive** - Object is to bury opponent. Shovels, casket, wheelbarrow, and tombstones used as weapons.
- **Empty Arena Match** - The arena is empty and wrestlers can fight anywhere.
- **Iron Man Match** - Person with the most pinfalls in a hour wins the match.
- **Towel Match** - A partner is outside and has a towel. He throws the towel in when he thinks you are finished and you lose the match.
- **Battle Royal** - Same as Royal Rumble but all wrestlers start in the ring at once.
- **Hardcore match** - Anything goes—no dq, no countouts, any kind of foreign object can be used.
- **Survivor Series Match** - Two teams of four or five are in a tag team style match. Match continues until all members of one team is totally eliminated.

Thanks to carnival traditions of years past, there's a name for everything in wrestling. In order to disguise the business from those who weren't meant to know what was going on, early promoters came up with code words for just about everything associated with the sport in order to deceive anyone looking where they shouldn't be. This practice is called "kayfabe," a word first used by carnies at the turn of the century, with origins that are lost to time. The phrase "breaking kayfabe" means exposing the secrets of wrestling to an outsider, while "kayfabing" someone means telling them a lie to further a story line in wrestling. That sort of behavior is so ingrained and accepted within wrestling circles that getting a straight answer out of someone involved in the business is a near-impossible task.

Wrestlers, for instance, aren't wrestlers—they're "workers." They don't wrestle, they "work." Most smart fans will use the term "worker" over "wrestler" because the latter denotes actual Olympic-style competition, and it's doubtful that anyone would confuse one with the other. "Smart" in this case doesn't refer to intelligence, it refers to being "in the know" about wrestling in general, which can range from simply knowing that it's fake to actually being in the business.

Speaking of fake, the popular word "work" is also used to mean "fake" in wrestling: If a promoter tricked you into thinking something, he "worked" you. Wrestling is fake—it's a "work."

Now, in wrestling, the opposite of something being a work is that it's a "shoot." That is to say, it's a real thing, whether it be a fight or a comment made by someone. To clarify, there have only been about eight such legitimate "shoots" in the entire history of pro wrestling, despite the frequency with which the word has been used since the Internet era of wrestling began in the 1990s. It should be completely clear by now that everything in wrestling is a work, although not as choreographed and scripted as Hollywood and popular legend would have you believe.

Want an example of a shoot? In a 1987 match between Bruiser Brody and Lex Luger, a hungover and grumpy Brody stopped cooperating with Luger at one point in the match, and the inexperienced Luger immediately called an end to the match and ran back to the dressing room. Despite anything you may hear to the contrary, that's about as ugly and violent as "real" situations ever get in wrestling. Any actual injuries that may happen, blood that doesn't come from blading, or even a guy getting a bruise on his leg, are unintentionally done. Shoots are so uncommon that 99.9 percent is a work—period!

During a match, the actual wrestling is faked by "selling." Even though your opponent might not be making contact with you, you act like he is and roll with the punch. Let's dispel one myth right now: Bad wrestlers do go out there and have six inches of space between the fist and the target, yes. Certainly there

PSST!
DON'T HURT ME!!!

have been many cases of there being so much air moved by a missed punch that the other guy's hair is blow-dried on the spot from the wind generated. However, that is absolutely the exception.

The whole concept of wrestlers stomping the mat while doing fake-looking forearms is an antique notion (antique in wrestling terms being 1985), and it was long ago abandoned for the practice of chopping the chest with the side of the hand, or simply punching the guy in the head—softly. The norm these days is a much stiffer style ("stiff" in this case meaning "real contact being made"), as opposed to the looser ("loose" in this case meaning fake punch, stomp, fake punch, stomp, fake punch, stomp) style of the '80s. Unfortunately, this new realism also means more injuries.

Talking about selling leads us into "psychology." The word has a totally different meaning in wrestling, although with similar origins to what you probably know it as. Psychology in this case means "If you get hit in the leg, you pretend your leg is hurt. If the match runs another 10 minutes, then you keep pretending your leg is hurt for those 10 minutes and adjust your selling accordingly." That's a pretty simple way to break it down. Suffice it to say that you'll score points with your buddies by watching a match and pointing out that a wrestler not being able to do his world-famous dropkick because his knee is still sore from earlier is "great ring psychology," and we'll leave it at that.

Let's blow another misconception out of the water right now: Wrestlers do not sit in their dressing rooms for three hours beforehand writing out move-by-move listings for their matches. Well, most don't, at least. For the most part, they have a general idea of how long they have for the match, with some highspots planned out, and what the ending of the match will be. The rest of the action is actually called during the match by the heel, who generally whispers moves to the babyface during slow points or when the wrestlers engage in a well-timed brawl into the crowd.

The whispering method has been the popular one for decades, but with the recent increase in TV wrestling, the microphones planted in the ring have made for more than one awkward moment of having the planning session captured on live television, so the "brawl into the crowd and plan there" method has become the de facto standard these days. In some cases, there have been wrestlers talented enough to improvise excellent matches, start and finish included, during the course of the match itself, but this is a rarity.

Okay, so we've established that the matches are completely worked and they're not actually trying to hurt each other out there. So what's the point of wrestling in the first place?

Money.

Long ago, more than a hundred years in fact, promoters learned that while displays of athleticism might entertain people in the short term, even more money could be made if they could control those displays. This simple leap of logic led to a complete reversal of what made a "good" worker. Whereas before success was measured by the actual skill level of the person in question, now it became measured by how many people the promoter could convince to watch that person wrestle. That's why most people refer to wrestling as a business rather than a sport. It's certainly not "sports entertainment," a slogan devised by the WWF to justify their own excesses of silliness in the '80s and to avoid medical costs and regulations by outside sports agencies.

The term "sports entertainment" was thought up by WWF owner Vince McMahon during the heyday of the WWF because certain states were pressuring him to man proper medical staff on site and make sure his wrestlers had licenses to compete as professional athletes. Vince's response was to essentially reply that it wasn't sports, it was sports entertainment, a genre that didn't exist until he created it, and thus the WWF couldn't be mandated by the government. Listen carefully whenever you watch a wrestling show from one of the major promotions: When referring to wrestling in general, the hosts will almost always refer to it as "our business" or "this business," because "wrestling" is actually a taboo word within wrestling.

But getting back to the original point, drawing money had overridden athleticism as the #1 motivator for wrestlers by World War II, and certainly by the time the television era began. As such, certain modifications to the rules became necessary.

As you probably already know, the main way to win a wrestling match is to "pin" your opponent, holding his shoulders down to the mat for a three-count. This is called a "fall," named as such because the Olympic form of wrestling, which evolved into the professional style started in Europe, with the win coming when one wrestler could hold his opponent down for the time it took for the referee to say the word "tomber" (the French verb "to fall").

You can also win if your opponent gives up, which is technically called a submission within both wrestling and more formal fighting ranks. This was fine for the first twenty years or so, then promoters began realizing that while decisive finishes to the matches would provide for a satisfying evening for the fans, if they could find a way to make the finish more open-ended, they could stage another match and make more money. Money motivates pretty much everything in wrestling. So in the early part of the century, disqualifications suddenly started popping up much more frequently than in the amateur wrestling ranks, with one wrestler doing something illegal and thus losing the match—but without really losing the match, because no one got pinned, right? He could then vow revenge and they could have another match.

Some variation of this theme has been going on for a hundred years now and still draws money. As an alternate method of having an indecisive finish, someone decided one day that if a wrestler left the ring area for a given amount of time (usually ten seconds) then they'd also lose the match, with that being called a "countout." So there's four basic finishes to a match: Pin, submission, countout, and disqualification. When a wrestler loses a clean match, it's called a "job," because, hey, they don't want to lose, but it's been predetermined, so it's their "job" to go out and lose. Job is also used as a verb: "He jobbed last night." Someone who loses often is a jobber. If you lose in a controversial or indecisive

manner, that's a screwjob. If you lose and go out on a stretcher, that's a stretcher job. It's a very versatile word.

In the 1940s, wrestling truly distanced itself from its more legitimate competitors in the sporting world by going truly over-the-top and devising bizarre variations on basic one-on-one competition. These are known as "gimmick matches" within wrestling jargon. The first such was the tag team match, originating in Australia of all places, featuring two-on-two competition with the action switching from person to person by "tagging" their partner into the ring. Southern promoter Paul Boesch provided the wrestling world with yet another innovation, putting a fence around the ring for a match with a hated rival, and thus giving birth to the "steel cage match." Today, there are literally hundreds of variations of matches, which most wrestling fans are able to grasp and accept with a minimum of worry about the realism involved.

By the time the television era arrived in the 1950s, another huge innovation was set to take over. Up until

LEX LUGER

that point, wrestlers were defined by what they did in the ring and said outside of it. Lou Thesz was just plain Lou Thesz, a great worker and all-around legend. That all changed with the introduction of Gorgeous George, a flamboyant blond who pranced around the ring with his valets and feather boas. This is generally regarded as the first-ever "gimmick" in wrestling.

A gimmick can best be described as the thing that makes a wrestler into a character beyond what he does in the ring. More than anything else in the history of the "sport," gimmicks changed the entire perception of wrestling. The biggest change was to formally introduce the whole good/evil paradigm into the sport. Before then, you had some people who were mean people in the ring, and some people who were nice, but really everyone played by the rules when it came right down to it. When gimmicks started ruling the day, that protocol went out the window completely. Pretty soon the entire roster of promoters everywhere was divided into the "babyfaces" (good guys) and "heels" (bad guys), and even sooner after that the promoters found out how much money was to be made by matching a popular babyface against an unpopular heel.

Babyfaces (or "faces" for short) always played by the rules, to the point where it became an exploitable weakness. They slap hands with the fans on the way to the ring, sign autographs without complaint, never initiate fights without provocation, stand by their friends, and drink a glass of milk every day to stay healthy. Heels curse at the fans, make themselves out to be better than their opponent, always look out for their own good, break every rule in the book (while the referee is distracted, of course), and generally don't try for a pin without putting at least one body part on the ropes for leverage. Fans picked up on all of this in record time, and the guys who make the big bucks in wrestling are the ones who get cheered or booed the loudest.

From that point, the entire promotional push of wrestling became different. Using the weekly TV shows as a basis for making money, it became apparent that there were two sure-fire ways to make big money: Create a hot feud, or a hot angle.

A feud is pretty straightforward: Joe Wrestler hates

Gary Grappler for whatever reason, and demands a match. It ends without a decisive finish, so they have another one, and another, and pretty soon everyone is making money off the deal. Feuds are the basis for everything in wrestling, because it's all based on two people fighting each other and there usually has to be a reason behind it. The better the reason, the more money is made. The more popular the babyface is and the more hated the heel is, the more money is made. If you really want to go for the big loot, get two really popular babyfaces and turn one of them heel against the other.

An angle is a little trickier. Essentially, it's the event that triggers a feud. Angles can be used very effectively, or very ineffectively. Always remember the golden rule of wrestling: If it makes gold, it rules. Story lines are only as good as the money they draw. Probably the most used (and overused) angle is the "turn." Someone is a babyface, and one day decides that those babies they've been kissing have actually been ugly and they've had enough of it, so they attack their best friend and become a heel. The ultimate example of this was when Paul Orndorff turned on Hulk Hogan and made

HULK HOGAN

millions for the WWF.

Sometimes a heel forms a partnership with another heel (not a friendship—heels are vile and heartless fiends who never have friends), but Heel A will make one mistake too many and Heel B will suddenly abandon him or attack him in a parking lot with five or so of his other associates. The crowd will generally sympathize with the one being attacked and a new babyface is born, like when Randy "Macho Man" Savage turned face after being rescued by Hogan from a gang attack by Honky Tonk Man and The Hart Foundation. Very few wrestlers have remained either babyface or heel throughout their entire career, but most often, a given wrestler will turn upwards of 5 or 6 times in an effort to keep his character fresh.

Once the line is drawn between the babyfaces and the heels, you have to know how well the crowd is reacting to them. This is called "heat." The louder a crowd is responding to a wrestler, or a match, or anything else going on, is the heat for it. If a heel wrestler is an especially dastardly fellow, he's said to have "a lot of heat on him" because the audience wants him to be beaten up by the territory's babyface more than usual. Heels having too much heat on them, like Bobby "The Brain" Heenan and "Rowdy" Roddy Piper in their heydays, have actually had death threats made against them and been attacked by fans. That sort of thing is just par for the course for a good heel.

The ultimate goal of anyone or anything in wrestling is to "get over." If the fans respond to a wrestler's entrance or a move they do or a catchphrase they use, then it's over. If a wrestler is generally believable in his position in the promotion and gets a good reaction, then he's over. If one guy rubs his butt in another guy's face during the course of the match and the fans react, then that's over too. Wrestling has no shame when it comes to making money.

A lesser goal is to make the fans "pop," that is, to make some noise. Cheering or booing, it doesn't matter. Heat and pops don't have any positive or negative forms: If they make noise, it's a success either way. The worst thing in wrestling is for the fans to make no noise at all.

Reactions achieved by doing things that don't require thought or effort are referred to as "cheap." Cheap heat is pushing over an old lady in the front row or insulting the hometown football team. These are things that any large group of people will react to, not just wrestling fans, and thus they don't make money for the promotion. A cheap pop is making the fans cheer by saying the name of the city you're in or having a female show skin. Again, there's no challenge to doing either of those things and it doesn't demonstrate that the wrestler in question is over one way or another. Doing those sort of things on a regular basis generally shows desperation on the part of those controlling the character, in that they can't find any other method of making the fans react. A good example is Charles Wright, most well known as the Godfather, who built his career on wrestling opening matches and getting a reaction by bringing out a large number of scantily clad women with him—his "ho's." The fans reacted well to that, but once he was in the ring, he had nothing that the fans cared about, and he soon became defined by the women with him until the fans only popped for the women and not for him at all. In this case, he became defined by cheap heat and suffered as a character because of it.

Now, as most wrestling fans probably know, there are essentially three levels of competition in wrestling: Undercard, midcard, and main event. The undercard is generally composed of people who are either not over (or over only on cheap heat) and inexperienced ("green") workers, and are thus positioned near the beginning simply to get the crowd involved in the event that heat will rub off on them. Once a wrestler finds a gimmick or angle that makes the crowd care about him, he usually advances to the midcard, which is the wrestling equivalent of purgatory. Once here, you're usually either a youngster on your way up or a has-been on your way down. If you're in the middle of those categories, the midcard is the worst possible place to be.

Wrestling fans, whether or not they're aware of it, form certain associations with wrestlers, and if they see someone who beats undercard wrestlers but loses to the stars, that person is labeled in their minds as a midcarder, and someone who they will not generally pay money to watch. No one wants to pay to see mediocrity, they want to see greatness, something special. If the fans think a wrestler is that something special, or they work hard enough in the ring to convince the promoter of that, then they're a main eventer and will find themselves in the final or second-to-last match of the evening and being given more focus and time to develop their matches. As you advance up the card you are being given a "push," as in the promoter is behind you and pushing you to the top.

Just to hit another couple of terms you'll want to remember: Ratings and buyrates are all-important to the discerning fan.

I'm sure you know what ratings are—there are such-and-such million people who have televisions, and such-and-such a percentage watching a given show. That's the rating. That's also an industry unto itself for millions of wrestling fans, who anxiously await the ratings

STING AND BILL GOLDBERG

numbers every Tuesday to back up their own arguments about the worth of the promotion they follow. Ratings really only matter when both of the big two promotions (WWF and WCW) are close in them, and since that hasn't been the case since 1998, feel free not to worry about them. Buyrates are the ratings for Pay-Per-View events.

In this case, there's roughly 30,000,000 homes (give or take 5,000,000) equipped with cable systems that can show the month's PPVs, and you get the buyrate for a show by dividing the number of people who actually purchased the show by 30,000,000. The "magic number" for a show to make money these days is 1% (called a 1.0 buyrate), which amounts to about 300,000 people buying your PPV. Why is this important? Multiply 300,000 people by $30 a show and you'll understand why there's so darn many PPVs every month.

At some points throughout the book, you'll come across star ratings for certain matches. Star ratings are the smart fan's best friend, because it's a (supposedly) universal way for wrestling fans to compare the quality of the matches, although it rarely works out that way. The basic premise is that a match is "rated" from DUD (0 Stars) to ***** (5 stars), using scary words like workrate, psychology, transitions, heat, and other intangibles to define just how good it was.

It was invented by manager Jim Cornette and Norm Dooley and has since been taken by the Internet community and modified for their needs. Here's a rough guide for you:

|  |  |
|---|---|
| ***** | Match of the Year candidate |
| ****1/2 | Almost perfect |
| **** | Excellent |
| ***1/2 | Extremely good, but with some important flaws |
| *** | Good, but lacking in many ways |
| **1/2 | Above average, but nothing special |
| ** | An average match—most of the wrestling matches on regular TV will top out here due to time constraints |
| *1/2 | Below average, but watchable |
| * | Bad match, but enough action to make it worthwhile |
| –* | Terrible match |
| DUD | No value whatsoever |
| NEGATIVE NUMBERS: | Completely offensive to the viewer in every way |

The fan is always free to make his judgments on the worth of a match and use whatever rating he wants. In the end, your own entertainment is the important thing, and one man's ***** classic is another man's boring DUD. That's what makes the discussion so interesting most of the time.

And now that you're armed with the essentials, let's head back to 1904 and examine exactly how we got from there to here.

RANDY SAVAGE

Pay-Per-View

# 3

THREE

# THE WWF GOLDEN AGE:
## THE ROCK AND WRESTLING CONNECTION 1984–1988

The WWF's first "golden age" began in January of 1984, as Hulk Hogan defeated The Iron Sheik in roughly 5 minutes to become the ninth man to hold the WWF World title. Hogan's star continued to rise, and the WWF rode a wave of mainstream success on Hogan's back to millions of dollars via the War to Settle the Score show on MTV and the first ever Wrestlemania, which was broadcast on closed-circuit TV. This era lasted four years, and ended in February of 1988, when Hogan lost the title to longtime friend Andre the Giant in front of the largest TV audience ever to watch a wrestling match. This move allowed the WWF to open the door for someone else to be champion for a while, but it backfired badly and they never quite recovered, losing the mainstream luster they once had with Hulk Hogan on top.

# HULK HOGAN

Love him or hate him, it cannot be denied that no one in the past twenty years (outside of WWF owner Vince McMahon) has had more influence on the sport than Terry Bollea, better known to fans all over the world as Hulk Hogan.

Born in August 1953, Hogan spent his younger years living in Venice Beach, California, where he tried everything from a career as a musician (reportedly his life's dream) to a career as a bodybuilder.

It was the latter that would attract the attention of a wrestling promoter who was scouting at Muscle Beach. Hogan's own story of why exactly he got into professional wrestling changes by the interview, but the fact remains that in 1978, a young and impressively physiqued Terry Bollea made his debut in Memphis as Terry Boulder.

This persona didn't exactly set the world on fire, but Hogan had an impressive work ethic and a strange charisma that others were lacking, and so he caught the eye of the WWF and was brought into that promotion in 1979, with the less-than-impressive name of "Sterling Golden" and with Classy Freddie Blassie as his manager. His most notable feat during this period was to shave his chest hair in the shape of a mushroom cloud. Obviously a repackaging was in order, and so as the '80s began, he was changed into "The Incredible" Hulk Hogan, based on the comic book character The Incredible Hulk.

Even as Hulk Hogan, he languished in the midcard for the first few years of his career, playing a cocky heel and feuding off and on with Andre the Giant. They had a notable match (6 years before their supposed first meeting) at Shea Stadium in 1981, which ended up being a quick win for Andre. An increasingly dejected Hogan left the WWF in 1982 and bounced between the WWF and Verne Gagne's AWA, hoping to find better fortunes there.

Once again, Hogan began as a heel, but then something very unexpected happened: Hogan was cast to play the evil wrestler "Thunderlips" in *Rocky III*, and shocked critics and fans alike by doing a remarkable job at it. Admittedly, playing a professional wrestler wasn't much of an acting stretch for him, but Hogan found his popularity suddenly increasing with the national exposure of the hit movie.

Verne Gagne was the first to attempt to capitalize on this, turning Hogan into a babyface and elevating him into the main event via a feud with hated manager Bobby Heenan. Heenan not only managed such top stars as Ken Patera, but also the World champion at the time, Nick Bockwinkel. It was only natural that Hogan would be in line for a title shot after plowing through the rest of Heenan's stable and in 1983, he began receiving them. And winning. But, as is often the case in wrestling, what the audience thought they saw was not what they actually saw.

Most of the matches, beginning with their first meeting in 1982, would see Hogan valiantly overcome Bockwinkel's offense, fighting back to his now-patented legdrop finisher to win the title—only to have it immediately overturned (or in some cases, overturned a week later) on a technicality—the original referee was knocked out, Hogan didn't read the fine print in the contract, etc. The goal, from Gagne's point of view, was to use Hogan's increasing popularity as a drawing card to lure tens of thousands of fans into the arena, send them home happy, but still have his favorite Bockwinkel as the champion at the end of the day. So far, so good.

However, in April '83, Gagne's AWA made their biggest mistake with Hogan. They promoted *Super Sunday,* taking place live in one arena in St. Paul and being shown closed-circuit in another, featuring yet another Hogan-Bockwinkel match for the title as the main event. Lord James Blears, legendary tag-team champion from the '50s, was brought in as the special referee to lend it an extra aura of something special, and both arenas sold out. This time, the fans figured,

Hogan had to walk out with the title, after more than a year of chasing it. Alas for them, it was not to be, as once again Hogan was screwed out of the title on a cheap non-finish featuring a ref bump and an overturned decision.

However, this time, the fans reacted in a different manner than their usual acceptance: They nearly rioted, pelting the ring with garbage and booing the decision for minutes. Verne Gagne failed to take the hint, but Hogan realized he was on the verge of something great and began openly campaigning to get the World title, or be allowed to go somewhere where he could get one. Gagne wasn't convinced of Hogan's drawing power as champion, and let him know that it wasn't happening.

Hogan left the AWA in May '83 for New Japan Pro Wrestling, taking part in the tournament to crown the first ever IWGP champion (the New Japan equivalent of the World title).

The tournament came down to Hogan and Antonio Inoki in the finals, and a finish was booked where it would appear that Inoki was "accidentally" knocked out and Hogan would be "forced" to pin him and win the title, thus making the whole thing look real. They did such a convincing job that many title histories actually list this as a legitimate occurrence. Hogan dropped the title back to Inoki a year later, to prevent conflicts with his WWF schedule.

# SUPERSTAR STATS:

**Hulk Hogan**
*Real name:* Terry Gene Bollea
*Height:* 6'7"
*Weight:* 275 lbs.
*Trademark move:* Running Legdrop
*Aliases:* Hollywood Hogan, Terry "The Hulk" Boulder,
   Sterling Golden

So in late 1983, Hogan departed New Japan a bigger star than when he came in, and rejoined the WWF. He made a surprise reappearance at a TV taping, saving World champion Bob Backlund from an attack by the Wild Samoans, and immediately cemented himself as a top babyface.

"Well, you know Mean Gene…"
—Hulk Hogan

Then one of those weird things that only happens in wrestling happened.

The WWF champion, Bob Backlund, had been in that spot for six years and was a very popular favorite with the fans. However, he had the stigma attached to him of being boring, a bland technical wrestler, and Vince McMahon had bigger plans. So in December '84, Backlund was signed to meet evil Iranian, The Iron Sheik in what was supposed to be a routine title defense. However, at one point, Sheik locked Backlund in his finisher, the Camel Clutch, and Backlund's manager Arnold Skaaland threw in the towel, the universal sign for submission, and the shocked MSG crowd saw the Sheik walk out with the WWF title. One problem: No one told Backlund that this was going to happen, or so he claims. He indignantly quit the promotion soon after and didn't resurface there until 1992.

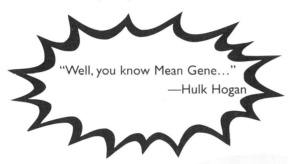

## WRESTLER SPOTLIGHT

# HULK HOGAN

### BIGGEST CONTRIBUTION
Spearheaded the WWF's national drive. Mainstream icon.

### BEST MATCH
Debatable, but most would favor either a match in Japan against Stan Hansen that was about ****, or one of his numerous house show battles with Randy Savage, most of which were also in the **** range.

### BIGGEST MATCH
Unquestionably against Andre the Giant at *Wrestlemania III*. Although terrible from a technical standpoint, it sold out the Pontiac Silverdome and drew more money than any other show in the U.S. to that point. It also stands in the minds of some as the symbolic "passing of the torch" from Andre to Hogan and features the biggest moment in modern history: Hogan bodyslamming Andre before pinning him.

### BIGGEST RIVALS
Pretty much every main event wrestler in the WWF, including The Iron Sheik, Randy Savage, Andre the Giant, and the Ultimate Warrior.

And so, in the moment the wrestling world had been waiting for since early 1983, Hulk Hogan got his shot at the WWF title in January '84 in front of a sold out crowd in Madison Square Garden, and crushed the Sheik in a little over 5 minutes with the legdrop to claim his first World title. The pop for the win was enormous, and sent shockwaves through the entire wrestling world. "Hulkamania" was born.

Hogan's star rose quickly, as he sold out arenas all over the country and had the fans eating out of his hand. 1984 itself was fairly uneventful for him, as he spent the entire year as champion without many serious threats to his title. Besides the usual rematches with the Sheik (and his cohort, evil Russian Nikolai Volkoff; these were the years of the Cold War, remember), Hogan mainly concentrated on taking on larger foes like Big John Studd and wrestling in tag matches with good friend Andre the Giant. The true leap in popularity for Hogan would come in 1985, as the WWF began promoting its inaugural *Wrestlemania* show. The setup was fairly straightforward: Hogan and rival "Rowdy" Roddy Piper had a famous match on an MTV special, called *The War to Settle the Score*.

It ended in a huge brawl, with Piper and cornerman Paul "Mr. Wonderful" Orndorff fighting Hogan and his cornerman, celebrity Mr. T. Since this is wrestling, a tag-team match was set up, and it would headline the first-ever *Wrestlemania*, live on closed-circuit TV all over North America from New York's Madison Square Garden. Hogan and T won that one, of course, and the event was a huge success, although had it not been one, the WWF would have gone bankrupt nearly on the spot.

1985 saw Hogan find yet another source of national exposure, as the WWF negotiated with NBC to air late-night wrestling specials on network TV, in place of weeks when a *Saturday Night Live* rerun would be aired. And so, May '85 saw the debut of *Saturday Night's Main*

Event (*SNME* for short from here on), with a main event of Hulk Hogan v. Bob Orton, a match that Hogan won without too much trouble. In fact, that was kind of a problem—there weren't any legitimate threats to Hogan's title at that point (outside of Piper, who even then was something of a clown to begin with), and so the WWF began a new formula for giving Hogan challengers, and it would make the WWF even more money than in previous years.

The first such attempt occurred on the March '86 *SNME*, as Hogan faced the Magnificent Muraco for the title. Hogan had things well in hand, when the mammoth King Kong Bundy ran in and hit Hogan with several of his "avalanche" splashes in the corner, "breaking" Hogan's ribs and forcing Hogan to be carried off on a stretcher. Not coincidentally, the WWF was in need of a main event for their upcoming sequel to *Wrestlemania*, the imaginatively titled *Wrestlemania 2*.

course of the past year, but Orndorff was starting to bore the fans as a virtuous babyface and look out of place toiling in the midcard. Hogan needed a new challenger, and Orndorff needed a new challenge, so the timing was perfect for everyone.

The setup was actually more soap-operatic than most of the story lines at the time, as Orndorff and Hogan engaged in a series of tag matches with the Bobby Heenan family, most notably Big John Studd and King Kong Bundy. Orndorff, in interviews to build up the feud, let it be known that he thought Hogan wasn't giving him enough credit as a member of the team, while Hogan told him that he was simply being paranoid. Things came to a head in May of '86 in the tag match setup, as Hogan & Orndorff took on Studd & Bundy on an episode of the WWF's syndicated program, *Superstars of Wrestling*.

Orndorff took a long beating in the match, refusing

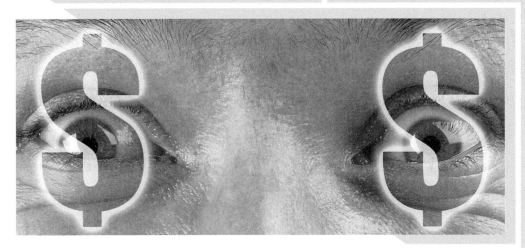

to tag Hogan in, until finally Hogan took matters into his own hands and brought himself in, getting the win for his team. The crowd was happy, but "Mr. Wonderful" was not, faking happiness for a minute before suddenly clotheslining Hogan

A cage match between Hogan and Bundy was signed, and Hogan won that one without breaking too much of a sweat, either.

So the formula was laid out: Evil heel lays out and injures Hogan, Hogan comes back and defeats him. Good enough. But something was missing, and once they found it, Hogan would draw millions more for the WWF. The answer was quite simple, really: Establish a friendship, and then violently destroy it.

Paul Orndorff, the spurned ex-partner of Roddy Piper, had joined into an alliance with Hogan in order to fight Piper and his bodyguard, Bob Orton, over the

out of nowhere and hitting him with his patented finisher, the piledriver. The crowd was in shock as Orndorff went back to the dressing room as the newest member of the Heenan Family and the newest challenger for Hogan's title.

You could almost see the little dollar-signs light up in Vince McMahon's eyes.

Hogan and Orndorff engaged in a seemingly endless series of matches, each one doing amazing business. Their first one was held in the CNE Stadium in Toronto, Ontario, with an attendance figure quoted by the WWF as 74,000. You may safely take any attendance figure quoted by any wrestling promotion with several grains of salt, but it was indeed an impressive number of people packed into the stadium. In that match, Hulk Hogan defeated Orndorff by a disqualification and a feud was born, as they sold out arenas all over the country, doing an absolutely mind-blowing run of shows that lasted nearly a year. The final culmination of the feud came on *Saturday Night's Main Event*, as Hogan defeated Orndorff in a controversial cage match that some still talk about today.

The finish was fairly unique, in fact: The standard object of a WWF cage match is to be the first person not to score a pinfall, but to simply exit the cage, either by going out the door or over the top. However, in this case, both men attempted to leave at the same time, and appeared to hit the floor simultaneously. It was ruled a tie, and Hogan went on to win by more mundane means and retain his title. Orndorff, as would be a trend for challengers to Hogan's throne, was actually left in a far worse position in the wrestling business than when he came in, and never again reached main event status.

But life continued in the WWF, and now something very big was on the horizon: *Wrestlemania III*, in the Pontiac Silverdome. In need of a main event to set attendance records and deliver the most bang for the viewer's pay-per-view dollar, Vince McMahon decided to take the now-established Hogan formula and take it up a notch.

And so, in December '86, Andre the Giant, Hogan's longtime partner and friend, appeared on a *Piper's Pit* interview segment, where WWF figurehead President Jack Tunney was to present him with a trophy for his long years of service with the WWF and devotion to the sport. Andre accepted happily. The next week, Andre was also present on that segment as Tunney presented Hogan with a bigger trophy for his three years as WWF champion, of which the easy-going Andre suddenly seemed a little upset about. His only

comment on the matter: "Three years is a long time." Hogan tried to find out what was wrong with Andre, but the only reply he got was a challenge from heel announcer Jesse Ventura to meet Andre in a debate the next week on *Piper's Pit*. Hogan accepted, but was shocked to see Andre standing not only with Ventura, but with Hogan's eternal nemesis, Bobby Heenan. Andre chided Hogan as though punishing a child, declaring that Hogan had been ducking him for three years and had never offered him a shot at the WWF title. Hogan protested that Andre had never asked, but it was too late to appease the giant, as Andre ripped the shirt, which was the ultimate symbol of Hulkamania, off Hogan's back, and the cross around his neck in the process. This was very heavy stuff for the time. The fans were shocked, and Hogan was left in tears. What else could they do but have a match?

And now in his glory, Vince McMahon unleashed a barrage of media coverage and hype for the third *Wrestlemania*, the likes of which had never been seen in wrestling before. A staggering number of households bought the PPV—nearly 10% of the available "universe." To put this in perspective, a PPV is considered an amazing success today if it does 1-2% of the available universe. The Silverdome was sold out—nearly 78,000 people, which magically became 93,173 in time for the media to report it as such, despite the Silverdome not actually being capable of holding that many people—and Hogan and Andre proceeded to engage in one of the worst-wrestled main events in the recorded history of wrestling.

It had the most amazing heat ever heard for a match, however, and ended with a stunning visual, as Hogan bodyslammed the 500-pound Andre and pinned him to retain the title. Revisionist history (a favorite of Vince McMahon) has since turned this match into the one where Andre "passed the torch" to Hogan, despite Andre's best days being 10 years behind him and Hogan having drawn millions on his own, with or without the benefit of Andre on the card. But it was historical enough on its own, even without the bogus significance.

This was truly the peak for professional wrestling to that point, and for the rest of the year it would end up being downhill. Hogan's final fate came a few years later, but until then, Hulkamania was running wild.

# "ROWDY" RODDY PIPER

The original hell-raising heel turned baby-kissing babyface, Piper was the thorn in Hogan's side for the Rock 'N' Wrestling years and made himself into a nationally known name by participating in the first ever *Wrestlemania* main event.

Born Roderick Toombs in April 1951 in Scotland, Piper moved to Winnipeg, Canada at a young age, where he pursued his dream to become a boxer. He actually won the Golden Gloves at age 15 before finding a calling more fitting to his off-the-wall sense of humor and manic demeanor: Pro wrestling. Starting at a young age in the smaller promotions of Canada, the newly renamed "Rodney Piper" (the silly-sounding Rodney was later miscalled as "Roddy" by an announcer and it stuck) quickly gained a reputation as someone who would do or say anything to get over.

His flamboyant style of dress, including traditional Scottish kilt, and obnoxious mannerisms annoyed fans everywhere to the point where he had death threats levied against him, and was actually stabbed on the way to the ring by a crazed fan in the early '80s. This terrified Piper, and he decided to try a new tactic in 1981 while working in the Georgia territories run by Ole Anderson. Piper at that point was a hated heel, with a

# SUPERSTAR STATS:

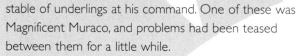

## "ROWDY" RODY PIPER

*Real name:* Roderick Toombs

*Height:* 6'2"

*Weight:* 235 lbs.

*Aliases:* Rodney Piper

men at the first ever *Starrcade* in November '83, the first acknowledged "supercard" for one of the major promotions. The two men were joined at the neck with dog-collars, which were then connected with a large chain. A huge amount of blood was spilled there, as Piper defeated Valentine in the non-title match. In fact, Piper lost much of the hearing in one ear as a direct result of that match.

However, all good things must come to an end, and in this case Piper's babyface run ended as Vince McMahon's rapidly expanding WWF came calling for him in 1984. There was, however, a slight problem. Piper was a popular babyface, but not nationally so and not massively so, both of which Hulk Hogan had covered well enough by himself. As a wrestler, Piper would be the first to admit that his specialty was more in the mid-level brawling area, and Vince didn't really need any more of those, which meant that Piper was stuck doing the one thing he could do better than anyone else in the WWF: Being an on-screen jerk.

And so *Piper's Pit* was reborn in '84, as Piper generally made an ass of himself and anyone else who wanted to risk going on the show. Notable segments included Piper interviewing his own favorite wrestler (himself, who else?) on a split screen, Piper interviewing

stable of underlings at his command. One of these was Magnificent Muraco, and problems had been teased between them for a little while.

During a broadcast where Piper was doing color commentary with main announcer Gordon Solie, Muraco came down to ringside and began harrassing the weakling Solie. When Muraco actually laid in a shot on him, Piper (who was evil but not a total scoundrel) suddenly jumped up to Solie's defense, laying a hellacious beating on Muraco and triggering a bloody feud between the two men. Piper was suddenly a top babyface, a position he enjoyed very much. This angle was actually re-enacted in August 2000 in the WWF as a tribute to the late Gordon Solie, using Jerry Lawler in Piper's role, and Tazz in Muraco's role.

Piper moved to the NWA in 1983, where he maintained his babyface status and engaged in a brutal feud with U.S. champion Greg Valentine, leading to a "dog-collar" match between the two

jobber Frankie Williams to give him a taste of fame (only to pound him into tiny pieces after a couple of minutes), and then one very famous interview that changed his career forever.

The point of *Piper's Pit* was for Piper to interview other heels and show them up, and on one of them he brought on a babyface for a change, in this case Jimmy "Superfly" Snuka. Rattled by Snuka's lack of English-speaking ability and general ignoring of Piper's insults, Piper snapped and smashed a coconut over Snuka's head, triggering an instant pull-apart brawl that destroyed the set of *Piper's Pit* and dragged Roddy, kicking and screaming, back into active competition as a wrestler in order to settle the feud.

Something interesting happened in that feud. Although Snuka had thoroughly beaten and bloodied Piper many times over by the time their feud was done in late '84, the fans came out of it perceiving Piper as the star, due to his weekly exposure on *Piper's Pit*, and the crowd reactions got louder and louder by the minute as Piper became more hated. Finally, Vince and the WWF decided to gamble and elevate Piper to main event status in the famous program with Hulk Hogan. To assist him, Piper was given a bodyguard in Cowboy Bob Orton and a major push to the top.

Piper and Paul Orndorff lost to Hogan and Mr. T at the first *Wrestlemania*, of course, and Piper split with Orndorff after that and they had a brief feud through 1985. Mr. T would return later in 1985 and engage Bob Orton in a series of forgettable boxing matches, one of which aired on *SNME*, which in turn led to a boxing match between Mr. T and Roddy Piper at *Wrestlemania 2*. The fixed nature of wrestling clashed with the whole purpose of boxing and the match was a wash, as Piper bodyslammed T to draw a DQ and lose.

Piper, seeing nothing in the near future worth his while, took some time off and decided to try acting. Hollywood recognized his charisma and cast him to play (what else) a wrestler in the movie *Body Slam*. The movie was a total bomb, but Piper's acting ability impressed critics—and fans. After taking six months off, Piper returned to the ring, getting something he hadn't heard in a while—cheers from the fans. Being Piper, he decided to return in style, defeating jobber AJ Petrucci on an episode of *Superstars* with one hand literally behind his back.

However, all was not as he'd left it. During his absence, *Piper's Pit* had been replaced with the *Flower Shop*, hosted by a stereotypical gay character named Adrian Adonis. Adonis (born Keith Franke) is actually an interesting case, as he spent much of his early career playing a "New York tough" street thug through the AWA and WWF, before suddenly gaining 100 pounds and becoming unmarketable in that persona. So the WWF decided to try a new gimmick with Adonis, turning him into a pink-wearing primadonna—like Gorgeous George but without the subtlety—in order to punish him for the massive weight gain. Adonis never recovered from the humiliation, and ended up dying on a lonely road in Canada in 1988 on the way to an independent show when the van he was riding in hit a patch of ice and fell off a cliff, killing all the passengers.

## "ROWDY" RODDY PIPER

**BIGGEST CONTRIBUTION**
Foil to Hulk Hogan and icon to many. Innovator of the "wrestling talk show segment" with *Piper's Pit*. General nuisance to all.

**BEST MATCH**
Probably something against Jimmy Snuka.

**BIGGEST MATCH**
Against Hulk Hogan on MTV, the so-called "War to Settle the Score," broadcast live in 1985, which in turn set up the first *Wrestlemania*.

**TRADEMARK MOVE**
Atomic Drop

**BIGGEST RIVAL**
Jimmy "Superfly" Snuka

At any rate, Piper had a verbal confrontation with former ally Adonis about getting his interview segment back from what he considered to be the disgraceful *Flower Shop*, and harsh words were exchanged. Piper was shocked to then learn that former bodyguard Bob Orton, and former underling Magnificent Muraco, were both now in the employ of Adonis. He was even more

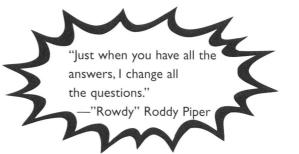

> "Just when you have all the answers, I change all the questions."
> —"Rowdy" Roddy Piper

shocked when all three of them brutally attacked him, broke his leg, and painted his face with makeup and lipstick to humiliate him.

This meant war.

The next week, Piper waited until Adonis was away from his interview set, before going ballistic with a baseball bat, smashing the set into pieces, and re-establishing *Piper's Pit* as the only interview segment on WWF programming. Piper was once again a huge babyface and now he had a new enemy: Adrian Adonis.

The two men had a series of inconclusive matches, until once again Hollywood came calling for Roddy—this time in the form of *Hell Comes to Frogtown*, a sci-fi movie. And so a "retirement" match was signed for *Wrestlemania III*, between Piper and Adonis. Adonis wanted another stipulation: Loser gets his head shaved.

Before that show, however, the men participated in a six-man tag match that had an interesting side effect. It was Adonis and the hated heel tag team of Greg Valentine and Brutus Beefcake against Piper and the British Bulldogs, and during the course of that match,

Adonis decided to give Piper a sneak preview by snipping off some of his hair. However, he accidentally cut the hair of ultra-vain Brutus Beefcake, who was noticeably upset with Adonis. And so at *Wrestlemania III*, Piper and Adonis had their blowoff match, which saw Adonis get the upper hand, locking on his sleeper hold until Piper passed out. However, Adonis released the hold too soon, allowing time for Brutus Beefcake (recently estranged from his tag partner) to run in and revive Piper, in turn allowing Piper to sneak up on Adonis and put him out with his own sleeper, for the win.

Beefcake did the honors of shaving Adonis's head, which turned Brutus into Brutus "The Barber" Beefcake, by far the most successful and long-lasting gimmick he would ever have. Although by nature of being Hulk Hogan's best friend, he would later cycle through more of them, including Brother Bruti, The Butcher, The Man with No Name, The Man with No Face, The Zodiac Man, The Booty Man, The Disciple, and finally back to Brutus Beefcake, none of them drawing a dime for WCW, the company that tried them all.

Piper then settled into retirement, from which he would emerge and retire again in 1989, 1990, 1991, 1992, 1994, 1996, 1997, 1998, and one last time in 1999 for old time's sake.

## "MACHO MAN" RANDY SAVAGE

Whereas Piper was the comic relief version of Hogan's rogues' gallery, Randy Savage was the psychotic loner who scared little kids and destroyed everything that got in his way.

Born Randy Poffo, November 1952, Randy Savage is the son of legendary old-time wrestler Angelo Poffo and brother of not-so-legendary poet laureate/wrestler "Leaping" Lanny Poffo. As with many of the people listed in this book, Savage's first career and goal was not to become a wrestler. In fact, Savage began his athletic career as a baseball catcher, playing with the Cincinnati Reds, St. Louis Cardinals, and Chicago White Sox during the '70s until a serious knee injury prevented him from doing the necessary squatting required to catch. So destiny interceded and his father trained him to do what he knew best: Wrestle.

Randy Poffo and brother Lanny debuted together in Memphis in 1973, impressing no one for the most part. Randy decided to distinguish himself from his family, taking on a more savage, brawling style of wrestling as opposed to an athletic, technical one. After one match with Ole Anderson, Ole quipped that the newcomer should be named "Randy Savage," and the new name was born. Savage traveled around the southern states, mainly staying in Tennessee, and doing battle with Jerry Lawler off and on until the early '80s, at which point he married business manager and love interest Elizabeth Hewlett, aka Miss Elizabeth. Seeing money in the duo, Vince McMahon signed both of them for the expanding WWF in 1985, and Savage's intital entrance involved him teasing several different choices as manager before rejecting all of them in favor of Miss Elizabeth. An instant chemistry existed on-screen between them, as Savage honed his "misogynist with a heart of gold" act, brutally attacking his opponents and treating Elizabeth like dirt, but acting fiercely protective of her should anyone else attempt to mistreat her.

Savage was an instant sensation in every sense of the word, rocketing up the card faster than the WWF could push him as the bloodthirsty fans in the audiences related to Savage's take-no-prisoners attitude and awesome finisher: the flying elbow smash from the top rope. Indeed, in some circles, Savage's popularity rivaled that of Hulk Hogan's—certainly no mean feat. In order to delay the inevitable meeting between the two (and to give them time to build a room large enough to hold all the money), the WWF instead re-routed Savage into a feud with recently turned babyface George "The Animal" Steele—he of the confused expression, green tongue, and turnbuckle-laden diet.

The story was as simple as Steele's character: Savage treated Liz like dirt and Steele was in love with her. Savage didn't appreciate that, and set out to destroy Steele at every opportunity. Along the way, Savage was featured in the *Wrestling Classic*, the first actual pay-per-view event for the WWF, as he wrestled four matches on the night in a tournament (defeating Ivan Putski, Ricky Steamboat, and Dynamite Kid, then losing to Junkyard Dog in the finals), and stole the show.

> "Dig it!"
> —"Macho Man" Randy Savage

By 1986, Savage's following was growing exponentially, and the WWF put the Intercontinental title on him in February of that year, as Savage defeated longtime champion Tito Santana in Boston with a foreign object. Savage disposed of George Steele in a mere formality at *Wrestlemania 2* to defend that title, and then the inevitable could no longer be stopped: Hulk Hogan v. Randy Savage was signed for Madison Square Garden shortly after that show, and the tickets sold out so fast that the WWF had to erect a TV screen in The Paramount Theatre, underneath The Garden, for closed circuit, packing another 5,000 or so people into that building in record time as well.

To top it off, Savage and Hogan proceeded to have a wild brawl, ending with Savage winning the title, only to see the decision overturned and Hogan come back to retain it in an exciting finish to the blood-soaked classic. The program was so great and drew so much money that the WWF put the feud on the shelf for three years, deciding instead to save it for something truly special. Instead, they gave Savage something else to sink his teeth into.

Savage was truly a fighting champion, defending his Intercontinental title against nearly anyone who signed on, including ex-champ Tito Santana, Jake Roberts, Billy Jack Haynes, and eventually Ricky "The Dragon" Steamboat.

An excellent wrestler, Steamboat was another NWA import from '84, who was somewhat over as a babyface but having trouble finding his niche in the muscle-oriented WWF. So it was decided that a sympathy angle might work, and in late '86, Steamboat challenged Savage for

the title on an episode of WWF *Supstars of Wrestling*. They engaged in a good TV match for the first few minutes, until Steamboat started to get uncomfortably close to winning for Savage's taste. Savage bumped the ref and tossed Steamboat out to the railing, draping his throat over the steel barricade and then dropping his patented double axehandle-blow from the top rope to Steamboat's neck, crushing his throat on the railing.

Steamboat did a superb job of selling the injury, convincing everyone in the audience that he was seriously injured. So Savage decided to really give them their money's worth, rolling Steamboat back in, then grabbing the bell

from ringside and jumping off the top with it, smashing it into Steamboat's injured throat and sending the crowd into shock.

Don't worry, it was all fake. Steamboat's wife Bonnie wanted a baby and Steamboat wanted a few weeks off to make one, so the WWF obliged and wrote the injury story line for him. There was one "real" twist in the story, however. As the dramatically twitching and thrashing Steamboat was being wheeled back to the dressing room on a stretcher, he accidentally kicked a fan in the head, costing the WWF a six-figure lawsuit and some bad PR.

Savage headed backstage to be interviewed by legend-turned-broadcaster Bruno Sammartino, which produced another twist in the story right off the bat, as Savage's arrogant celebrating of the injury caused Sammartino to fly into a rage and attack the Macho Man. Sammartino and Savage would have a series of house show matches over the next few weeks (which served to give Savage "the rub" from the elder, but still popular, Sammartino, and make him into a bona fide superstar) while Steamboat

# WRESTLER SPOTLIGHT

## "MACHO MAN" RANDY SAVAGE

### BIGGEST CONTRIBUTION
Sold out arenas around the country fighting Hogan; co-headlined *Wrestlemania III* against Ricky Steamboat.

### BEST MATCH
Against Ricky Steamboat at *Wrestlemania III*, which became the defining match of the era and a true show-stealer in every sense of the word. A true ***** classic.

### BIGGEST MATCH
Defeating Ted Dibiase for the WWF World title in the main event of *Wrestlemania IV* and solidifying his role as a top babyface.

### BIGGEST RIVALS
Heated feuds with both Ricky Steamboat and Hulk Hogan.

during a match with George Steele, and the title match was officially announced for *Wrestlemania*. Steamboat and Savage did a series of house show matches leading up to *Wrestlemania*, with Steamboat "losing his temper" and getting disqualified in all of them. The real purpose of the matches was to test out the individual parts of the big match and hone each one to a fine point. And when the time came to perform, the combatants were delivering the Match of the Year (and the decade, some say), as Steamboat pinned Savage to win the title after 15 minutes of non-stop action by reversing a simple slam into a rollup. One person, however, was not happy about the match:

Hulk Hogan.

Hogan, unhappy about being upstaged by workers he considered midcarders, used his clout to bury Savage in a losing streak for months after that show. But Hogan's actions had an unexpected side effect!
Savage, generally the most hated heel in the WWF, was stuck in a humiliating feud with fluke Intercontinental champion The Honky Tonk Man in a quest to regain that title. However, Honky wasn't just one of the most hated heels in the WWF, he was by far the most despised person in all of wrestling at that time.

"Ooooooh yeah!"
—"Macho Man" Randy Savage

and Bonnie made babies. Meanwhile, Savage and Steamboat knew their big rematch for the title was going to be at *Wrestlemania III*, so they began planning out the match move-by-move over the course of the three months they had to build up to it.

Steamboat made a dramatic return to the WWF on a *Saturday Night's Main Event*, distracting Savage

Compared to Honky Tonk, a bloodthirsty and mentally unstable psychopath like Randy Savage was a breath of fresh air, and so the fans began cheering Savage, despite the lack of an actual babyface turn for him. Further, the more cheers Savage got, the more people paid to watch him chase Honky Tonk's title, and the more money the WWF made off him. Later in 1987, Hogan decided to take time off to film a movie, and the WWF needed a new main event babyface to fill the void, and Savage was the logical candidate. And so Randy Savage was put into a main event match against One Man Gang on a house show and given the blessing of Hulk Hogan before that match.

One month later, Savage met Honky Tonk Man again, on *Saturday Night's Main Event*, now firmly into the babyface role without ever making an official turn. Honky's allies, the Hart Foundation—Brett "the Hitman" Hart and Jim "the Anvil" Neidhart—stormed the ring and pounded on Savage for the DQ, until Elizabeth came in to plead for mercy. The cowardly Honky Tonk shoved her to the mat, and she ran to the back for help as the beating continued. She emerged shortly after, followed by Hulk Hogan, as the fans erupted. Hogan ran off the heels, and in one of the more famous moments in WWF history, offered a hand of friendship (because while heels have allies, babyfaces have friends) to Savage, and the Megapowers were thus born. In reality, Hogan saw Savage's star rising rapidly and wanted a piece of the action, but bigger plans were afoot for the team.

Savage, now a full-fledged babyface, continued his chase of the Honky Tonk Man, leading to a final showdown with him on the *Main Event*, the first-ever prime-time WWF special on NBC—a showdown that would alter the course of the WWF's financial destiny for years to follow.

# THE BRITISH BULLDOGS

David "Davey Boy" Smith and Tom "Dynamite Kid" Billington both got their start in North America as a part of Stu Hart's Stampede Wrestling in Calgary, in the early '80s. Something that newer fans would probably be shocked to see is a tape of the early stuff featuring the two men, each weighing no more than about 150 pounds, at most. As with many of the teams widely recognized as great, Davey Boy Smith and the Dynamite Kid started their tenure as bitter rivals— Dynamite the cocky heel and Davey Boy the sympathetic babyface.

Tom Billington, born December 1958, and raised in the slums of England, got his start in wrestling as a teenager doing underground wrestling matches for small paydays. Dynamite was always very sure of his career as a wrestler, and it showed in his spectacular matches and willingness to take any risk to get over. After winning several mid-heavyweight titles in his home country, he met Bruce Hart in 1978 and impressed him so much that Hart decided to recruit him for his father's Stampede Wrestling in Canada, long regarded as one of the highest-quality promotions in terms of "real" wrestling action.

The Kid spent five years there, amazing audiences with his suicidal bumps. Example: Bruce Hart is out on the concrete floor, and Dynamite comes off the top rope with a headbutt attempt that misses. He lands face-first on the concrete with no protection, then proceeds to repeat that same spot night after night on a tour of small towns in Alberta. The one thing that held back the Kid was his lack of size, which he unfortunately attempted to compensate for by bulking up with anabolic steroids. He also began using drugs regularly to ease the pain that his bumping caused him. While it temporarily allowed him to continue his high-energy style in the short term, later on it would cost him dearly.

The Kid departed for a tour of Japan in 1979, and soon began a series of matches in New Japan with another up-and-coming superstar: Satoru Sayama, who wrestled as the first Tiger Mask. Fans today who are accustomed to seeing the lighter wrestlers flying around the ring might not realize that the style simply didn't exist before these two essentially invented it as they went along. The Kid and Tiger Mask thrilled audiences with their matches for the NJPW junior heavyweight title, until finally Dynamite returned to Stampede to a new international reputation.

In 1982, Davey Boy Smith came along for the ride. Billington's younger cousin (born November '62) and another British import for Stampede, Smith was less of a sensation than the Kid, choosing a more conservative style within the light heavyweight division. Soon the two men had matched up as bitter enemies, with Dynamite playing the heel. This proved to be successful enough in elevating Dynamite (in addition to his rapdily increasing size) that he was given a run as North American champion before beginning a team with Davey Boy Smith. Dynamite convinced him to bulk up as well, and soon the newly named British Bulldogs were dominating Stampede.

All-Japan Pro Wrestling quickly saw their potential and convinced them to return to Japan as a regular team, where they worked out their incredible timing and double-teams before returning to the States upon getting another offer.

Much like many of the other stars of the Rock 'N' Wrestling era, the Bulldogs were signed by the WWF in 1985 in an effort to massively expand the roster, and were intended to be used as special attractions due to their lack of size. However, two factors reversed this decision:

1) The Bulldogs were now heavily on steroids and wrestlers in The States had access to a huge supply of them.

2) The Bulldogs did things that no one had ever seen before, anywhere, and as a result the fans began doing something that WWF fans didn't traditionally do—react to the in-ring performance rather than the pre-made personality of the wrestler.

The Bulldogs' amazing moves electrified audiences everywhere. On many occasions, while wrestling jobbers, Smith would powerslam one of them, then put another over his shoulders. The Kid would climb to the top rope, jump onto the poor guy still sitting on Smith's shoulders, and hit a diving headbutt from that position onto the guy who just got powerslammed. The crowds went crazy for stuff like this, and the Bulldogs obliged by doing more and more of it every night, all the while not needing to cut a single interview. Dynamite Kid raised some eyebrows by being booked in the *Wrestling Classic* tournament and doing three matches in one night, going over Nikolai Volkoff and Adrian Adonis before bowing out to Randy Savage in the semifinals. Davey Boy was also entered, doing an injury angle in the first round to explain his early exit to Ricky Steamboat.

The Bulldogs, after disposing of early rivals in the Hart Foundation (fellow Stampede alumni Bret Hart & Jim Neidhart) were given a title shot at the tag champs, Greg Valentine & Brutus Beefcake. Despite Valentine's best efforts to carry his tag-team partner on his back, the pairing with Valentine was mainly a star vehicle for Hulk Hogan's friend Beefcake, and the match quality suffered as a result. The Bulldogs gave Valentine/Beefcake some much-needed hot matches to wow the crowd and, more importantly, gave them credibility as champions, something that had been sorely missing. The Bulldogs then began a lengthy chase of the tag titles.

Finally, figuring that more money could be made with the Bulldogs as

champions, the WWF gave the Bulldogs a manager—in Captain Lou Albano—to cut promos for them, and put them over Valentine & Beefcake for the titles at *Wrestlemania 2* in what was generally considered the best match of the show. To give the team an additional bit of star power, rocker (and native Brit) Ozzy Osbourne was in their corner. Although he didn't figure into the match, Ozzy's appearance endorsed the Bulldogs as champions. Sadly, this match would prove to be the Bulldogs' peak in the WWF as a team.

The Bulldogs held the tag title for nine months, a very healthy reign, and spent the majority of the time defending it against old rivals like the Hart Foundation and the Dream Team (Valentine and Beefcake). However, tragedy struck the duo as 1986 drew to a close: During a match with Magnificent Muraco & Bob Orton, the Kid attempted a hiptoss on Muraco, only to feel his back give way. The problem, it seemed, was that years of steroid abuse had deteriorated the Kid's back to the point where he shouldn't even have been able to walk. However, the other drugs that Kid took for everyday painkilling blocked the back problems from him so effectively that he was in traction by the time he realized the severity of them.

OZZY

The situation worked out somewhat well for the WWF, as the huge number of babyface teams working in the promotion at the time (Killer Bees, Can-Am Connection, and the Islanders) meant that a strong heel champion in the tag division was preferred anyway. So in January 1987, Dynamite was literally dragged out of his hospital bed and ordered to defend the tag belts in Tampa, Florida, against the Hart Foundation for a TV taping. Dynamite couldn't walk, so Davey Boy piggy-backed him on his shoulders to the ring and helped him to stand on the apron long enough for the heels to "knock him off" and allow him to rest on the floor. Davey Boy then wrestled the entire match alone and lost the titles, to the heel. He was finally "fired" before a match on national TV and "suspended for life" from refereeing (life, of course, being until 1989, in this case), thus giving him the shot he needed to become a real wrestler.

The six-man was, not surprisingly, a very good match, featuring Davis getting the living daylights beaten out of him by the Bulldogs and Santana before heel tactics on the part of the Harts allowed Davis to nail Davey Boy with manager Jimmy Hart's ever-present megaphone and get the upset pin. This pretty much put the final touches on the Harts-Bulldogs feud, as Dynamite Kid took some much-needed time off, before getting bored and reforming the team again in November of 1987.

However, with Lou Albano having left the promotion and Dynamite Kid wrestling as a shadow of his former self, the WWF felt they needed something to distinguish them as a tag team. So they gave the Bulldogs a bulldog. Named Mathilda, the WWF immediately went in the direction that everyone feared and had a heel team kidnap the "beloved" dog so the Bulldogs could seek revenge. In this case, it was the newly heel Islanders who did the evil deed, and it led to a six-man match at *Wrestlemania IV* with the Bulldogs and Koko B. Ware taking on The Islanders and evil manager Bobby Heenan. Amazingly, the WWF went with almost exactly the same booking as the year previous, as Heenan scored the upset win with the help of nefarious heel tactics. The move didn't help elevate the Islanders, and team leader Haku soon split off on a solo career.

The Bulldogs got into a feud with hot tag champs Demolition, which was comprised of wrestlers Ax and Smash, as 1988 dragged on for them, but were never in serious consideration to actually win them, merely being used to give the champs the rub they were lacking. The Bulldogs continued their descent down the card, doing the opening match with the Rougeaus at the first *Summerslam* in '88, then closing out their WWF career by quietly losing out in the tag-team elimination match at *Survivor Series '88*. Dynamite Kid

shock of the fans. The whole thing took 90 seconds total, if that. Dynamite returned to the hospital, where the doctors informed him that he would never wrestle again.

But Dynamite Kid was nothing if not stubborn, and only two months later he was back in the ring. After wrestling the Hart Foundation in a memorable 2-of-3 falls rematch on an episode of *SNME*, a six-man was signed for *Wrestlemania III* with the Bulldogs and Tito Santana against the Hart Foundation and evil referee Danny Davis. The story with Davis was fairly straightforward: He was a middling wrestler with little talent who was forced to go into refereeing, but he still wanted to wrestle. So a story line was created where Davis would start being biased toward heels, leading up to him "screwing" the Bulldogs out of the tag title by ignoring all of the Hart Foundation's cheating.

It was later established that Davis had been biased when refereeing the match that put the Intercontinental title on Randy Savage, thus giving wronged ex-champion Tito Santana a reason to hate him too. And make no mistake, Davis was amazingly over as a

was rapidly falling apart physically, and the relationship between the personable Smith and the injury-ridden Kid fell apart with it.

# WRESTLER SPOTLIGHT

## THE BRITISH BULLDOGS

### BIGGEST CONTRIBUTION
Introduced the Japanese high-flying style to U.S. audiences, while the Bulldogs' jaw-dropping double-team moves influenced teams for years to come.

### BEST MATCH
Sadly, the Bulldogs never had a truly great breakout match on a nationally televised show, although they did have some amazing matches with Greg Valentine & Brutus Beefcake (including the best match of *Wrestlemania 2*), and later some epic battles against the Hart Foundation (which were weighed down by Dynamite's injuries).

### BIGGEST MATCH
Defeating the Dream Team at *Wrestlemania 2* for the tag titles and stealing the show in the process.

### BIGGEST RIVALS
Too close to call between the Dream Team and the Hart Foundation

## SUPERSTAR STATS:

**Dynamite Kid**
*Real name:* Tom Billington
*Height:* 5'8"
*Weight:* 228 lbs.
*Aliases:* None

The Bulldogs made one last try to salvage things by returning to their roots in Stampede Wrestling. They won the International tag team titles from Makhan and Vokhan Singh, and things seemed better between them. But now, without the money from the WWF coming in, they were fighting constantly in real life. Stampede tried to salvage the situation as best they could by turning Dynamite into a heel and setting up a match between them, but before that could happen Davey Boy was seriously injured in a car accident. Dynamite Kid and new partner Johnny Smith (either the cousin or brother of Davey Boy depending on who tells the story) left for All-Japan while Davey Boy went solo upon his return.

Davey Boy eventually returned to the WWF under the British Bulldog name and forged a successful singles career; Dynamite's injuries proved too much to overcome, and he broke down completely mere weeks into the Japan tour. After several abortive attempts at a comeback years later, he retired completely and today is confined to a wheelchair as a result of his injuries. His legend, however, lives on in Japan to this day.

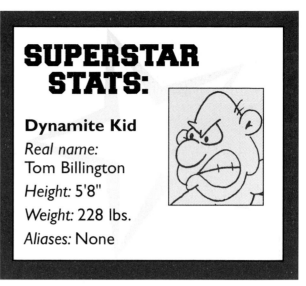

# THE HONKY TONK MAN

Born Wayne Ferris in January 1953, Honky Tonk first broke into the sport in Memphis, with the help of cousin Jerry "The King" Lawler, reigning deity of that territory. His image was one that would be unfamiliar to people who would watch him later: He sported long blond hair and had a Hollywood sensibility as part of a team called the "Blond Bombers" with partner Larry Latham. Ferris' biggest contribution to the wrestling scene at that point was his participation in the famous "Tupelo Concession Stand Brawl," as the Bombers and the team of Lawler & Bill Dundee engaged in a wild and chaotic battle on live TV that ended up literally in the stands, and into an unsuspecting concession stand.

Ferris left Memphis for Stampede Wrestling in the early '80s to try an entirely different gimmick. Dyeing his hair back to its original jet black, Ferris combed it into a pompadour, à la Elvis Presley and began playing up his southern roots, calling himself "Honky Tonk" Wayne Ferris, and then Honky Tonk Wayne. Surprisingly effective as a singles competitor, Honky Tonk Wayne captured the North American title in 1986 (the top title in the promotion) and held it for two months before the WWF noticed his unique gimmick and obnoxious personality and made him an offer.

Renamed the Honky Tonk Man, he vacated the North American title and immediately left for the WWF. For reasons never adequately understood by anyone in the business, the WWF felt that Honky Tonk Man had appeal as a babyface, despite there being zero evidence to prove it. And so, in September of '86, the flamboyantly dressed Honky Tonk Man appeared in a series of pre-taped interviews claiming to be a friend of Hulk Hogan's, and letting the fans know how much he loved them all.

No one bought it.

Maybe it was because Hogan never actually said that he'd endorsed Honky Tonk, or maybe it was because Ferris was just so naturally obnoxious, but for whatever reason The Honky Tonk Man's initial tour of the house show circuit saw him meet with resounding boos. But all was not lost, because fans' boos are just as desirable as cheers—it's the silence that kills wrestling careers. All that was required was a change of perspective, so the WWF ran an angle whereby Honky Tonk decided to run a "poll" of fans to determine whether they wanted him in the WWF after all. The results were roughly two-thirds against him. The week that the results were announced, Honky Tonk cut a bitter promo against the fans, declaring that he was sick of kissing babies, and that longtime heel manager Jimmy Hart would now guide his career, as "Colonel Jimmy Hart," clearly a spoof on Elvis' right hand man, Colonel Tom Parker.

The effect was dramatic: Honky was instantly booed out of the building now that fans were "free" to do just that (as opposed to playing along with the babyface image built by the WWF), and the WWF began the slow process of elevating him up the card.

The major problem, however, was credibility—

Honky Tonk had none. His major ticket to heel heat was his deliberately bad Elvis impersonation and tendency to never shut up, ever! Before matches, after matches, DURING matches, during interview segments, during other people's interview segments—Honky had an unlimited stream of banter about how great he was and it never ceased. In the ring, however, he was regarded by smarts and marks alike as a boring wrestler with a limited moveset and a lame finisher (a swinging neckbreaker) who was unlikely to give anyone a run for their money. Obviously something drastic was needed.

And so, after blindsiding Jake "The Snake" Roberts with a guitar to the head early in 1987 and turning the Snake babyface in the process, Honky was given his biggest win ever, upsetting Roberts at *Wrestlemania III* to the shock of millions. There was no method to the madness—the WWF simply wanted to put more heat on Honky Tonk and solidify Roberts's sympathetic babyface status. However, two months later, something interesting happened.

Intercontinental champion Ricky Steamboat, fresh off defeating Randy Savage for the title at *Wrestlemania III*, was looking for a few weeks off to help his wife tend to their new baby. Vince McMahon gave it to him, along with another six weeks to show him exactly who was boss, and didn't pay him for it. Steamboat was also informed before a TV taping that he would be dropping his newly won title to "The Natural" Butch Reed that night in an effort to get Reed over with his "black man with blond hair" gimmick that was supposed to draw huge money for the WWF.

Sadly, the world was deprived of "Intercontinental champion Butch Reed" that night, because Reed no-showed and was fired soon after. Honky Tonk Man, feeling confident after getting monster heat by beating Jake Roberts, quickly talked the WWF bookers into giving him a run with the belt instead as a fluke champion. They agreed, and Honky upset Steamboat in a surprisingly decent match with a horribly convoluted finish: Both men rolled around in the corner on a roll-up attempt by Steamboat, ending with Honky getting the eventual pin on what appeared to be only a two count. Steamboat left on his vacation, and Honky was immediately inserted into a series of matches with rival Jake Roberts for the title.

The assumption was that beating Honky was merely a formality for Roberts, and indeed the matches that resulted were completely one-sided, with Honky getting no offense and taking a hellacious beating for about five minutes, before simply walking out of the match and taking the countout loss.

"Okay," the fans collectively thought, "he got lucky that time, but next time he's screwed." And when the WWF realized that mentality was out there from the fans, they knew exactly what to do about it: prolong the process.

The next step was to announce a series of matches where there were no countouts allowed. Honky added to his cheap finish repertoire by attacking the referee to draw a disqualification. By now, fans were becoming incredibly annoyed with his antics and started putting down more and more money to watch him "get his," which ironically ensured that it would be longer before he got it.

When they finally advanced to the stage where Honky would cheat and get a pinfall victory to retain his title, he had been champion for longer than Steamboat, and had managed to piss off nearly everyone in the northern hemisphere. Management then decided to take the heat off him and have him lose to satisfy the fans. And so a program with a somewhat demoted Randy Savage was started in September 1987, with Honky's astounding title reign at 6 months and counting. The motivation for Savage was simple: He had been removed from "his" title and wanted it back.

The progression of finishes was the same as before, with Savage destroying Honky in their initial series of matches, only to see Honky walk out late in the match and get counted out. Then, on an edition of *Saturday Night's Main Event*, a match with Savage that ended in a disqualification triggered the formation of the Megapowers and Savage becamed a full-fledged babyface. The matches between Savage and Honky became even more one-sided, as Savage would quickly wipe the mat with Honky and Honky would get himself disqualified, sometimes in under two minutes. Finally, as 1988 began, it was decided that enough was enough and they needed to take the title off Honky and let Savage have it again.

And then came the moment that altered the financial destiny of the WWF from that point forever. The fateful match with Savage was to be broadcast on the *Main Event*, the first prime time wrestling special since the '50s. It was live and expected to draw an audience on par with most major sitcoms. Sensing the tension everyone was feeling, Honky Tonk went to Vince McMahon before the show and made what could have been considered either an incredibly bold or an incredibly stupid move: He threatened to go against the planned finish in the match, and then show up on WWF rival Jim Crockett's TV show with the belt that weekend if he wasn't allowed to keep the title.

Suddenly, everything was thrown into disarray. Even

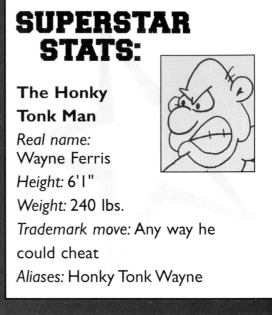

## SUPERSTAR STATS:

**The Honky Tonk Man**
*Real name:* Wayne Ferris
*Height:* 6'1"
*Weight:* 240 lbs.
*Trademark move:* Any way he could cheat
*Aliases:* Honky Tonk Wayne

though it was probably an empty threat, Vince couldn't take that chance with something as huge as that show, and he gave into Honky's demands, changing the finish

"These people came to see the Honky Tonk Man sing!"
—The Honky Tonk Man

from Savage getting a pinfall win to Savage winning by countout, which would thus keep the title on Honky Tonk Man. However, this had larger repercussions than that one match. The big plan for the upcoming *Wrestlemania IV* was a tournament for the WWF title, which was to be won by Ted Dibiase in an effort to legitimize him as a main event heel and build to a Dibiase-Hogan match at the first-ever *Summerslam* PPV. However, in order to appease Savage, who was made to look weak in front of tens of millions of people ("He couldn't even beat Honky Tonk Man?"), the WWF decided to go with a new gameplan and put the World title on Randy Savage instead at that show and build to a Hogan-Savage match for the next year.

Honky was put into a feud with Hogan's friend Brutus Beefcake and fought him for the title at *Wrestlemania IV*, with the usual finish resulting. However, it was obvious that the end of Honky's reign was nearing. The finishes were becoming more involved, more people were having to run in, and Honky was generally losing his heat. However, the main reason was simpler: With a title reign of 14 months and counting, he was now the longest-reigning Intercontinental champion in the history of the promotion, a feat which has yet to be topped and likely never will. But whereas with almost anyone else credibility is a good thing, with Honky it had become a detriment.

The basic idea behind his insanely long title reign is that fans were to believe that he could lose the title on any given night, but now they were conditioned to instinctively know that the end wasn't going to come in their hometown, because surely it would have happened by now. The money stopped coming as the fans no longer bought the basic concept behind the Honky Tonk Man character, and soon the title matches were reduced to comedy matches with Brutus Beefcake and the title was an afterthought. This was clearly a waste of the title, and with the first-ever *Summerslam* PPV approaching in August '88, a change was needed.

Honky was set to defend his title on that show, and the general feeling was that whoever got the shot, it was over for the Honky Tonk Man's title reign, now at 18 months and clearly 6 months too long. The slot was given to Brutus Beefcake, but fan reaction to yet another Beefcake-Honky match (after months of Brutus being unsuccessful in his chase) was lukewarm to say the least. So instead the WWF decided to go with a more satisfying and spectacular finish to the Honky Tonk Man saga.

On the last TV show before *Summerslam*, the stale Beefcake was suddenly attacked by "Outlaw" Ron Bass, and "injured" by him with a pair of spurs, so badly that when *Summerslam* began, it was announced that Beefcake would not be there to compete for the title. Honky, ever confident despite being hopelessly overmatched in every situation, calmly grabbed the microphone and issued an open challenge to anyone in the dressing room to come beat him for the title.

The result of that challenge was hardly a secret to anyone with access to "insider" newsletters. Back in the '80s, the WWF produced two hours of syndicated programming a week, in the form of *WWF Superstars of Wrestling* and *WWF Wrestling Challenge*. These shows generally consisted of one or two notable happenings, and five or six squash matches with the pushed stars destroying jobbers in short order to showcase their finisher or work out new characters or whatever. Because no one in their right mind would pay to see a one-hour live show consisting of just that, the WWF taped four hours of programming at a time, to be split up over a given month. In the days before well-coordinated PPV and TV, the placement of the tapings during the year was fairly arbitrary.

In the case of *Summerslam*, the schedule was that the first week of the "fresh" tapings would air before the show, and the following three weeks would air after the show. This made for a somewhat sticky situation, because Honky was to drop the title at *Summerslam*, but also had to appear on three weeks' worth of matches following that, all of which were to be taped before he lost the title. Ditto for the new champion, who had to appear without the title in the week before *Summerslam*, but with the title afterwards. Aren't you glad you weren't the guy who had to keep track of this stuff?

In order to explain this to the fans in attendance at the TV taping, Honky Tonk Man threw out an open challenge to anyone in the back at the start of the evening, which was answered by the Ultimate Warrior, Vince McMahon's new golden boy. Warrior destroyed Honky and took the title belt, but WWF President Jack Tunney quickly declared that it wasn't a real title match and Warrior had the belt illegally. Warrior did another three matches wearing the belt, and Honky stole his belt back at the end of the evening.

So quite a few people were in the know about the situation when Ultimate Warrior once again answered Honky's open challenge at *Summerslam*, and this time it was a real title match. Warrior went through his entire set of moves (three clotheslines, a bodyslam, and a big splash) in a 30-second slaughter of Honky Tonk Man to win the title, and the crowd exploded in relief after 18 months of listening to Honky Tonk Man sing and cheat his way to victory.

Honky's brush with fame proved to be indeed a fluke, as his stock fell rapidly in the WWF following that loss. Before he could be rebuilt, he first had to repay all the victories he held over people in the last 18 months, and he did so with gusto, dropping completely clean pinfall losses to everyone in the WWF. After six months of this, however, with still more people wanting to go over Honky, the credibility was gone, and Honky was regarded as little more than a comedy figure. A tag team with Greg Valentine helped somewhat, but Honky was never again to achieve the heights of notoriety he rose to during his glory days as the "greatest Intercontinental champion of all time—thank you, thank you very much."

# WRESTLER SPOTLIGHT

## THE HONKY TONK MAN

### BIGGEST CONTRIBUTION
Defined the cowardly heel act that Hulk Hogan later used as Hollywood Hogan.

### BEST MATCH
Getting squashed in 30 seconds by the Ultimate Warrior at Summerslam '88. A terrible match, to be sure, but it sticks in the minds of everyone who had to put up with his nonsense for 18 months leading up to it.

### BIGGEST MATCH
Defeating Ricky Steamboat to win the title 18 months previous to the above match.

### BIGGEST RIVAL
Randy "Macho Man" Savage.

# TED DIBIASE

Hand-picked by Vince McMahon to play the wrestling equivalent of himself, Dibiase shot to the top of the heel ranks in the late '80s by becoming scummier than anyone else in the promotion, and he helped keep the WWF alive during tough times. It's somewhat fitting, and ironic at the same time, that this ultimate representation of capitalism would signal the end of the WWF's first big financial run.

Born in January 1953, Dibiase was another future wrestler influenced by family, in this case his stepfather,

> "Everyone's got a price for the Million Dollar Man!"
> —Ted Dibiase

"Iron" Mike Dibiase. Mike Dibiase died of a heart attack in the ring when Ted was 15, prompting Ted to start in wrestling himself as a tribute to his late father. Soon, however, it became apparent that the younger Dibiase was even more talented at his chosen craft than the man who inspired him.

Ted Dibiase spent much of his early years wrestling in the southern states promotions, including Georgia and Tennessee. His most famous angle in wrestling involved the mysterious "Mr. R." Ted Dibiase had beaten Tommy Rich in a "loser leaves town" match, then a mysterious stranger appeared, calling himself "Mr. R." This was obviously Tommy Rich under a mask, but of course the only person in the promotion not to be in on the joke

was Dibiase. A frustrated Dibiase put his Georgia National title against Mr. R in the big payoff match—and lost when Tommy Rich came to ringside to cheer Mr. R on, distracting Dibiase long enough to be rolled up and pinned. A confused and angry Dibiase unmasked Mr. R as Brad Armstrong. Curses, foiled again. This sort of angle would go on to happen again several times over the years in other promotions, but this one was considered the prototype for them all.

Dibiase was to achieve his most noteworthy successes in Bill Watts's Mid-South promotion, however, with the "Rat Pack" trio of Dibiase, Jim Duggan, and Steve "Dr. Death" Williams. Dibiase was one of the top heels, and his gimmick was to pull a loaded black glove out of his tights and hit his opponent with a punch for the victory. What he could possibly load the glove with that was enough to secure a knockout and still fit in his tights is a mystery still unsolved to this day.

By 1986, the Mid-South promotion was renamed the UWF, and once that happened, Vince McMahon began considering them as a threat, and raided the talent as a result. Gone were top stars Jim Duggan and One Man Gang, and Dibiase was next on the shopping list. Dibiase made his interest in leaving known to Bill Watts and asked for the UWF World title to keep him in the territory, and when the answer was "no," Dibiase lost the ever-popular "loser leaves town" match and went to seek his fortunes up north.

Vince McMahon had big plans for Dibiase from the start. Seeing his talent, Vince decided to give him his greatest gimmick idea to date: An on-screen version of Vince himself, the super-arrogant multimillionaire playboy with no scruples and an "ends justify the means" philosophy.

Dibiase immediately established his character as a class-A jerk, employing a bodyguard whom he abused incessantly (Mike "Virgil" Jones, named as such in a petty shot at Virgil "Dusty Rhodes" Runnels—a big man in WCW, WWF's rival promotion) and showing no regard for the fans. His most famous shtick was simple but incredibly effective: He would pick an audience member at random from the crowd, and offer them some enticing amount of money to perform a demeaning task on national TV. Oddly enough, the more humiliating the task, the more

enthusiastically the audience members would jump at the chance to perform it.

The genius of the gimmick, one that carnival operators have used for decades, is that

Dibiase would let the poor fan get so close to fulfilling the goal needed for the $500 payoff, then yank it away. He would bring out a young fan and have him bounce a basketball 10 times to earn the money, but would kick the ball away on the ninth bounce. He would get a fan to do 10 pushups, but push them over on the ninth. The lure was the key, making the fans think they could get something (money) for nothing (silly exercises). And when Dibiase cheated and won his own little game, it infuriated the fans that much more.

Dibiase truly lived the part as well, being given spending cash by the WWF to throw around when out on the town in "real life," in order to further the character in the minds of the fans and make it seem like he really was a millionaire. Dibiase also flew first class while the rest of the comparable stars on his level flew coach. He soon began to believe the lifestyle, however, becoming addicted to drugs and nearly destroying his marriage in the process.

Meanwhile, back in the wrestling world, all the buildup with Dibiase paid immediate dividends, as he bypassed the midcard entirely and became a main event heel without doing anything more strenuous than wrestling a few squash matches. He was put into a program with WWF champ Hulk Hogan, but not in the usual sense. Being money-oriented, Dibiase had a different plan for acquiring the title.

He announced on WWF TV in late 1987 that he would pay Hulk Hogan outright whatever he wanted in exchange for Hogan turning the championship over to him. Hogan immediately refused, being the good person he was, infuriating Dibiase into action. He decided to purchase the contract of Andre the Giant from manager Bobby Heenan for $1,000,000 to use as a weapon against Hogan. As a sidenote, Heenan's

678911

pay to the order of BOBBY HEENAN
One Million Dollars

$ 1,000,000
Dollars

Ted D'Biase
The Million Dollar Man

Memo Andre the Giant's Contract

:788340749342: 14 12 77 43 2

00678911

character later bought the contract back for $100,000, thus making $900,000 profit on the deal and truly proving himself to be "The Brain."

Andre had lost at *Wrestlemania III* in his first bid to defeat Hulk Hogan for the World title, but with Dibiase behind him he was set to give it another go after pissing and moaning for months afterwards about a near-fall that he thought was three. The contract for the rematch was signed at *Royal Rumble '88*, and the match was set for The *Main Event*, broadcast live on NBC in prime time.

Here's the back story: First of all, the Hebner who referees in the WWF today (Earl) is not the Hebner (Dave) who refereed in the WWF during the glory years. Dave and Earl, however, were twin brothers, and in the days leading up to this

show, the WWF made a very strange promotional move by hiring Earl away from the NWA. At the time, no one thought anything of the move, because who really cares which promotion hires which referees, right?

The finish to the Hogan-Andre match was one of the best-kept secrets in wrestling history, as almost no one had any clue what was going to happen. The general feeling was that Hogan's title reign was about to end, for no other reason than it would be instantly memorable as a TV show, but how do you beat a guy who hasn't been beaten in four years? Like this: Andre and Hogan did their usual terrible match for five minutes, before Hogan got the big boot and legdrop to finish Andre.

Referee Dave Hebner was distracted by Virgil, and Andre was able to get back up and sneak up on Hogan, giving him something vaguely resembling a suplex. Hogan lifted his shoulders at the one-count very clearly, but Hebner simply ignored that and counted to three.

The crowd and millions at home were in total disbelief. Hogan threw a temper tantrum but the decision was final. And almost before Andre could even get the belt over his shoulder, he got on the microphone and announced that he was surrendering the title to the new champion—Ted Dibiase. But even after all that, another twist happened: Out of the dressing room emerged—Dave Hebner? The twin referees argued as the crowd grew more confused, before Hogan finally picked one and tossed him out of the ring like a javelin. But the damage was done, and Hogan's four-year title reign was history.

To confirm this the next week on the weekly TV show, Jack Tunney gave a famous speech, consulting the mythical "rule book" to find that:

a) The referee's decision is final, so Hulk Hogan was not the champion.

b) A champion can surrender his title at any time, so Andre was not the champion.

c) A title may only be won from the previous champion in a match, so Dibiase was not the champion.

Of course, b) and c) contradict each other, but the ratings for this stuff were so high that it didn't matter. A tournament for the belt, the first one ever, was set up for *Wrestlemania IV* in an effort to top *Wrestlemania III*. It didn't work, as most people thought *IV*, at a mind-numbing four hours, was perhaps the most boring wrestling show ever, but that's another issue. The actual tournament saw Savage defeating Butch Reed, Greg Valentine, One Man Gang, and finally Ted Dibiase (thanks to the help of Hulk Hogan) to capture his first World title. As an interesting sidenote on the tournament, Savage's second-round match was with Greg Valentine. Valentine defeated Ricky Steamboat in the first round to earn that slot, a move that most fans found downright puzzling, as Valentine had little or no credibility and Steamboat winning would have set up a rematch of the classic Steamboat-Savage match from the year before. Steamboat considered this booking choice the final slap in the face to him after years of service, and he left for the rival NWA later that year.

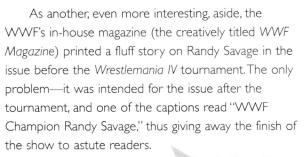

**Ted Dibiase**

*Real name:*
Theodore Dibiase
*Height:* 6'3"
*Weight:* 245 lbs.
*Aliases:* The Million Dollar Man

As another, even more interesting, aside, the WWF's in-house magazine (the creatively titled *WWF Magazine*) printed a fluff story on Randy Savage in the issue before the *Wrestlemania IV* tournament. The only problem—it was intended for the issue after the tournament, and one of the captions read "WWF Champion Randy Savage," thus giving away the finish of the show to astute readers.

Dibiase and Savage spent the next few months tearing up the house show circuit with rematches for the title, while Hogan took increasingly large amounts of time off. Hogan's absence started hurting revenue, despite the awesome matches being put on by Dibiase and Savage. That was the first small sign that everything was no longer wine and roses for the WWF, and the effect slowly built from there. The WWF never truly got behind Randy Savage as the #1 babyface, always leaving him in the shadow of Hulk Hogan, whether as a cornerman or a tag-team partner. Hogan and Savage (the Megapowers) teamed up against Dibiase and Andre (the Megabucks) at the first ever *Summerslam* PPV in

August '88, in a match won with Hogan's legdrop.

Hogan's (or the WWF's) refusal to move the Hogan character away from Savage and allow him to stand on his own as World champion was doing serious damage to Savage's drawing power at that point, and as 1988 drew to a close, they began to turn Savage heel in order to kill him off as a top babyface once and for all.

Dibiase, meanwhile, out of title chances and stuck in career limbo (too over for midcard, but not in line for the main event) was given a strangely inspired new angle: He would simply buy his own championship. So he went to a jeweller and had a championship belt made out of gold and diamonds, in the shape of interlocking dollar-signs, and dubbed it the "Million Dollar belt." As dumb an idea as it might sound, it actually got him newly over, and gave him another few years of life to his character. He was never again to approach his peak from '88, and he retired completely in 1993 after winning three tag titles with Mike Rotundo and suffering a career-ending back injury. He switched into the managerial role, and had runs with wrestlers such as Bam Bam Bigelow, and even a "fake" Undertaker he introduced, who was defeated by the real Undertaker at *Summerslam '94*.

# 4
# THE END OF THE NWA, BIRTH OF WCW: 1983-1991

O nce Vince McMahon went national in 1984, the major NWA promoters also got it into their heads to do the same. Most notably, Mid-Atlantic promoter Jim Crockett Jr., whose Mid-Atlantic Championship Wrestling occupied a prime spot on Ted Turner's upstart WTBS "Superstation." With main star Dusty Rhodes doing the booking, however, disaster after disaster followed, as Crockett bought out rivals left and right until he himself was out of money and forced to sell to Ted Turner in 1988.

By that time, ego clashes between Dusty and Ric Flair over the use of Lex Luger eventually caused Flair to flee for the WWF, and Dusty's repetitive booking killed all the usual house show stops for the NWA, until finally, the renamed WCW became a TV company in 1990 and left the NWA high and dry in 1991. The official end of the era is generally regarded as Lex Luger's lame duck title win over Barry Windham at Great American Bash '91, widely regarded as the worst show ever.

# RIC FLAIR

Or so the doctors thought.

Because in 1976, amazingly only a little more than a year after the initial injury, Flair returned to active competition, and the near-death experience seemed to have made him better than ever, as he was immediately pushed up the card again, capturing the U.S. title for the first time in

The 60-minute man. The Man. The Nature Boy. No one carried an entire promotion, and indeed the entire NWA, on his back with the grace and style of Ric Flair.

Born Richard Fliehr in February 1949, the son of a doctor, Ric entered Verne Gagne's wrestling camp at the age of 23 after playing football at the University of Minnesota, and was deemed too fat and not talented enough to make it as a wrestler. Flair was persistent, however, and failed the camp two more times before finally making it out of the class of '75 along with fellow graduate Ricky Steamboat. Flair's career was showing promise as a solid midcard wrestler and he won the Mid-Atlantic version of the NWA TV title before a plane crash ended his career out of the gate in 1975 by breaking his back.

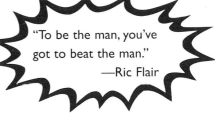

"To be the man, you've got to beat the man."
—Ric Flair

1977. Flair won his first NWA World title in 1981, defeating Dusty Rhodes. Flair was an immediate sensation as champion, traveling around the world to defend the title, including to the northeast U.S. for

a rare title v. title match against WWF champion Bob Backlund, a match that ended in an unsatisfying double-countout. Flair technically held the title for two years, although it has recently come to light that the NWA members in

RIC FLAIR

# WRESTLER SPOTLIGHT

## RIC FLAIR

**BIGGEST CONTRIBUTION**
You name it, he did it.

**BEST MATCH**
Too many to mention, but a 45-minute draw with Sting in 1988 was the most widely seen of his great matches, with honorable mention going to a 45-minute TV match with Barry Windham. Both were strong contenders for Match of the Year at the time.

**BIGGEST MATCH**
Probably losing the World title to Kerry Von Erich in Texas in front of 40,000 fans.

**BIGGEST RIVAL**
Flair had heated feuds with Sting and Luger.

Some sources count this as another Flair reign, giving him five at that point. On the other hand, the overriding rule of wrestling—"if it didn't happen on TV, it didn't happen"—pretty much puts all of these to rest, because none of them was acknowledged as a title change at the time. The first three were later acknowledged by NWA descendant WCW, but that's opening a whole other can of worms.

Flair officially lost his first World title to Harley Race, setting up a cage match for the title at the NWA's first supercard, *Starrcade '83*. With legend and former champion Gene Kiniski as the special ref, Flair defeated Race in the Match of the Year to reclaim the title for a second time. It was one of the true "passing the torch" moments, and it began one of the most amazing runs in wrestling history for Ric Flair, as Race departed for the WWF soon after and left Flair to carry the territory on his own merits.

Flair was immediately established as the dominant star of the entire NWA, but primarily of Jim Crockett's Mid-Atlantic Championship Wrestling, which was to be renamed World Championship Wrestling in short order. Flair's first big gate came in a co-promotional move with Fritz Von Erich's WCCW, which was based out of Texas. He was supposed to be defending the NWA World title against prodigy David Von Erich, largely

Trinidad, Dominica, and Puerto Rico did title switches with Victor Jovica, Jack Veneno, and Carlos Colon, respectively, and simply didn't tell anyone in the U.S. about it. This effectively meant that Flair was a four-time champion when everyone in the U.S. still thought he was on his first reign!

In the States, there was also a controversial title switch, as Dusty Rhodes (in his guise as the "mysterious" Midnight Rider) won the title from Flair cleanly, but refused to unmask for NWA president Bob Geigel, and was therefore stripped of the title and it was returned to Flair.

considered to be the next big superstar in the business, but a sudden bout of toxic shock syndrome killed David before the match.

In tribute to his late brother, Kerry Von Erich took David's spot for the main event at the *Parade of Champions* in front of 40,000 fans and defeated Flair to win the NWA World title. It was a huge emotional moment for the Texas fans, but it would prove to be a short-lived one, as Flair would regain the title in a 2 of 3 falls match in Japan a few weeks later. Politics dictated that someone from one of the "fringe" NWA territories, like Texas or Alabama, would never have a long reign, for fear of the big NWA members like Harley Race and "Wildfire" Tommy Rich losing power as a result. It was this attitude that forced the Texans to split off from the NWA and go on their own.

Flair held onto the title for the next two years, feuding off and on with the other major star of the promotion, Dusty Rhodes. Flair and Rhodes engaged in the "million dollar challenge" at *Starrcade '84*, with the special referee, boxer Joe Frazier, stopping the match when he deemed that Rhodes had lost too much blood. In story line terms, however, Rhodes was getting close to the title—too close for Flair's liking, so as 1985 began, he introduced an angle that would change wrestling forever.

The idea of a heel stable had been done before, but Flair's group, the Four Horsemen, served a very specific purpose: To protect Ric Flair's title at all costs.

Flair had previously been established as a "cousin" of the Anderson brothers (Ole and Arn) and so began going to them for help. The little group soon added midcard heel Tully Blanchard, and imported manager and longtime Rhodes nemesis JJ Dillon out of Florida. The Andersons and Blanchard immediately became established as Flair's personal thugs, running in to cause a disqualification when Flair's title was in trouble. Although the Horsemen concept was brilliant in theory, the actual execution of the constant run-ins annoyed fans more and more as it went on. The problem then wasn't the wrestling, it was the

ARN ANDERSON & TULLY BLANCHARD

booking by Dusty Rhodes.

The most direct example of self-destructive booking using the Horsemen occurred at *Starrcade '85*, as the main event saw Flair defending his title against Dusty Rhodes for what seemed like the millionth time. This time there was no special stipulation—it was simply another title shot for Dusty. The finish of the match was very confusing: Flair controlled most of the match (a necessity due to Dusty's lack of in-ring talent), only to see Dusty mount a heroic comeback. As Rhodes did so, the ref was bumped and Dusty proceeded to get what would have been the winning pin on Flair—if the referee was awake.

But he wasn't. As the referee woke up, the Four Horsemen ran in and beat up Rhodes, and the ref was knocked out again in the process. A second referee came into the match as the Horsemen's interference proceeded to backfire, and Rhodes scored what looked to be the winning pin on Ric Flair to capture the title; and indeed Rhodes left with the belt. However, the next week on the NWA's TV shows, it was announced that the first referee actually saw the Horsemen interfering and decided to disqualify Flair for outside interference before the second referee counted the winning pinfall.

Now, those of you who are still following all this may notice two things:

1) This situation bears an uncanny resemblance to the Hulk Hogan–Nick Bockwinkel AWA title match discussed in depth earlier on—and that didn't lead to good things for anyone.

2) It makes Ric Flair look exceedingly weak for him to constantly need three guys protecting him when he's supposed to be carrying the territory.

Whereas Flair had spent most of 1984 traveling from territory to territory and defending the title against whoever the local promoter wanted to put against him, now Jim Crockett (who owned the contract of Flair) was getting touchy about lending out "his" NWA World champion, so he kept him mainly in his own Mid-Atlantic territory, keeping the title on him with cheap finishes like the Rhodes one above. Whether intentionally done or not, weakening the champion like that weakened the entire NWA, and the fewer dates that Flair worked for the smaller members, the smaller their attendance, and the less money everyone took in.

Jim Crockett's basic plan was to become Vince McMahon, a successful promoter who took his territory and went national. But here's where the ugly politics begin. The first step that Crockett took in 1985 was to merge the relatively small Mid-Atlantic Championship Wrestling promotion with Ole Anderson's rapidly failing Georgia Championship Wrestling into a name that is familiar today: World Championship Wrestling, or WCW.

RIC FLAIR VS. DUSTY RHODES

However, because of NWA membership, the shows had to be promoted under the NWA name in order to keep Ric Flair (a WCW wrestler) as NWA World champion. And since Crockett didn't yet have enough power to split off from the NWA like McMahon had done a few years previous, he had to play ball with the NWA. However, Dusty Rhodes's booking of Ric Flair was rapidly eroding the total influence of the NWA and making that a moot point. To make matters worse for the smaller members, the NWA's flagship show was *World Championship Wrestling* on TBS, and that show almost exclusively featured Jim Crockett's talent, making national exposure now impossible for anyone outside of the "Charlotte clique."

As Crockett expanded, Ric Flair's title defenses became more and more limited to Crockett's shows, defending against the same core group of people: Dusty Rhodes, Nikita Koloff, Magnum TA, and the occasional singles match with tag wrestlers like Ricky Morton or Road Warrior Hawk. Flair was a master of using a job to put another wrestler over—by simply allowing himself to be pinned by the much-smaller Ricky Morton in a tag match, for instance, he immediately made Morton into a threat for his title and allowed the promoters to sign a series of matches between them where the fans actually believed that Morton had a chance to win the title.

The more Flair defended against that core group of talent, the more the fans in general perceived them as the top stars of the NWA and not whoever was the star of the hometown NWA promotion, a problem that has plagued wrestling for years and will continue to do so for years more.

1986 saw Flair's group consolidating their power, as Rhodes defeated Flair for the title in July in a cage match, only to lose it a week later in the rematch. Flair was building to a *Starrcade* showdown with hot challenger Magnum TA, but a car accident ended Magnum's career prematurely and thrust equally hot Nikita Koloff into the slot. Koloff had engaged Magnum in a heated best-of-seven series and brutalized him to win the U.S. title, but dedicated his career to Magnum after the car accident. His English suddenly improved, too. Flair managed to carry the extremely limited Koloff to a shockingly excellent double-DQ at *Starrcade '86*,

but the writing was increasingly on the wall: The 50-year old NWA was dying and Crockett's WCW was becoming the only member worth anything to the fans.

As 1987 began, Jim Crockett wanted to bring his featured attraction, Flair, to the world of pay-per-view to compete with the WWF. At the same time, down in Florida, a former football player named Lex Lugar, yes Lugar, was turning heads, being over enough to win the Southern title only a week into his career. In between battling hot challenger Barry Windham in awesome 45-minute draws, Flair defended his title against Luger in Florida for the *Battle of the Belts III* TV special. It was a 2 of 3 falls match that went to a time-limit draw at one fall apiece.

## SUPERSTAR STATS:

**Ric Flair**

*Real name:* Richard Morgan Fliehr

*Height:* 6'1"

*Weight:* 245 lbs.

*Trademark move:* Used the classic figure-four leglock as his finisher

*Aliases:* The Nature Boy, The Black Scorpion

Luger made enough of an impression on the Crockett promotion there that he was signed almost immediately, and Ole Anderson was kicked out of the Four Horsemen unceremoniously to make way for the renamed Lex Luger. That Horsemen combination—Flair, Anderson, Blanchard, and Luger—is generally considered to have been the best. At the *Great American Bash* shows of 1987, Flair had some unnotable title defenses against Jimmy Garvin, one of which ended with Flair getting a submission victory and thus being allowed one night with Garvin's manager/wife, Precious. This resulted in Garvin's story line brother (in reality his stepfather), Ronnie Garvin, dressing up as Precious to attack Flair in his home and set up a title match between them in September.

The ugly politics continued. Ronnie Garvin was in reality being set up as a patsy for Ric Flair. *Starrcade* had "traditionally" been an event to showcase Ric Flair (despite Flair only ever getting one clean win at a *Starrcade*—the first one in '83) and the plan was to have Flair lose the title and then regain it at *Starrcade* to a big pop. So the challenger not only had to be a babyface who was credible enough to beat Flair, but had to then be made to look like a complete fool by dropping the title to Flair, a huge heel, at the biggest show of the year. But wait, it gets better!

Ronnie Garvin was chosen as the lucky winner, and defeated Flair for the title in a good match in Detroit with a sunset flip off the top rope. Garvin was a

marginal main-eventer at best, and putting the title on him was a huge risk in terms of credibility. The feelings of the rest of the NWA weren't even a consideration, showing how far the relationship had deteriorated by that point into "WCW v. The NWA World."

However, once Garvin was champion, it was assumed that he would have to beat some contenders to make the *Starrcade* match look like a challenge for Flair. Those contenders didn't agree with that idea, though, and every major heel in the promotion refused to lose to someone who was so obviously a lame-duck champion. So it was explained on TV that Garvin was taking a 45-day sabbatical to "train" for the big title match, and wouldn't defend the belt until then.

To make matters worse, *Starrcade '87* was supposed to be the NWA's debut foray into the world of PPV. Just to mess with them, the WWF scheduled their own show on PPV that same night—*Survivor Series*—and forced cable companies to choose which one they wanted to carry. Given the WWF was in the midst of their hot period, almost every carrier north of the Mason-Dixon line went with the WWF show, and a humiliated Crockett was forced to move his Thanksgiving tradition to December the next year to avoid competition.

As for the show itself, Flair easily regained the title from Garvin to the shock of roughly no one, and by now the fans had so completely turned against Garvin (who they perceived as a "chicken champion," ducking all his challengers) that Flair was the babyface in the match. Ironically, Garvin's career never recovered from the experience of being World champion for two months.

RIC FLAIR VS. RON GARVIN

Lex Luger turned babyface and left the Horsemen on that same show, and after the NWA ran a disasterous test PPV show in January in the form of the *Bunkhouse Show* (countered by the WWF with a free show on the USA Network, the first ever *Royal Rumble*), they decided to go with Ric Flair v. Lex Luger as their next big drawing card. New blood was the theme of the year, in fact, as newcomer Sting took Flair to the limit in a 45-minute draw in March, on the first ever *Clash of Champions* event on TBS. It seemed that Jim Crockett was a fast learner of dirty pool, as the WWF's *Wrestlemania IV* was on PPV at the same time.

And in fact, that first Clash drew a record rating for wrestling on cable, and was seen by roughly 20 times the number of people that *Wrestlemania* was. Not coincidentally, Vince McMahon stopped scheduling events to compete with WCW after that. As a note on the *Clash* match, it had a stipulation whereby there must be a winner, because if there wasn't, three judges at ringside would decide a winner. In the eternal quest for wrestling to find a way to make any finish indecisive, one judge voted for Sting, one voted for Flair, and one voted for a draw, thus completely negating the point of the stipulation. The match itself drew a 7.1 rating, however, making it the most-watched match in cable wrestling to that point, a record that held for some 10 years.

Flair v. Luger was on tap for the first real try at PPV for Crockett, however, in the form of *Great American Bash '88*. Flair's credibility as champion, already in bad shape, was either badly in need of a boost by decisively beating the young challenger, or it was time to try Lex Luger as World champion. The show did a fairly good buyrate compared to the WWF, so obviously interest in the match was there amongst the fanbase.

Dusty Rhodes, the booker, made his intent well-known: He wanted Luger to win the title. Flair, who had a very smartly negotiated long-term contract, had veto power over his own bookings, and refused to job in this case, feeling Luger didn't have the drawing power and would sink the NWA; Flair wanted to "pass the torch" to Sting, who Rhodes liked but didn't think was ready to carry the ball yet. The general plan from all involved was to retire Flair to someone and get the title off him at the earliest convenience, since everyone (except Flair) felt he no longer had what it took to carry the promotion.

In the case of Luger, a compromise was reached: The finish would see Luger making the comeback and getting ready to

DUSTY RHODES

defeat Flair, but he would open a huge gash over his own eye in the process and bleed all over the ring until the doctors would have no choice but to stop the match. It sounded good in theory, but it didn't work out that way. In fact, the match went off mostly as planned, and was the best of Luger's career to that point, but Luger messed up the blade job and instead of opening a huge gash, he opened a tiny paper cut above his eye.

A small trickle of blood could be seen if you looked hard enough, and at that point a representative of the "Maryland State Athletic Commision" stepped in and stoppe the match, royally pissing off the entire crowd and making everyone involved look incredibly weak in the process. The finish did nothing to protect Luger or help Flair, and Rhodes kept booking Luger-Flair title matches in house shows across the country. Rhodes wanted a title change, Flair didn't, and they kept playing cat-and-mouse, with title changes scheduled every night and Flair turning the job down every night, all through the summer.

RIC FLAIR
VS. RODDY PIPER

In late 1988, the NWA died and no one noticed because the Flair-Rhodes backstage soap opera was too interesting to pass up gossiping about. Jim Crockett had expanded rapidly starting in 1986, buying up the Florida territory (and taking champion Mike Rotundo with him), then Bill Watts' UWF under a guise of partnership (taking top star Sting with him), then many of the minor southern territories who couldn't oppose him.

The end result was Jim Crockett controlling almost all of the NWA members under the WCW banner. The problem now was that Crockett was out of money and Dusty Rhodes had driven the Flair-Luger matchup so far into the proverbial ground that the house shows were no longer drawing significant money, and with the destruction of the smaller territories there wasn't any new source of hot talent to challenge Flair.

So Crockett did the only thing he could—he sold all his interest in WCW to Ted Turner and TBS, who in turn, could use it as a tax writeoff and a source of cheap programming. Crockett was quietly shuffled out of the mix and Turner executive Jim Herd was brought in as the first (of many) Executive Vice-President of Wrestling Operations. There was no President, as that was a title that would place the holder on par with other Turner heads, and that was an unheard of idea at the time.

Starrcade '88, the first show under the new management, was approaching, and Dusty Rhodes was rapidly losing control of the booking situation. Flair immediately befriended Jim Herd, and in retaliation, Rhodes booked Flair against Lex Luger at Starrcade. When Flair (again) refused the job, Rhodes changed the booking to Flair losing the title to midcarder Rick Steiner in a five-minute squash, at which point an infuriated Flair quit the company on the spot and announced he was leaving for the WWF.

That was enough for Herd, who stepped in and ended the squabbling once and for all by announcing that Flair would in fact defend against Luger, and retain, with a clean pinfall win. Dusty was removed as booker and Flair was given the job instead.

Dusty departed for the WWF early in 1989 in true Dusty style, leaving Flair free and clear to run the promotion, with the help of Jim Ross (the promotion's premier color commentator at the time), as he saw fit. In fact, the way Dusty left was worthy of a wrestling story line in itself: After being given specific orders to tone down the violence in the product, Dusty had his partners, the Road Warriors, turn heel on him during an episode of *World Championship Wrestling*. The beating concluded with Animal driving a steel spike into Dusty's head and opening up a five-alarm gusher that turned the ring mat red. This all aired during the dinner hour, and it infuriated WCW management so much that Rhodes was fired and thus free to head to the WWF.

Flair's first move as the new booker was to convince Turner to bring in a WWF malcontent and push him to the top.

As a word of explanation, the Four Horsemen were basically in a shambles as 1989 began. Barry Windham had turned on partner Lex Luger to take his place in the team early in 1988 before wining the U.S. title, but as 1988 ended so did his contract, along with Tully Blanchard's and Arn Anderson's. With JJ Dillon having jumped ship for a front office job in the WWF, Blanchard and Anderson were in the WWF almost immediately upon the expiration of their contracts, and Windham was rumored to be interested in jumping as well. Flair and Windham were left to be managed by Hiro Matsuda, and they began tormenting Eddie Gilbert—a former booking assistant to Dusty Rhodes—as their first new target.

Gilbert challenged the ex-Horsemen to a tag match against himself and a mystery partner on *World Championship Wrestling* early in 1989. Flair and Windham arrogantly agreed, and, as is often the case, their hubris came back to bite them, as the mystery partner was revealed to be Ricky Steamboat. Gilbert and Steamboat prevailed in an excellent match, as Steamboat pinned Flair with his patented top rope bodypress, and suddenly Flair had a new #1 contender and the first big feud of the new era.

Flair and Steamboat met for the title at *Chi-Town Rumble '89*, with Steamboat scoring a clean pinfall by reversing Flair's figure-four leglock to win his first World championship. It was called the best U.S. pro wrestling match ever by a number of notable people who followed the business, but amazingly the duo would top that performance not once, but twice.

The rematch for the title came at the sixth *Clash of the Champions*, broadcast live on TBS in April of '89, opposite the WWF's *Wrestlemania V*. In this case, the competition didn't affect either side, as the *Clash* drew a strong

RIC FLAIR
VS.
JIM GARVIN

TV rating and the *Wrestlemania* show set a record for buys that held up until 1998. It was to be a 2 of 3 falls match, with a one-hour time limit. It had been ages since anyone had "gone Broadway" (the term used to describe a one-hour match), but if anyone could pull it off, it was Flair and Steamboat—two men hitting their strides as wrestlers against each other.

It was especially sweet for Flair, who had been written off by Herd, after an unexplained falling out between the two, as over-the-hill when Herd had come onboard a few months earlier. The match itself was excellent, voted Match of the Year by readers of the *Wrestling Observer Newsletter*. Flair won the first fall by pinning Steamboat, then Steamboat evened it up (making history in the process) by becoming the first person to make Ric Flair submit—the move was a flying double chickenwing. This set an important precedent for their third match, as Flair was now established as being vulnerable to that move.

In the third match, Steamboat went for the move again, only to see Flair fall back on top of him to try and get the pin. But Steamboat lifted his shoulders leaving Flair's on the mat for the winning pin at the 55-minute mark to retain the title. An irate Flair (who also had his feet on the ropes during the pin) demanded, and was granted, one last shot at the title, at *WrestleWar '89*.

RIC
FLAIR

Believe it or not, that final match was even better than the first two, lasting nearly 35 minutes before Flair came from behind to reverse a Steamboat slam into the winning pinfall; it was Flair's sixth World title. The finish to the match was, ironically, how Steamboat won his biggest match ever against Randy Savage two years prior. The Flair/Steamboat match was notable, however, for starting an even bigger feud. In the case of a draw, there were three judges at ringside to "score" the match: Lou Thesz, Pat O'Connor, and Terry Funk. The score at the time of the match finish (which was probably just made up by the announcers) had Steamboat winning on points. Funk had been in semi-retirement, doing movies like Sylvester Stallone's *Over the Top*, but new booker Flair still saw his money-drawing potential, despite his largely comedic run in the WWF with endless matches against Junkyard Dog.

Immediately following Flair's victory, he was interviewed by Jim Ross, and Funk joined them in the ring to congratulate the new champion. Funk humbly asked for a title shot, but was (rightly) rebuked by Ric Flair for not even being a contender. Funk, never stable under the best of circumstances, snapped and attacked the exhausted Flair. Another bit of brilliant booking: The match was specifically booked to be long enough so that Flair wouldn't have the energy to defend himself against Funk.

Funk spent the better part of 10 minutes brutalizing Flair. Flair was a heel at that point, and had no allies left to save him with Windham having gone to the WWF, and so the attack continued unabated until Funk finished it off by piledriving Flair onto the judges' table and "breaking his neck." Flair was turned into a total babyface by this attack, and Funk went on a rampage through the NWA in classic monster heel style. You just knew that when Flair returned from the injury, there was going to be hell to pay.

In fact, that ended up happening at *Great American Bash '89*, as Flair returned from his injury to take on Funk for the World title. This show is generally regarded as the greatest PPV of all-time, featuring match quality that was untouched before or after. Flair and Funk both bled buckets, but no "Maryland State Athletic Commission" stopped the match this time around. The match ended as Flair went for the figure-four, Funk reversed it, and Flair reversed it again to get the winning pinfall. As usual in wrestling, though, the war was not yet over, as Funk and new ally the Great Muta, a Japanese wrestler who mimicked the face paint and green mist of '80s Japanese wrestler The Great Kabuki, attacked Flair and left him laying for dead until Sting came in to make the save. Can you say "tag match?"

At *Halloween Havoc '89*, the first so named event for the NWA, Flair and Sting took on Funk and Muta in the first-ever "Thundercage" match, featuring the unique idea of having a cage with an electrified top surrounding the ring. Bruno Sammartino was the special guest referee, and the match would continue until either Ole Anderson (in the faces' corner) or Gary Hart (in the heels' corner) threw in the towel for their team.

Complications arose as a piece of decoration caught on fire due to the electricity, and referee Tommy Young had to scurry up the cage to put it out, but for the most part the match went off smoothly. The finish saw Ole Anderson hitting Gary Hart hard enough to send his towel flying into the ring, which Sammartino counted as a submission on the heels' part. This of course didn't sit well with Terry Funk, who demanded one final match with Ric Flair, this one a retirement match.

It happened at *Clash of the Champions IX*, and it was an "I Quit" match. Quite simply, the winner had to make the loser say "I quit" into a microphone. Considered the best match of Terry Funk's career, the two destroyed each other for the better part of 20 minutes before Flair wore down Funk's knee enough to put on the figure-four and get the submission. Funk went into retirement (which turned out to be about as long-lasting as Roddy Piper's) and Flair went on to something else entirely.

For whatever reason, Ole Anderson had been brought back in to help with the booking and to take an on-screen role, and Arn Anderson had just left the WWF. So it was decided that a reformation of the Four Horsemen was in order. This time, however, they would be babyfaces, so the coveted fourth position after Flair and the Andersons was offered to, and accepted by, Sting. Everything was going great until *Starrcade '89*, which featured an "Iron Man" round-robin tournament with Flair, Sting, Lex Luger, and the Great Muta.

Each man would wrestle each other over the course of the evening (20 points for a pinfall win, 15 for a countout, 10 for a DQ, and 5 each for a draw) and the person with the most points would win. It came down to a match between Sting and Ric Flair at the end of the show, with Sting needing a pinfall to prevent Lex Luger from taking the tournament. Sting got it, reversing Flair's figure-four for the win. He asked for a title shot after that, and you might as well have painted a bullseye on his back.

The match was set for *WrestleWar '90*, and at the tenth *Clash of the Champions* show, the other three Horsemen officially gave Sting the boot from the team and turned heel again. The Horsemen were in the main event of the show against Gary Hart's J-Tex Corporation, and Sting charged the ring and tried to climb over the cage around the ring for that match. Unfortunately, Sting fell and legitimately blew out his knee, which essentially sunk Ric Flair's days as a booker in one fell swoop.

The money match between Sting and Flair, where Flair would finally pass the torch and move down to the midcard, was not an option for at least six months while Sting rehabbed his knee after surgery. With only a couple of weeks until the show, U.S. champion and eternal Flair challenger Lex Luger was turned babyface and stuck into the slot. With Luger's U.S. title defense canceled, the match had to fill nearly an hour of airtime.

Despite being a really good match, it couldn't possibly fill the expectations fans had for the Sting-Flair match. It ended with Sting limping out on crutches to lend support for Luger, and getting jumped by the Horsemen. Luger left the match to help him, and was counted out. The angle was not what you'd call a huge hit with the fans, and now backstage sentiment was swinging against Flair, as he was accused of

using his power to put himself over at the expense of the other talent. Jim Herd, always looking for the opportunity to demote Flair, pounced on the situation and removed Flair as booker, inexplicably putting Ole Anderson (whose basic mismanagement of Georgia Championship Wrestling had caused that promotion to go under) in charge of the ship. This coincided with another change, as announcers were instructed to refer to the promotion as "WCW" at all times, phasing out the NWA name once and for all.

Anderson's first big show as booker saw Flair defending the title against Lex Luger in a cage match. But once again, it was Flair v. the booker backstage, as Anderson booked a title change but Flair refused, instead wanting to wait until Sting was ready to get the title. The compromise saw the ridiculous ending of Barry Windham (back from the WWF) running in and disqualifying Flair in a no-disqualification match, a start that didn't bode well for Ole's run as booker. Flair's next challenge came at *Clash XI*, as he faced washed-up

RIC FLAIR VS. JUNKYARD DOG

Junkyard Dog in a non-title match—and lost! Soundly panned by critics as one of the worst matches in Flair's career, Flair was growing increasingly dejected with his position and desperately wanted that epic match with Sting to restore his credibility.

Sting did return soon enough, and finally Flair agreed to drop the title at *Great American Bash '90*. However, the match was booked to run short and with lots of outside interference, so when Flair lost the belt to Sting in roughly 14 minutes, it left fans feeling less than overwhelmed. Flair meekly took a demotion to the undercard and was put in a program with partner Arn Anderson against new tag champs Ron Simmons & Butch Reed. Flair & Anderson made the most of a bad situation, engaging the champs in a memorable brawl at *Halloween Havoc '90*, before fate once again intervened on Flair's behalf.

Due to Ole Anderson's booking, Sting was a total failure as champion, and to make matters worse, the big angle leading up to *Starrcade '90* was supposed to be Sting v. The Black Scorpion. Problem: They had no one to play the role who was credible enough to challenge for the title once he was revealed. So they asked Flair to take the humiliating role, and Flair agreed

with a price: He wanted the title back in exchange. Jim Herd reluctantly agreed, and fired Ole Anderson soon after.

Flair regained the title, his seventh, in January of 1991, as WCW officially changed their name from the NWA and split off the lineage of the World and tag team titles. Herd had no intention of keeping Flair as the #1 man in the company, however, this time being determined to bury him at all costs. As Flair's contract neared expiration, Herd played a game of financial hardball that would ultimately cost him his own job and give Flair an even bigger place in the history books.

But that comes a little later.

# LEX LUGER

Heralded as "the next Hulk Hogan" when he debuted, Luger never quite worked out the way bookers wanted. In fact, Luger's biggest contribution is being the catalyst for the end of the NWA due to the Flair-Rhodes squabbles backstage, and later, as the first WCW World champion.

Born Lawrence Pfohl in June of 1958, Lex Luger had zero intention of going into pro wrestling early in life. A career in football enticed him more than anything, as he did well enough in college ball to earn a look from the NFL. A look was all he got, however, not actually signing with any teams and eventually signing with the Montreal Alouettes of the CFL at 19. He played briefly with the Green Bay Packers before he concluded that his career wasn't going to happen in the NFL, and moved to the USFL's Memphis Showboats. At a celebrity golf tournament in 1985, he met longtime Florida wrestler Bob Roop. Roop liked Luger's look and sent him to Hiro Matsuda to be trained as a wrestler, convinced that Pfohl could draw serious money with his physique alone. Initially, he was correct.

Luger debuted late in 1985, and was an instant sensation and one of the most over wrestlers in the Florida promotion. Luger was put over Ed Gantner for his debut (Gantner was a top star in Florida at the time) and only a week into his career was put over wrestling legend Wahoo McDaniel to capture his first title—the Southern title. The buzz on Luger (initially spelled "Lugar" for you nitpickers out there. The "Lex" part came as an homage to Superman's nemesis Lex Luthor) was immediate and

**LEX LUGER**

far-reaching, as people very high up in the NWA began getting in Jim Crockett's ear about signing the hot young prospect, despite his total lack of experience.

As an experiment, Ric Flair was sent down to Florida to give Luger a shot at the NWA World title in a 2 of 3 falls match, broadcast live on local TV as the *Battle of the Belts III*. Luger was hugely impressive in being able to keep up with Flair (although Flair could carry the proverbial broomstick to a good match at that point) and snowed enough people into believing him to be a legitimate superstar in the making that he was offered a lucrative contract less than a year into his career. Luger, who was already approaching 30 at that point, quickly signed the deal to cash in while he was young.

Before leaving for the bigtime, however, Luger had one very famous confrontation with Bruiser Brody, who had a short run with the promotion, jumping back and forth from Japan. Luger and Brody were in a feud, and were scheduled for a cage match to settle it. Brody, a veteran wrestler and a legitimate worldwide superstar, didn't think Luger was ready for his push and resented it somewhat. To make matters worse, he was hungover from the night before and in an extremely bad mood. The result was a weird match where Brody suddenly

stopped selling for Luger, shrugging off all his punches, and suddenly revealing to Luger that he had prepped every finger for blading. The terrified Luger shoved the referee down for an immediate DQ and climbed out of the cage and back to the dressing room as fast as he could move before Brody could do any damage. Luger showed up in the NWA soon after that incident. That, by the way, was about as real as wrestling ever gets from straying from the "script."

Luger, still a raw rookie as 1987 dawned, was suddenly thrust in the major angle of the entire NWA, as he was brought in as a "Horsemen Associate" for Flair, Blanchard, and the Andersons. The logic being that if he were an official Horseman, then it would be the Five Horsemen and that would just sound stupid. Luger proved to be over enough, thanks to efficient use of squash matches, that Ole Anderson

was soon kicked out of the group for skipping a show to watch his son compete in an amateur wrestling tournament, and Luger was officially

LEX LUGER VS. NIKITA KOLOFF

inducted in the spring of 1987.

Luger's mind-bogglingly fast rise up the card saw him programmed into a feud with U.S. champion, Russian Nikita Koloff (how ironic until Koloff turned babyface and embraced the U.S.A.), that culminated in a mind-numbing 40-minute cage match that saw Luger win the title with help from manager JJ Dillon.

Luger and compatriot Tully Blanchard were entered in the Jim Crockett Senior Memorial Cup Tag Team Tournament (simply called "The Crockett Cup" by most sane people) for 1987, and made it all the way to the finals before meeting up with booker Dusty Rhodes and his partner Nikita Koloff. The booker's team won the tournament, to the shock of no one.

Luger and Dusty spent most of 1987 feuding on and off, with the story line being that Dusty needed lessons from legend Johnny Weaver about the proper way to do a sleeperhold (one of the most basic moves in the business), which he then started using as his finisher. This feud ended up with a cage match at *Starrcade '87*. It was Luger's U.S. title v. 90 days away from the sport for Dusty. Dusty of course won the title in a horrendous match, making a heroic comeback and foiling Luger's evil schemes in the end. The match was notable for someone tossing a chair in the ring, and, with Dusty being out of position for the finish, Luger was forced to bend over and spend 10 seconds picking up the chair until Dusty was ready to come over and DDT him on it for the pinfall. In order to justify the win over the younger, hotter, and more over Luger, Dusty decided to push him to the main event.

After the cage match, Luger did his first babyface turn by giving the semi-famous "I Am An Athlete" speech, effectively quitting the Four Horsemen and, not surprisingly, telling the world what a great guy Dusty Rhodes really was. That sort of thing happened a lot when Dusty was booking. Many people feuding with Dusty tended to give interviews that contained the phrase "Dusty Rhodes is a scum-sucking pig, but he's the toughest guy I've ever faced" or some variation thereof. This in turn led to Luger being entered in a series of Bunkhouse Stampede battle royales in the early part of 1988, many of which ended when it came down to Luger, Blanchard, and manager JJ Dillon in the ring. The finish would see Blanchard voluntarily eliminating himself to give Dillon the win, only to see Luger rebel and eliminate Dillon himself to take the match. Simple but effective. Luger was now a full babyface, and the target was clear: Ric Flair's title.

In reality, Flair wasn't so

DUSTY RHODES VS. HAWK

# WRESTLER SPOTLIGHT

## LEX LUGER

**BIGGEST CONTRIBUTION**
Flair refused to put him over, causing Rhodes to be fired as booker.

**BEST MATCH**
Against Ric Flair at *Starrcade '88* (****1/2) and against Ricky Steamboat at a house show in 1989 (****3/4)

**BIGGEST MATCH**
Against Flair at *Great American Bash '88,* the NWA's first "real" PPV.

**BIGGEST RIVAL**
Ric Flair

That shot came at *Great American Bash '88,* and featured the infamous "Maryland State Athletic Commision ending," where a paper-cut on Luger's forehead caused the ref to stop the match. Luger wrestled Flair almost every night after that, throughout 1988, leading up to *Starrcade '88* and his "last title shot ever" where he finally lost once and for all—"once and for all" being "about six months" in this case.

Luger finally had that big match with Barry Windham (only a full year after the fact!) at *Chi-Town Rumble '89,* for Windham's U.S. title. In what can only be termed a shockingly excellent match with a clichéd finish, Luger lifted his shoulder on a belly-to-back suplex attempt by Windham and won the U.S. title for a second time. Windham accidentally punched the ringpost during that match and broke his hand, then departed for the WWF shortly after. As for Luger, his title reign would prove to be short-lived.

Before Windham left, he teamed with his brother Kendall to take on Luger and Michael Hayes in a tag team match. Kendall's only real claim to fame is being arrested and jailed for counterfeiting in the early '90s, a refreshing change of pace from the usual assaults and drug charges plaguing most wrestlers. Michael Hayes, before he was turned into the corporate announcer you see today, was a loud-mouthed, hard-

thrilled about that idea. He preferred to give the rub to Sting, and so the first *Clash of the Champions* featured Flair v. Sting as the main event, while Luger and best friend Barry Windham faced tag champs Tully Blanchard and Arn Anderson for the titles. Luger and Windham won the belts, to one of the loudest crowd reactions in wrestling history. But there was a problem: The Horsemen needed a new fourth man. The solution? The next week, Barry Windham shocked everyone by turning on Luger and joining the Horsemen, allowing Blanchard and Anderson to regain the titles. Luger bypassed the obvious Windham feud and headed right for the top, finally getting his shot at the title.

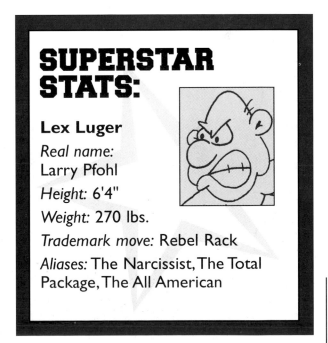

# SUPERSTAR STATS:

**Lex Luger**
*Real name:* Larry Pfohl
*Height:* 6'4"
*Weight:* 270 lbs.
*Trademark move:* Rebel Rack
*Aliases:* The Narcissist, The Total Package, The All American

drinking southern bad-ass heel turned babyface. It didn't fool anyone, and Hayes inevitably turned on Luger during that tag match, setting up a match between them at *WrestleWar '89*. Hayes had roughly zero chance of winning that match, but the NWA was determined to make a singles wrestler out of the tag specialist Hayes to fill the heel void, and Hayes scored the huge upset with the help of partner Terry Gordy to win the title, his only major singles belt. That particular experiment lasted less than a week before irate fans convinced them to switch it back, and Luger regained the title in the "Blufield Moon" match a few days later, so named because Luger rolled Hayes up and grabbed hold of such a huge handful of tights that Hayes mooned the crowd.

With the Hayes experiment dead and buried, Luger was turned heel again to fill the void. In this case, he attacked Ricky Steamboat at *Clash of the Champions VII* and once again became the arrogant and narcissistic jerk that people loved to hate. Steamboat then pulled off a minor miracle, getting the best matches of Luger's career out of him and some of the best of the '80s, period. The two met at *Great American Bash '89* for Luger's U.S. title and put on an amazing match that ended with Steamboat getting disqualified and thus not getting the title. However, now Ric Flair was a babyface and Lex Luger was a heel, so for lack of any better ideas they were once again programmed in title matches throughout the summer. Luger didn't fair any better this time around.

In the fall, Luger was put into a program with hot newcomer "Flyin'" Brian Pillman. Newer fans may know Pillman for the tragic death that marked the end of his career in 1997, but in 1989 he was one of the most exciting wrestlers to watch in America.

LEX LUGER
VS.
BILL
GOLDBERG

Luger and Pillman had two notable and excellent matches, one at *Clash of the Champions IX* and one at *Halloween Havoc '89*, both won by Luger, both very hard-fought wins. They served to elevate Pillman, but now Luger was starting to hear cheers again. And when Ric Flair turned heel in early 1990 and Sting was injured, it was Lex Luger to the rescue again, as he got plugged into yet another feud with Flair over the World title. Luger had the title won at *WrestleWar '90* but elected to help Sting and thus lost; later, he won by disqualification at *Capital Combat '90*. With Ole Anderson in as booker and Flair out, it was back to defending the neglected U.S. title for Luger.

Luger had a notable title defense against rookie "Mean" Mark Callous at *Great American Bash '90*, defeating him fairly easily with a clothesline to retain the title. Well, it wasn't notable as a match, sure, but Mr. Callous was soon to jump to the WWF and become—the Undertaker. Now almost 18 months into his U.S. title reign, Luger was beginning to look unbeatable. So they beat him.

Enter Stan Hansen, the loose-cannon cowboy who was never seen without a hunk of chewing tobacco in his mouth. Figuring they could use Hansen's name to elevate Luger to the final plateau, the NWA put the U.S. title on Hansen at *Halloween Havoc '89* in clean fashion, ending Luger's long reign. Luger regained the title in a screwy bullrope match at *Starrcade '90* after a ref bump and massive controversy. However, with yet another management change on the horizon, bigger things were ahead for Luger.

Luger retained his title against Dan Spivey at *WrestleWar '91*, but now an old foe reappeared with a new twist: Nikita Koloff. Bitter over being left behind by the wrestling business and feeling that Luger's U.S. title win years before had sunk his career (all story line—in reality Koloff's wife Mandy had died from Hodgkin's Disease and Koloff was so devastated that he left the business entirely), Koloff blindsided Luger with the newly redesigned U.S. title belt (the same one that is still in use today by WCW) and began a bitter feud with him. However, it was never settled in the ring, as Luger was intended for the main event, so that feud was transferred to Sting.

At the next PPV, the first *Superbrawl*, Luger & Sting met the tag champs, Rick and Scott Steiner, in what was one of the greatest matches of the decade. Koloff tried to slug Luger with a chain, but Sting sacrificed himself and was knocked out and pinned by Rick Steiner. Koloff and Sting thus began a feud. Two weeks later, Lex Luger squashed the Great Muta on *Clash of the Champions XV* to earn one last, final, this-is-really-it title shot at Ric Flair at the *Great American Bash '91*.

Complications arose, however (which will be covered the next time we get to Ric Flair later on) and Flair was fired from WCW and did not show up at the *Bash*. He also took the belt with him, which presented another problem for the people running the show. So they did the only sensible thing: They found an old regional title belt, slapped a plate on the front that said "World Champion," and took midcarder Barry Windham out of an intergender tag match and put him into the main event as Luger's opponent, winner gets the title. This, more than anything, truly symbolized the transition from the NWA to WCW and the way business was to be conducted from that point on. Luger not only won the title, but also turned heel again for no conceivable reason in the same match (presumably to fill the slot left by Ric Flair), taking Harley Race on as a manager and kicking off the Post-Flair era of WCW.

Oh, and in case you're wondering, they did eventually get a new belt made.

LEX LUGER

# ◀STING▶

Truly the prodigy of the NWA's later years, Sting was plucked from the faltering UWF and turned into a major star with Ric Flair's help. His youthful enthusiam and brash actions turned him into an overnight sensation.

Born Steve Borden in March 1959, Sting was discovered in Venice Beach in 1985 by trainer Rick Bassman and recruited for a part in his new project: Powerteam USA, a group of bodybuilders who would invade wrestling and take it by storm, or something like that.

Unfortunately for Rick, the only two members of the team with any talent appeared to be Borden and Jim Hellwig. They were cut loose from the team and left to seek their fortunes in the Memphis territory as the Freedom Fighters—Steve "Flash" Borden and Jim "Justice" Hellwig. Despite a noted lack of mobility due to their size and muscled physiques, they were over enough for a look and repackaging in the Alabama territory. As both lost weight, they sped up, and soon Steve was renamed Sting, and Jim was known as Rock, and they were the Blade Runners. Internal friction split the team in 1985, and both men would go on to greatness, taking completely different routes to the top. You might know Mr. Hellwig as The Ultimate Warrior.

As for Sting (his given name

STING

was dropped entirely, and in fact he had the Sting name trademarked before the singer even attempted it), he signed with Bill Watts' UWF and began learning his trade faster than anyone thought possible for a former weightlifter. Initially used as a henchman for top heel Eddie Gilbert, Sting—after a crewcut, blond dye-job, and addition of facepaint—and Gilbert captured the UWF World tag titles on two occasions early in Sting's UWF run, and Sting later won the title again with partner Rick Steiner.

His fast-paced, high-impact offense was rapidly turning him babyface without the help of the promotion, however, and he was let loose from the Gilbert "family" midway through 1987 and turned into a singles star. His finisher was the simple "Stinger Splash," a running splash on an opponent in the corner, but his cocky interviews more than made up for his lack of technical expertise.

By the end of 1987, the UWF was all but dead and bought out by Jim Crockett, and Sting was introduced to NWA audiences in December, as Crockett salvaged a few stars from the UWF and left the rest to fend for themselves. Sting made his PPV debut at *Starrcade '87*, teaming with Jimmy Garvin and Michael Hayes to take on Eddie Gilbert, Larry Zbyszko, and Rick Steiner in a match that ended in a 15-minute draw. Sting was shockingly over, however, and a major effort from WCW's braintrust began to push him to the top as soon as possible. The first order of business? Come up with a new finisher. The Stinger Splash wasn't seen as effective enough, so a submission move was added—the Scorpion Deathlock. Taken from Japanese star Riki Choshu, the move was an

immediate hit with the fans and solidified him as a top-level star.

Taken under the wing of Ric Flair, Sting was pushed into an immediate feud with the Four Horsemen via a confrontation with JJ Dillon, and before you could say "Ratings Ploy," a match was set up between Sting and Flair for the first ever *Clash of the Champions* on TBS. The show was invented as counterprogramming for the WWF's *Wrestlemania IV* PPV, and WCW figured that Sting v. Flair was the money match they needed to get a big audience. And in fact, it was.

The show drew a huge cable rating (a 5.8) and the Sting-Flair match itself was voted Match of the Year for 1988, no small feat for Sting in his first three months in the big leagues. It ended in a 45-minute draw, with Sting on the verge of winning the title when time ran out. Sting was immediately boosted to the main event level in the eyes of the fans. Flair loved him, but booker Dusty Rhodes didn't, so Sting got demoted into a tag title match with stale Nikita Koloff against Anderson & Tully Blanchard at the *Great American Bash '88* PPV. That one went to a 20-minute draw, doing nothing to elevate Sting.

Sting was entered in what would be the last Crockett Cup tournament in 1988 with partner Ronnie Garvin, but Garvin had turned heel. Lex Luger was entered with Barry Windham, but Windham also turned heel. And so in one of the most brilliant things Dusty Rhodes thought of during that period, Sting & Luger, the hottest two talents in the NWA, teamed up to blow through the tournament and defeat Anderson

LEX LUGER

"It's Showtime!"
—Sting

& Blanchard in the finals to win it. However, Luger was the one getting the title shots, while Sting was involved in a program with the Road Warriors and Dusty Rhodes.

Dusty, knowing a good thing when he saw one, used his usual modus operandi and made sure to be seen with the hot newcomer in situations where he would look good. Sting and Rhodes challenged the Road Warriors for the tag titles at *Starrcade '88* to settle the Sting-Warriors feud, and Sting managed to do the impossible and get Rhodes involved in an excellent match. Clearly this was the star of the future, but before Rhodes could use him to further his own career any more than he had, he was fired and Sting was on his own again.

And not a moment too soon, as new booker Flair decided to pump him back up as a singles threat for the future by putting the TV title on him and

letting him squash jobbers to his heart's content. Like magic, Sting's credibility was restored, and suddenly he had one of the hottest feuds in the NWA—with Japanese sensation The Great Muta. Muta is fondly remembered for his stuff in 1989 and not for anything that came after, and with good reason. Pulling out moves (like his patented moonsault) that no one had even attempted before (and doing them with ease) and shooting his deadly green mist at opponents, Muta was a phenomenon that took the midcard of WCW by storm.

Sting got a chance to see if he could hang with the big boys of international wrestling by getting into a feud with Muta over the TV title, and the two men had an awesome match at *The Great American Bash '89* PPV that ended with a controversial double-pin and a held-up TV title. They battled throughout the summer to resolve the vacancy (with Muta eventually winning) before both men were moved into the main event picture at *Halloween Havoc* in the Thunderdome cage match.

Flair was now primed to invite Sting into the Horsemen, turn on him, and put him over clean to make him into the biggest drawing star that the

**STING VS. BOBBY EATON**

NWA had ever seen, with Flair booking his every move.

Then everything went to hell.

With Arn Anderson jumping back to WCW from the WWF in late 1989, it was decided that a Four Horsemen reunion was in order. Ric Flair and the Andersons (Ole and Arn) formed the core team, and they invited Sting into the fold as the fourth Horseman. Things were rocky for the alliance almost immediately, as Sting defeated Flair in the finals of the Iron Man tournament at *Starrcade '89* and asked for a title shot as a result. The Horsemen's nemesis was Gary Hart's J-Tex Corporation, consisting of Buzz Sawyer, the Dragon Master, and the Great Muta, and a cage match between the two teams was set up for *Clash of the Champions X* in January, and a Flair-Sting title match was signed for *WrestleWar '90* in February.

Early in *Clash*, the Horsemen proceeded to turn heel by calmly firing Sting and declaring him to be a Horsemen target as punishment for challenging Flair. An irate Sting charged the ring during the cage match main event and went after the Horsemen—and disaster struck. Sting slipped and fell off the cage, blowing out his knee and injuring it so severely that he suddenly needed major surgery on it. While this fit into the story line of the Horsemen as remorseless career-killers, it also meant that there would be no Flair-Sting main event at *WrestleWar*.

Sting forged an alliance with friend/enemy Lex Luger (they always had something of a love/hate/love/hate/love relationship, in character and out of it), which allowed Luger to be inserted fairly seamlessly into the story, taking Sting's place until he was healed.

**STING**

In the time between the injury and the recovery, however, the great WCW tradition continued, and they switched bookers again. This time, the winds of change brought Ole Anderson into the big chair, and he had some decidedly unorthodox ideas about what was going to get over. For instance, in order

# WRESTLER SPOTLIGHT

## STING

### BIGGEST CONTRIBUTION
Lured in a younger audience and excited them with his moves.

### BEST MATCH
Against Ric Flair at the first *Clash of the Champions*, winner of Match of the Year.

### BIGGEST MATCH
Same as above.

### BIGGEST RIVAL
The Great Muta and Nikita Koloff in the earlier years, but with Ric Flair in one of WCW's hottest rivalries ever

with Attitudes," consisting of Paul Orndorff, the Junkyard Dog, and the Steiner Brothers. In the case of Orndorff and JYD, Anderson had fired higher priced (and more talented) wrestlers in order to bring in his friends at bargain-basement rates to save the company money. Again, to the shock of no one, this team didn't thrill anyone. Finally, with Sting recovered from the knee injury, the big Sting-Flair title match was set for *Great American Bash '90*. But there were a few stipulations:

1) El Gigante would be handcuffed to Ole Anderson.
2) If Ric Flair was disqualified, he would lose the World title.
3) The Four Horsemen were barred from ringside.
4) The Dudes with Attitudes would be at ringside to keep the Horsemen away.

OLE ANDERSON

to attract a younger audience, WCW not only hired an actor to portray the "real" Robocop (as opposed to some schmuck just portraying a generic law-enforcing cyborg), but then had him make an appearance on their *Capital Combat* PPV to save Sting from the Horsemen by bending the bars of an iron cage that he was locked in. Why the Horsemen would lock Sting in an iron cage in the first place remains a mystery, but thank god Robocop was at least there. To the shock of roughly no one, Robocop failed to give Sting any kind of rub.

Next strategy: A cool babyface team to oppose the Four Horsemen. Solution: Sting leading "The Dudes

"Owwwwwwwwwwwwww!"
—Sting

This struck a great many people as just a little bit overbooked, although Sting and Flair managed to overcome the limitations of the booking and have a pretty good match for the 14 minutes given them. Sting reversed Flair's figure-four into a small package to win the title for the first time, and received a huge ovation for it.

There was one problem, though: Ole Anderson didn't like Ric Flair. Now, this normally wouldn't be a big deal, but the problem here was a distinct lack of credible challengers for Sting's title, and of that select group, Flair was the undisputed leader of the pack. But with Flair being put into the midcard as fast as humanly possible, only the very green Sid Vicious remained as someone who might draw money against Sting. The solution? WCW invented a new challenger for him. Note: They literally invented a challenger— the mysterious Black Scorpion, whom no one had ever heard of before. The "character" was played on TV by Ole Anderson (with his face shrouded in darkness) and voiced with a distortion box, because if people knew the Scorpion was just Anderson, they might think it was a lame idea or something.

Don't worry, that joke gets funnier as the story unfolds.

The Scorpion's introductory promo saw him reveal himself as someone from Sting's past, with vague references to Venice Beach included. The intention was to cause fans to instantly think of the reigning WWF World champion at the time, Ultimate Warrior, and go "Wow, maybe he's gonna jump ship and join WCW." The real intent was to bring in Dave Sheldon (who used to be called The Angel of Death) and have him play the role. Sheldon was an associate of Sting's in the early days of his career. You're probably wondering just who this Angel of Death guy was, anyway? But that question was just one part of the problem. There were a few more.

First of all, they didn't actually have Sheldon under contract, so all they could do was produce increasingly mysterious promos until they actually had someone to play the part. Then, at *Clash of the Champions XIII*, the mysterious Black Scorpion made his first appearance, making his mark in the wrestling world by—attacking Sting? No, that would have been too obvious, right?

So WCW decided to go completely the opposite route and have The Black Scorpion earn his spot as #1 heel by maliciously turning an innocent audience member into a tiger! That's right—a tiger. How could the all-time great heels like Dick the Bruiser, Baron Von Rashke, and even Ric Flair himself compete with the evil incarnate that saw a man subject a helpless audience to badly done magic tricks? The Scorpion, of course, never even touched Sting, preferring to wage psychological warfare on the viewers who were unfortunate enough to tune in that night.

Could it possibly get worse? Yes, it could.

Sting and the Black Scorpion actually had a match at the next *Clash* show because they thought they

could get a good rating out of it. And they did. Of course, you're probably thinking to yourself, "But how could they have a match if they didn't even have a Black Scorpion?" And the answer is: They put Al Perez in the black suit and had Sting squash him. Never mind that Perez was roughly half the size of the guy who had been doing the magic act in the previous appearance. Ah, but WCW had already thought of that, so they had another Scorpion emerge and taunt Sting, with the idea being that this was the real one and Perez was just an imposter.

The Scorpion showed up again to make Sting's life miserable at *Halloween Havoc '90*. That show actually was a personal best for Sting, giving him two miserably failed angles to

STING

## SUPERSTAR STATS:

**Sting**

*Real name:*
Steve Borden

*Height:* 6'2"

*Weight:* 252 lbs.

*Trademark move:* Scorpion
Death Lock

*Aliases:* Stinger, Flash

work with in the same night. First: The Scorpion appeared during a Sting interview, pulled a "fan" out of the audience, brought her to an adjacent stage area, and made her disappear. Sting stood in place (despite being maybe 15 feet away) as though transfixed by some kind of mystical forcefield.

Second: Sting was defending his World title against Sid Vicious in a match WCW was actually desperate enough to attempt, but they didn't want Sid to go over. At the same time, they didn't want him to job either. So they came up with the unique solution of having the Horsemen kidnap Sting during the match, and then Barry Windham, dressed as Sting, would run back into the ring and lie down for Sid. Sting would then return to reveal his kidnapping ordeal and roll up a stunned Sid for the actual pin. Does this even sound like a good idea to you? WCW apparently thought it was because they went through with it.

The really amazing part is that after all this, someone then came to the conclusion that the fault for them losing a ton of money could be attributed to Sting and his lack of drawing power. Those same people also decided by that point to rid themselves of Ole once and for all, but first they had a Sting v. Black Scorpion main event at *Starrcade '90* to set up—still with no one to actually play the Scorpion.

Obviously the Scorpion had to lose and be unmasked to make the angle work in the slightest, but then that led to another problem: If you stick The Angel of Death under that mask, then no one has a clue who he is. That might have been fine six months before, when the angle began, but this was now a major angle spanning the entire year and the hopes of the show were resting on the identity of the mysterious Black Scorpion being someone the fans would pop for.

So who else did they call to save the company again—but Ric Flair? Flair struck a deal whereby he would take on the humiliating role in exchange for getting the title back again shortly into 1991. And so, the main event of *Starrcade* saw a tastefully done ring introduction featuring four flying saucers dropping four different versions of the Black Scorpion into the ring, followed by the mothership leaving Flair (dressed as the Scorpion) in the middle. Sting beat Flair to retain the title, and the Scorpion angle has not been spoken of on WCW television since then.

Despite Sting's eventual winning of an additional 9 World titles, the stigma attached to him by 1990's poor financial showing and the Black Scorpion angle haunted him for years following and prevented him from achieving the success that he should have been due. As one final note on the ironic nature of wrestling, Sting is today best-known for dressing all in black, with a big scorpion on his tights.

He has, to date, not changed anybody into a tiger.

# 5

## THE DARK AGES: 1990–1996

**1989** was a good year for both promotions. In 1990, however, the WWF, with Hogan's unbeatable aura gone, tried a series of stand-in champions, most of whom failed badly in the role. The defining moment of the era came when Hulk Hogan was unceremoniously humiliated, beaten with his own finishing move, and dumped from the WWF in June of 1993, only to sign with rival WCW a year later. The WWF changed wrestling, again, with the introduction of Monday Night RAW in 1993 and used a radical new approach by having better wrestlers on top, in the form of Bret Hart and Shawn Michaels. But political grandstanding backstage nearly sunk the promotion in 1995.

Meanwhile, WCW was the laughing stock of the wrestling world with its revolving door of Vice Presidents and money-pit attitude. Signing Hulk Hogan and Randy Savage in 1994 was a signal that things were changing, but it took a bigger step to erase the negative perception in the fans' eyes. The "dark ages" officially ended in September of 1995 when WCW Monday Nitro hit the airwaves as a competitor to the WWF's RAW, and a war began.

# HULK HOGAN
## PART II

Things went from good to really bad to good again for Hogan during this time, as he began by ousting Randy Savage from the World title picture in the most successful PPV to date at that time, *Wrestlemania V*. As mentioned during the discussion of Ted Dibiase, Savage's title reign from '88-'89, although intended to create

a new main-event babyface, in fact was essentially sabotaged from the start by the WWF's lack of confidence in him. Savage's character began acting jealous of Hogan in late '88, feeling that Hogan was "lusting" after Miss Elizabeth and his title. Ironically, while the latter was certainly true, even the former may have some basis in reality.

Savage and Hogan, having dispatched of the Megabucks threat, were now dealing with the problem of the Twin Towers (Akeem and the Big Bossman). Akeem is the wrestler who was also known as One

Man Gang—a 400 pound mohawked monster with a loud bellow and not much wrestling skill. In order to get him over, the WWF trashed the successful Gang gimmick—which he'd had since the beginning of his career—and gave him a sillier new one: Akeem the African Dream. The idea was Gang, a white man, would "find himself" on a trip to Africa and realize that he was a black man trapped in a white man's body. It wouldn't have mattered whether he was Gang or Akeem, as the WWF was pushing him to the main event regardless of heat, but the gimmick was given as yet another juvenile shot at Dusty Rhodes, as a play on his "American Dream" gimmick.

An angle began whereby one of the Megapowers' team members would be wrestling one of the Twin Towers' team members in a singles match, and the heels would suddenly turn it into a 2-on-1 beatdown. The other Megapower would run in to "make the save" by chasing off the heels..

## WRESTLER SPOTLIGHT

### HULK HOGAN

**BIGGEST CONTRIBUTION**
Moving to WCW was a major story both in wrestling and out.

**BEST MATCH**
His matches with Ric Flair in WCW were pretty amazing, by Hogan's standards.

**BIGGEST MATCH**
His first match in WCW against Ric Flair drew the highest buyrate in the history of the company to that point.

However, the twist was that while Hogan would be grateful for Savage's help, Savage would not be grateful for Hogan's help, insisting that he had matters in hand and could have done it alone. Remember: Faces have friends, heels have allies. This led up to the second prime-time WWF show, as *The Main Event* returned to NBC in February 1988.

The featured match was the less-than-inspiring tag match of Hogan & Savage v. Bossman & Akeem, and during that match, Savage finally snapped and attacked Hogan, walking out of the match and leaving Hogan to face both 400-pound heels by himself. Hogan, of course, won, thus proving Savage's point about them not needing each other. The WWF failed to pay attention to small story line flaws like that one until it was too late.

But the bigger point was that the Megapowers were set to explode, with Randy Savage defending the WWF title against Hulk Hogan at *Wrestlemania V* in a match with a conclusion so foregone that they might as well have advertised it on the promotional materials. And in fact one enterprising wrestling magazine picked up on that and actually published the results of the show (with about 90% accuracy, give or take a double-DQ that couldn't really be predicted) well in advance

**WRESTLING MAGAZINE**

RESULTS OF THE SHOW:

Hulk Hogan:
WINNER

Randy Savage:
LOSER

of it happening!

The match itself was shockingly good, as Hogan of course defeated Savage to win his second WWF title and send the crowd home happy. In the process, the increasingly jealous and unstable Savage fired manager Elizabeth and joined with Sherri Martell instead, solidifying him as a heel. But there was now a problem—Martell had never managed in the WWF before, and thus had no main-event credibility as a manager. Savage's increasingly cartoonish character didn't help matters, and as Hogan dispatched Savage time after time in rematches, Savage fell farther down the card.

Hogan, meanwhile, had other plans for his career at that point, choosing to focus on his acting career in Hollywood instead of the World title that he had destroyed Savage's main event potential to win. He signed to do a movie called *No Holds Barred*, to be produced and distributed on PPV in association with the WWF themselves, playing a champion wrestler who is opposed by a large black man with a bad eye named Zeus. High concept stuff, to be sure, but the WWF decided to take it a step further—by actually signing the actor who played Zeus to become a real wrestler (albeit in the loosest possible sense of the word) to oppose Hogan in "real life." Even the more mark-ish publications like *Pro Wrestling Illustrated* had a hard time swallowing that one.

To put this in perspective, the only thing Zeus (played by actor Tony Lister) had going for him was his enormous size and imposing demeanor. He had no formal training, no real idea of selling or pacing, and was completely unproven as a box-office draw, let alone a wrestling draw. The movie itself was a huge flop, but the WWF went ahead with their plan to push Zeus as a serious wrestler anyway, as he injured Hogan with his crippling nerve hold to the neck and set up a tag match for *Summerslam '89* in the process with Hogan and lackey Brutus Beefcake against Zeus and Randy Savage.

This was clearly the Hogan Show, as he dispatched both heels without too much effort. Savage's star was falling fast, as he had been demoted to a feud with Jim Duggan over the bogus "King of the WWF" title and had taken to calling himself "The Macho King" as his new nickname after "winning" the crown from Duggan.

Once *No Holds Barred* sped to PPV after leaving the theaters, the WWF packaged the movie with a special cage match featuring the above tag teams, as Hogan and Beefcake once again defeated Zeus and Savage, with Hogan pinning Zeus for the win. Most people were dreading the upcoming *Wrestlemania VI*, because the only viable main event for the 60,000 seat Skydome seemed to be Hogan v. Zeus for the title, something that no one wanted to see.

But Zeus disappeared for good soon after, because the WWF had something else in mind. At the *Royal Rumble* in January 1990, Hogan won the Rumble match itself for reasons escaping most people. At one point in the match, the only two people left in the ring were Hogan and Intercontinental champion Ultimate Warrior, the man who finally ended Honky Tonk Man's title reign. The two men had a pretty epic shoving match, and ended up knocking each other out on a clothesline. Okay, so it wasn't exactly Ali-Frazier, but the crowd was electrified by the thought of the two biggest stars in the WWF going at it, and suddenly the main event for *Wrestlemania VI* became apparent.

But there was one problem: Hulk Hogan wanted to retire to make another movie. But he wasn't 100%

sure that he wanted to officially retire, so the WWF wanted to keep him strong for his eventual return or in case they decided to have him keep the title. So in building up the match, they made sure to balance both guys out 50/50 in terms of crowd support and heat, and didn't do anything to make one of them into a heel, which would jeopardize the support for the winner after the match. But face v. face matches, while a good short-term money draw, don't really do anything for the promotion in the long run because eventually the fans have to choose sides.

What this essentially means is that whoever walks out of the match as the winner is going to have their total fanbase cut in half, because the other group's favorite just lost. Unless, of course, the loser is an extraordinarily unselfish person who does the job gracefully *and* endorses the winner after the fact. Since this is Hulk Hogan we're talking about, the WWF had a problem.

Leading up to the match, Hogan defended the WWF title against Randy Savage on the third *Main Event* program on NBC, and Vince appeared ready to bail out on the Hogan-Warrior match and put the title back on Savage. But scheduled special referee Mike Tyson was knocked out by Buster Douglas shortly before this match, thus instantly ruining his star power. He was replaced as ref by Douglas, and the WWF felt that it would be silly to use an unproven boxing champion like Douglas in such a prominent role, so the

title change that would have involved Mike Tyson (8 years before his historic appearance at *Wrestlemania XIV*) was switched to Hogan retaining the title when Douglas interfered and knocked out Savage.

**Face vs. Face MATCH short-term $$$**

The Hogan-Warrior match finally came and went with media crackdowns approaching the levels of East Berlin, as no reporters were allowed out of the pressboxes until the show was finished, to make sure results weren't leaked before the WWF was ready. Hogan and Warrior had a match that most people very generously called "very good," keeping in mind the extreme limitations of both men and the incredible heat for the match. Warrior won the title by splashing Hogan after Hogan's legdrop missed, and ended up with both the Intercontinental and World titles in the process.

After the pin, referee Earl Hebner accidentally handed the World title belt to Warrior when the plan was for Hogan to do the honors himself. The camera hastily cut away as Warrior gave the belt back to Hebner, who in turn gave it back to the timekeeper in time for the camera to pick up on Hogan taking it from there again and giving it to Warrior. Warrior was the man to lead the WWF into the next decade, and everyone lived happily ever after.

Well, not quite.

While people *seemed* ready to give up Hogan as their hero and savior, people also *seem* ready to give up smoking on a regular basis, too. But neither one was likely to actually happen. More on that when we cover the Ulimate Warrior.

As for Hogan, he shot an angle where newcomer John Tenta, dubbed The Earthquake, injured him with a butt-splash and put him out of action for six months. Hogan swore revenge and the usual rematch happened at *Summerslam '90*, with Hogan winning by countout to set up another match. For his part, however, Hogan was losing interest in the wrestling business and began sleepwalking through his matches, even more so than usual, as Hollywood kept asking him to make movies.

As 1991 approached, the U.S. started the Gulf War with Iraq and the WWF decided to capitalize. Longtime patriotic wrestler Sgt. Slaughter was made into an Iraqi sympathizing turncoat, and got the WWF title at *Royal Rumble '91*. Who else could oppose him but the "Real American" himself, Hulk Hogan? Vince booked the 100,000 seat L.A. Coliseum and waited for the money to start rolling in. After three months of waiting and barely 18,000 tickets sold, it was apparent that they had a problem. To make matters worse, the Gulf War ended in a heartbeat, turning Slaughter into little more than a joke.

So wrestling's natural tendencies took over, and Vince (who was being raked over the coals by the legitimate media for exploiting the Gulf War) came up with a "bomb threat" that was looming, and for "security reasons" the event would be moved to the L.A. Sports Arena at the last minute. How this increased security is anyone's guess, but one thing was for sure—the only bomb that night was the show. The WWF's sudden desperation was evident during the show itself, as the announcers played up how *Wrestlemania VII* was the "most-watched PPV of all time."

However, given that buyrates usually take 4-6 *weeks* to be calculated, this was an obvious lie on their part. And indeed, the show's eventual buyrate proved to be half that of the previous year's show, and set a trend of lowered buyrates for the next few years. Hogan was once again losing interest in being an active wrestler, as he half-heartedly did a main-event match with Ultimate

Warrior to take on Sgt. Slaughter, Col. Mustafa (a repackaged Iron Sheik), and General Adnan (their manager) at *Summerslam '91*. Again, the buyrate was not exactly what the WWF had hoped for, and to make matters worse, the Warrior left the WWF entirely after that match, leaving them short of top babyfaces. Ironically, to fill that void, Randy Savage was brought out of retirement and elevated back to the main event again, this time making sure to avoid the shadow of Hulk Hogan completely.

The first real sign of cracks in Hulkamania's armor came at *Survivor Series '91*, as Hogan defended the title against newcomer The Undertaker in what, even 3 years prior, would have been a routine matter of dispatching him with the big boot and legdrop. However, the lowered buyrates and drastically lowered attendance figures spoke of a decline in Hogan's popularity, and as a result Hogan was made to lose the title in the middle of the ring after being hit with Undertaker's "tombstone piledriver" finisher. An assist was provided by new WWF entrant Ric Flair, but the result was still viewed as a huge shock, given the previous tendency for Hogan to escape such situations unscathed in the past. Hogan briefly regained the belt a week later on another PPV (good thing they had that other timeslot lined up so far in advance) but was stripped of it on a technicality.

Meanwhile, Ric Flair came into the WWF and immediately went after Hulk Hogan, something that puzzled many people. Hogan and Flair were the two biggest-drawing World champions of the '80s and had never met before, and the WWF simply put them out there on a show in Dayton one night and gave it away. They did other matches over the course of the next two months, going through the usual progression of finishes in a Hogan feud (heel wins by DQ, Hogan wins by DQ, Hogan wins by pinfall), as more and more people wondered why this wasn't being saved for a PPV instead. When Flair cost Hogan his WWF title, many thought this would be the catalyst for that match.

The vacated WWF title was put up for grabs in the *Royal Rumble* of 1992, and of course Hogan was entered. It came down to Flair, Savage, Hogan, and Sid Justice (aka Sid Vicious), and after Savage was eliminated, Sid tossed Hogan out. However, Hogan began to whine and complain to the referees about the perfectly fair elimination, causing the smart New York crowd to turn against him, something that had never happened on that scale before. He then cheated and pulled Justice out after him, giving the World title to Ric Flair. Hogan and Sid had a pull-apart brawl with the crowd very clearly siding with Sid. Judicious editing on the part of the WWF made it sound like the opposite in every later broadcast of the incident, since they wanted Sid to be the bad guy in this situation.

A World title match between Ric Flair and Hulk Hogan was announced for *Wrestlemania VIII*, which everyone thought made perfect sense, but that proved to be a red herring. Hogan wanted to retire (yes, again) after this match, and since there was no way he was

$1,972,072,882,391.73

going to lose to Ric Flair in his retirement match, that would mean winning the WWF title and then retiring with it, something that even Vince McMahon was unwilling to let go down. So the match was changed to a "double main event": Ric Flair defending against Randy Savage and Hulk Hogan taking on Sid Justice.

That way Hogan could vanquish Justice and retire. Things didn't go so smoothly even then, as the match was supposed to end on a disqualification with Papa Shango (you might know him as The Godfather) running in. However, Shango misjudged the time it would take to run down the aisle in the 80,000 seat Hoosierdome and missed his cue, leaving Hogan and Justice to improvise a new finish. Justice was forced to kick out of the devastating legdrop (another nail in Hogan's WWF coffin, intentional or not) and some people attributed this to Sid "shooting" on Hogan. Eventually Shango made it out and Ultimate Warrior made his triumphant return to make the save, and Hogan left. Finally.

But he came back again.

In January of 1993, the WWF launched a new program to replace the *Primetime Wrestling* show on USA. At the same time, Hogan had finished shooting his latest movie and wanted back into the main event scene yet again. However, things had changed significantly in the WWF in the 8 months since Hogan had last left. Unlike his other absences, where the WWF had left a Hogan ally (Randy Savage) or a Hogan clone (Warrior) to fill the space he left, this time a totally different approach to things had come about.

Throughout 1992, Ric Flair and Randy Savage were having a hot feud over Miss Elizabeth and the WWF title, and were drawing just fine without a trace of Hulkamania. In fact, their feud helped sell out the 80,000 seat Manchester Stadium for *Summerslam '92*, and when Flair left the WWF in October, longtime employee Bret Hart was elevated into his place as champion and was put into a feud with Shawn Michaels. Both men were superb technical wrestlers and completely opposite the kick-and-punch philosophy

that had carried Hogan and his ilk for the past 10 years, and both men were bigger draws of money and ratings than Hogan had been in recent years. Both also worked for less money combined than Hogan made, something that pretty much sealed Hogan's fate.

In order to provide a quick boost to *RAW*'s ratings and make it seem important, the WWF shot an angle whereby Hogan and Brutus Beefcake would get into a confrontation with tag champs Money, Inc. (Ted Dibiase & Mike "IRS" Rotundo) and adopt Jimmy Hart as a manager. The idea was to build to a tag title match at *Wrestlemania IX* and phase Hogan out of the main event and into the midcard by placating his ego with the tag titles. Hogan had other plans, pitching instead that he be given the WWF title again. Vince reluctantly agreed at the last minute, literally just before the show started, and the finish of the tag title match was changed to the challengers winning by disqualifcation instead of winning the titles.

However, in the main event of the evening, WWF champion Bret Hart was defending against the 600-pound Yokozuna, the up-and-coming monster heel of the year. The finish that was told to Bret leading up to the show was that he would defeat the undefeatable monster and move onto other things. Suddenly, the ending was made into Yokozuna cheating and winning the title from Bret, at which point Hogan would come in, challenge the new champion on the spot, and win the title back in 20 seconds. This would also bury Bret Hart in the process, but Hogan was determined to get his way. Vince agreed to this scenario on one condition: Hogan would defend the title against Bret Hart at *Summerslam* that year, and put him over big enough to endorse him as the new generation of wrestler, before leaving for good. Hogan agreed, and walked out of *Wrestlemania IX* as the new champion.

Almost immediately after the show, Hogan changed his mind.

Now the champion, he decided to take nearly two months off, and also informed the WWF that he would no longer be doing the job to Bret Hart at *Summerslam*. Given the anemic buyrate and horrible reviews for Hogan's title victory—when he wasn't even in the title match!—it was apparent that Hogan had

**Undefeatable Monster?**

made the single biggest mistake of his WWF career: He had dared Vince McMahon to call his bluff.

So at the inaugural *King of the Ring* PPV, Hogan was set to defend the title against Yokozuna, and originally was going to win before moving onto Bret Hart. Instead, the finish was changed to Yokozuna completely manhandling Hogan and pinning him with his own finisher: The legdrop. Hogan, Beefcake, and Jimmy Hart were fired immediately after and essentially told never to come back.

Humiliated and no longer in a good bargaining position, Hogan took nearly a year off to lick his wounds and shoot another movie, telling anyone who would listen that he was done with wrestling, for good this time.

Meanwhile, down south…

WWF rival WCW had been bought out by Ted Turner's media conglomerate in 1988, essentially as a plaything and a tax writeoff that provided cheap programming for Superstation WTBS. The cycle of ineffective vice presidents had put former junior announcer and Verne Gagne coffee boy Eric Bischoff in command of the ship, and as 1994 began, he was in serious danger of being removed from that position less than a year into it. After a financially disastrous 1993, the company needed anything to justify the expenses that Turner was pumping into it. So Bischoff made his last-ditch pitch to his superiors for money: He wanted several million dollars to go out and sign some big-name stars and finally make WCW competitive with the WWF. Ted Turner agreed to that and more, because when Ted Turner did something, he did it big.

Bischoff was given permission to sign Hulk Hogan, Randy Savage, Jim Duggan, the Nasty Boys, Brutus Beefcake, Jimmy Hart, the Honky Tonk Man, John Tenta, and just about everyone else associated with Hulk Hogan from the WWF who was available. A ticker-tape parade for Hogan was staged by WCW and fans were paid to act like they were excited to see him. While some certainly were, there was a much larger percentage of fans who were not, due to the long-standing belief from NWA (and later WCW) fans that their promotion was the "real" one, featuring "real" wrestling action and hard-hitting effort from the wrestlers. Hulk Hogan represented the circus of the WWF and was a slap in the face to longtime supporters of the promotion.

WCW went for the throat immediately, putting longtime dream match Ric Flair v. Hulk Hogan on the first PPV of their "new era," *Bash at the Beach '94.* The rather odd-sounding name was a combination of the two former shows that ran in the July slot: *The Great American Bash* and *Beach Blast. The Great American Bash* show in 1991, in fact, was considered such a disaster and deemed so bad that the name itself was retired for four years following. Hogan, in his first match in the promotion, defeated Ric Flair to capture the WCW World title and become only the third person (after Flair and Buddy Rogers) to win the World titles of both major promotions.

WCW instantly time-warped back to 1985 as all of Hogan's friends overran the promotion, forcing out longtime WCW loyalists such as Mick "Cactus Jack" Foley, Steve Austin, and Vader, and moving popular stars like Lex Luger and Sting from the main event into the midcard or behind Hogan's shadow again.

Hogan's first big title defense was against Ric Flair at WCW's *Halloween Havoc* show in October, and Flair's eventual defeat there meant "retirement" for him. Having killed off the homegrown WCW talent, Hogan main evented WCW's showcase PPV, *Starrcade,* against best friend-turned-traitor Brutus Beefcake in an exact repeat of every stale story line from 1984-1988 that had worked before.

Except this time, it didn't. The show was a total failure, drawing an embarrassing buyrate and low attendance. Hogan stepped up his efforts, moving himself into a feud with resident monster Vader, but again he completely miscalculated. In the WWF, Vader would be a strong heel who lost out to the American hero Hogan, but WCW worked under a different dynamic. Heels were built up big until there seemed no way for the face to win, at which point the face pulled off a miracle comeback and did so. This usually entailed the heel beating the face for his title in the first match and dominating the rematch, only to lose. Vader had in fact done this very formula to tremendous success with both Sting and Ric Flair in recent years, and Hogan looked to be no exception. A match between them at *Superbrawl V* was booked, with Vader set to win the WCW World title and set up a rematch.

Hogan, not understanding the southern booking mentality, changed the finish to him retaining the title on a big double-DQ; the match also included Hogan no-selling Vader's crippling powerbomb. To give you an idea here, Vader actually did cripple a man with the powerbomb, breaking the back of jobber Joe Thurman by accident and thus turning the move into a match-ender in every sense of the word in the minds of the fans from that point on. Hogan killed that in one fell swoop and Vader's career never recovered. The best was yet to come, though, as Hogan and Vader did a strap match gimmick for their rematch at the inaugural *Uncensored* PPV.

The match was a decent brawl, won by Hogan after fulfilling the winning conditions by dragging the special participant, Ric Flair, to all four corners in succession. The fact that Flair wasn't a real participant in the actual match was apparently less important to

Hogan than beating Flair again. During that match, another Hogan brainchild debuted, as he had promised "The Ultimate Surprise" for Flair and Vader, leading most fans to think that Ultimate Warrior was about to debut for WCW. Instead, it was Rick Williams, dubbed "The Renegade," and given mannerisms and dress that were a direct imitation of the Warrior. The WWF quickly sued to put an end to that little bit of plagiarism, but Hogan kept up the manic pace.

Next, debuting wrestler Paul Wight (better known as The Big Show these days) was given the gimmick of being "Andre the Giant's estranged son" and simply dubbed The Giant, and put into a feud with Hogan in an attempt to duplicate the money drawn by the original Hogan-Andre feud. That also failed miserably and now Hogan was starting to feel the heat from WCW higher-ups who wanted some sort of return on their investment in him.

About that time, with Hogan's star falling rapidly and WCW losing money again, WCW head Eric Bischoff did yet another last-ditch pitch for money, this time in the form of an opposing TV show for *Monday Night RAW* to be shown on Turner's TNT network. The show was called *WCW Monday Nitro* and Hogan was going to be featured prominently fighting Kevin Sullivan's "Dungeon of Doom," which included Kevin Sullivan, Hugh Morrus, and Konnan. WCW began pitching a change in Hogan's character to him to freshen it up as the year came to a close—and no one, not even WCW themselves, could have predicted what sort of long-reaching effects that change would have on wrestling as a whole.

But more on that later.

# RIC FLAIR
## PART II

Dissatisfied with his treatment in the new WCW in 1991, Flair shocked the wrestling world by jumping ship to the circus-like WWF, where he immediately made a huge impact.

Well, when we last talked about Flair, he was starting the 1991 season by beating Sting to win his seventh World title, tying Harley Race's record. But Jim Herd was plotting the downfall of Flair.

This is the deal: Flair had a big contract. A holdover from the NWA days, Flair's deal stipulated not only huge amounts of money, but creative control over his finishes and title reigns and such. However, in one of those weird leaps of logic that only wrestling executives ever seem to make, it was felt that Flair's worth to the promotion was diminished and his contract, when it expired in June, would not be

renewed unless it was drastically reduced and Flair's power with it.

This despite WCW literally begging Flair to save the company by taking on the Black Scorpion role a few weeks earlier, thus showing how truly fickle the sport can be. Now, Flair had leverage for two reasons: 1) He was World champion and scheduled in the main event of the next show and; 2) He owned the title belt

itself, in a manner of speaking.

How did Flair get to own his own title belt? Well, strictly speaking, he didn't. But he thought he did, and WCW didn't know any better. See, in 1985, to really give Flair the superstar image, the NWA commissioned a brand new, gigantic title belt (the one still used today) with tons of gold and jewels and stuff. It cost roughly $10,000 to make, and by a strange coincidence that was almost exactly how much Jim Crockett owed Flair in certain bonuses due from his contract. So they struck a deal: Flair keeps the belt and waives the right to those bonuses. Everyone was happy.

So, Flair is pretty insulted by the treatment he's receiving and threatens to quit, just like he's done seemingly hundreds of times before in order to leverage a better deal. Jim Herd decides to call his bluff this time and fires him outright. Big mistake.

Instant locker room rebellion springs up, since everyone loves Flair. Fans nearly riot at house shows leading up to the *Bash* with the sudden absence of Flair. Vince McMahon pounces like a blood-crazed predator, signing Flair almost immediately and prepping him for a main-event entrance into the WWF. Rumors fly about Flair jumping ship—with the title belt.

*Hold up*, says Herd, *no one said anything about THAT*. Oops, apparently the brass forgot about Flair's "ownership" of the gold, which was confirmed when Bobby Heenan knocked on Hulk Hogan's door at WWF's *Summerslam '91* carrying the WCW World title. This was the equivalent of wrestling armageddon, the worst-case scenario for any promotion, and here it was happening to WCW only 8 months into their existence. To compound the pain, the few remaining members of the NWA itself were throwing fits upon seeing the title belt representing 50 years of heritage being used as a prop for the WWF. Just because they could, the WWF started billing Flair as "The Real World's Champion" to set up a match between him and WWF champ Hulk Hogan. This was too much for the NWA, and they stripped Flair of NWA title recognition in September of 1991.

But wait, didn't Lex Luger already get the World title in July of 1991? Yes and no. The problem with ugly politics is that they're so ugly. Just look at the NWA and WCW.. WCW went solo in 1991, yes. But they still had to recognize the NWA World champion to be an NWA member. But they wanted their own champion, too. Solution: Jim Herd was made president of the NWA, and it was decided that reigning champ Ric Flair would be both the NWA and WCW World champion at the same time, and for the sake of everyone's sanity they would use the same belt, and just conveniently forget to mention on TV that Flair was still NWA World champion.

This situation led to a *really* complicated argument in Japan over whether or not Tatsumi Fujinami had won the title(s) one night. As it turned out, since the rules of WCW and the NWA were different, circumstances dictated that he was NWA World champion, but not WCW World Champion, despite pinning Flair. Stuff like this happens all the time in wrestling, and it's best not to dwell on it too long or else you might start thinking like a booker. This problem of semantics became amplified when Flair left for

the WWF with the NWA World title belt. In fact, although WCW had the power to strip Flair of the WCW World title, the other NWA members saw no reason to strip Flair of the NWA World title until he actually started appearing in the WWF.

So let's get back to where we left off: Flair in the WWF is carrying around a title he thinks belongs to him and calling himself the Real World's Champion. Two lawsuits immediately pop up: WCW sues Flair for ownership of that belt, while the NWA sues the WWF for insinuating that Flair is still the NWA World champion by use of that distinctive belt. The WWF loses both of them, and two things happen: WCW buys back their belt from Flair for $28,000, and the WWF gives Flair a new fake title belt, which is then "video distorted" by WWF President Jack Tunney as a convenient way to keep fans at home from noticing that it's not the same belt anymore. The NWA sues again, pointing out that even the new fake belt resembles theirs, so that one gets taken away and Flair just uses a tag team title belt instead.

Ric Flair officially made his WWF debut in October of 1991, facing Hulk Hogan for the WWF title right out of the gate, and winning it. Unfortunately for him, the decision was reversed, but the fans in attendance were ecstatic for a few moments. After a month of Flair-Hogan matches, Flair cost Hogan that title at *Survivor Series '91*, throwing a chair into the ring for Undertaker to tombstone Hogan onto for the winning pin. Due to the controversial nature of the match between Hogan and Undertaker (and the rematch), the WWF title was vacated and put up for grabs in the 1992 *Royal Rumble*, with the winner receiving the title.

At this time, Flair had replaced the retired Bobby Heenan as his manager (or as Flair called him, "Financial Advisor") with the semi-

WORLD TITLE JULY 1991

retired Curt "Mr. Perfect" Hennig ("Executive Consultant"). Flair put in the performance of his WWF career to that point, going more than sixty minutes and surviving 30 other men to help Hulk Hogan eliminate Sid Justice at the end. Left alone in the ring, Flair was the new WWF World champion.

Next, everyone expected Flair to defend his title against Hulk Hogan at *Wrestlemania VIII*, but because of the things discussed in the previous section on Hogan, the match became Ric Flair v. Randy Savage for the title. Fearing that a straight wrestling match wouldn't sell (probably justifiably so), the WWF decided to add an angle to spice things up. And so, soon after the title match was announced, Ric Flair suddenly produced photos of himself and Savage's wife Elizabeth from "years before" in compromising positions. Flair's claim, "She was mine before she was yours," became a very successful selling point of the match, even after it was revealed that Flair doctored the photos. Flair and Mr. Perfect promised one last photo of Liz for the show, this one featuring her wearing "just the staples where the magazine folds," which sadly was never produced.

Savage became even more incoherent and maniacal leading up to the event, guaranteeing a good time for all. As is the case in "wronged husband" angles, Savage got his revenge, defeating Flair for the WWF title with a roll-up after fighting off interference from Mr. Perfect. A massive brawl erupted after the win, ensuring that Flair would continue to make Savage's life miserable. Now the Ultimate Warrior would enter into their little soap opera, as Savage was announced as defending his title against the Warrior at *Summerslam* in a face v. face match. Flair played both guys against each other leading up to the show, claiming to be in the corner of one of them, but really just being there to screw Savage over rather than help Warrior.

Savage was counted out due to Flair's interference, and one last match between Savage and Flair was signed soon after that. Ric Flair (and new buddy Razor Ramon, aka Scott Hall) defeated Savage to capture his second WWF title, but there was a hitch: The first match between them on the evening was so bad, they actually had to retape it at the end of the night to keep it from looking like amateur hour.

Flair's second reign was to be less eventful than his first, however, as he still had to settle the issue with Randy Savage and Ultimate Warrior, and that would

## WRESTLER SPOTLIGHT

## RIC FLAIR

### BIGGEST CONTRIBUTION
Carried WCW on his back in 1993.

### BEST MATCH
Against Vader at *Starrcade '93*, probably his last great one.

### BIGGEST MATCH
Hogan v. Flair drew the money WCW was looking for.

come in the form of a tag match signed for *Survivor Series* between the new Flair/Ramon tandem and Savage/Warrior. However, just as the match was building nicely, Warrior suddenly weirded out and left the promotion a week before the match, leaving the WWF in the lurch.

Luckily, a backup plan was in place and a new story line was concocted: On the episode of *Primetime Wrestling* before *Survivor Series*, it was quickly announced that Warrior was gone (which was the last mention of him before his 1996 return) and that Savage would be free to pick a new partner by the end of the show. Flair's manager Mr. Perfect was one of the roundtable panelists for the show, and when Savage was contacted "via satellite" to ask him who he wanted for a partner, he picked—Mr. Perfect. An indignant Bobby Heenan sputtered that it was ridiculous to pick Perfect, which prompted Perfect in turn to ask if that was because he was friends with Flair, or because Heenan didn't think he could get the job done? Savage egged on the argument until Perfect finally turned on Heenan and agreed to be Savage's partner.

The match itself turned out very well, despite Perfect's still-healing back problems, but it ended in an inconclusive finish.

However, change was the order of the day for the WWF, and Ric Flair wasn't part of the plan any longer. Vince felt that Flair had no long-term potential as a main eventer because of his age and wanted to move him into the midcard, so Flair asked to be let out of his contract so he could jump back to WCW. Since Flair was a friend of Vince's, a deal was struck whereby Flair would drop the title to Bret Hart, then put over Mr. Perfect in a retirement match on the way out. Flair dropped the title to Bret Hart in Saskatoon, Saskatchewan, Canada, then did a ***** 60-minute Iron Man match with him in Boston for an untelevised house show that he later called his best WWF match ever. He drew entry #1 in the 1993 *Royal Rumble*, being eliminated by Mr. Perfect in fairly short order, and lost to Perfect on an early episode of the new *Monday Night RAW* program to finish out his WWF career.

Things had changed drastically in WCW during Flair's WWF stay, however. 1991 saw Lex Luger reign as WCW champion to empty arenas, prompting the firing of Jim Herd, booker Dusty Rhodes, and eventually Luger himself at the end of 1991. Turner suit K. Allen Frye had a brief run as Vice President, using a spectacularly successful system whereby he would pay a cash bonus to whoever had the best match on a given show. The effort that resulted from the workers was impressive, but he had no one who could book. So WCW went to its past and brought in Bill Watts, whose UWF promotion had been bought out in 1987 during the formation of WCW. Watts was given the reigns as both booker and Executive Vice President, and he immediately started implementing a bizarre throwback style, banning top rope moves and removing the mats from the concrete floor surrounding the ring.

Watts favorites Steve Williams and Terry Gordy were brought in and pushed all the way to the tag titles in short order, and Big Van Vader was elevated to a monster heel, squashing Sting and becoming World champion. This change in attitude for the promotion provided some good old-style wrestling, but didn't do much for the bottom line. Watts's refusal to be a corporate yes-man cost him in the long run, however, as he was fired for insubordination with 1992 limping to a close, and replaced with junior announcer Eric Bischoff early in 1993.

At the same time, the NWA was desperately trying to re-establish its name in the sport, and they went to their biggest member, WCW, for help in doing so. An NWA World title tournament was run in Japan, with Masahiro Chono defeating Rick Rude in the finals to win the belt. Here comes the complicated part: They were using the big gold belt that WCW bought back from Ric Flair in 1991. They were essentially lending it to the NWA for use as their World title. WCW had their own World title. The NWA World title was defended on WCW programs, with the Great Muta winning in Japan late in 1992, then dropping it to Barry Windham on the *Superbrawl 3* PPV back in America in February 1993. So as 1993 began, WCW had essentially two World champions: WCW World champion Vader and NWA World champion Barry Windham.

Ric Flair signed with WCW immediately upon his WWF release, but couldn't wrestle for 90 days due to a no-compete clause, so instead he was given a talk segment, "A Flair for the Gold," where he interviewed various WCW wrestlers. He was also given a "maid" named Fifi as a valet. No one is quite sure why. At

*Slamboree '93*, Flair was put in the unfortunate position of reforming the Four Horsemen yet again, this time with Arn Anderson, estranged and washed-up Ole Anderson, and lifetime jobber Paul Roma (who was "replacing" the born-again and absent Tully Blanchard, who smartly wanted nothing to do with the whole deal). The fans immediately turned on Roma in vicious fashion, despite Flair's best efforts to rub his stardom off on him.

One notable interview segment later on saw the hottest tag team in the business, the Hollywood Blonds (Steve Austin & Brian Pillman) doing their own version of the show, called "A Flair for the Old," with Austin dressed up as Flair and doing his impersonation of him. This set up a tag title match between the Blonds and the team of Ric Flair & Arn Anderson once Flair was legally cleared to wrestle. The Horsemen team won by disqualification, and Paul Roma was phased into the feud to take Flair's place. An angle was set up whereby Flair had asked NWA champion Barry Windham to join the Horsemen team, but was snubbed by Windham, leading to the inevitable title match. Flair won the title, beating Windham with the figure four.

There was, however, a complication.

With a WCW-contracted wrestler holding the NWA World title, the NWA's bargaining power with WCW was essentially gone, and so to save money WCW simply stopped paying dues to the NWA and left the organization cold in June of 1993. This now had the bizarre effect of leaving the NWA with no World champion, while WCW had an extra World champion with no organization to back it. This normally would be a trivial matter to deal with: You have Flair lose a unification match to Vader (the WCW World champion), end of problem.

However, in the case of 1993 WCW, even the complications had complications.

Here's the back story: Sticking with the money-saving motif, someone high up in WCW decided that booking arenas for syndicated shows like *WCW Worldwide* was an expensive proposition, and maybe for those sorts of shows they should just book a TV studio down in Orlando somewhere and get three months of programming in the can and be done with it. Someone actually thought this was a good idea and implemented it, and in May of '93, WCW sent most of its roster for a marathon taping session in Orlando, comprising three months' worth of squash matches and happenings. It was that "happenings" part that complicated things, as they decided to give away all their title changes in one shot. At the tapings it was revealed that Ric Flair would defeat Barry Windham at *Beach Blast* for the NWA World title, then go on to feud with Rick Rude and lose that title to him at *Fall Brawl* in September.

After all of this was taped, WCW pulled out of the NWA, meaning that the already-filmed Rude-Flair feud was over a meaningless belt. WCW's solution to the problem: Call it "The Big Gold Belt." And indeed, *Fall Brawl '93* saw the match being promoted in a serious fashion as being for "The Big Gold Belt." Flair continued feuding with Rude for that title as WCW tried to fix the problem by forming a ficticious "WCW International Board of Directors," who then backed Rick Rude as the "WCW International World champion," by which point most fans had ceased paying attention to the whole thing anyway.

Flair was settling into a nice upper-midcard groove

when once again disaster struck and WCW needed him to bail them out. At the Orlando TV tapings, it had been revealed that hot babyface Sid Vicious would defeat Vader for the WCW World title at WCW's biggest show of the year, *Starrcade '93*, and be the guy to carry the company. As you can probably guess, there was a complication.

In this case, Sid and Arn Anderson were doing a house show in England, and got into a fight in the hotel room following the event. Words were exchanged, and finally Sid grabbed a pair of safety scissors and attacked Arn with them, nearly puncturing Arn's kidney and taking an eye out. WCW had no choice but to fire Vicious only two weeks before putting their World title on him. Left with no main event and facing the loss of his job as a result, Eric Bischoff asked Flair to take Vicious's place in a title v. career match at *Starrcade*, with a bonus: Flair could take over as booker again following the match.

As usual, Flair delivered, getting a brutally entertaining match out of Vader in front of Flair's hometown crowd in Charlotte, North Carolina. Flair won with a fluke roll-up and the crowd erupted. Flair again defeated Vader in a rematch at *Superbrawl IV*, where there was some controversy backstage as Flair was waffling on the booking almost up to the day of the show, undecided as to let Vader have the title back or not. In the end, he wanted to build to a match with himself against Ricky Steamboat, so he chose to keep the title.

However, external forces were aligning against Flair. Hulk Hogan was now on the way in and wanted the top spot in the promotion ASAP. Flair defended the title against Ricky Steamboat at *Spring Stampede '94* in a match called a classic by most viewers, and due to its inconclusive double-pin finish, they did another match to settle the dispute, with Flair winning that rematch.

Despite being hugely over as a babyface, Flair was nothing if not a team player, and he stepped aside as booker midway through '94 and did a hasty heel turn to set himself up as Hogan's first opponent. Flair solved the double-World-title situation once and for all by beating Sting in a unification match, leaving him with the big gold belt as the WCW World champion, just in time for Hogan to win it in his first match.

Flair and Hogan had a rematch on the *Clash of the Champions* following that match, with Flair being booked to regain the title. However, now Hogan turned the tables on Flair, using the same veto power that Flair had used for years before to reverse the booking and keep the title (despite a "crippling knee injury" inflicted by a mystery man earlier in the show). Increasingly paranoid about Flair's popularity, Hogan asked Flair to step aside, and Flair agreed, dropping a retirement match to Hogan at *Halloween Havoc '94*.

However, retirement rarely means anything in wrestling, and indeed by early 1995 Flair was back in the mix, returning at the *Uncensored '95* PPV, dressed as a woman to sneak into the audience and attack Randy Savage. At *Slamboree '95*, Flair interrupted the "legends reunion" and attacked Savage's father, Angelo Poffo, triggering a blood feud between the men.

Flair was "reinstated" soon enough, and Flair and Savage proceeded to do a surprisingly entertaining series of matches in the early part of 1995, trading wins at *The Great American Bash* and *Bash at the Beach* PPVs in June and July respectively. Flair was on a losing streak, however, and his best friend Arn Anderson let him know, in on uncertain terms, about how unhappy he was that he was having to help Flair out all the time. Tensions mounted between the men, and they ended up taking on a face-turned Vader in a handicap match at the *Clash of the Champions* show in August. Vader pinned Anderson, and Flair laid the blame squarely on Arn's shoulders, and vice-versa. Suddenly, the unthinkable was happening, as Flair and Anderson appeared to be ready to fight.

It happened at *Fall Brawl '95*, as Arn Anderson v. Ric Flair happened for the first time, and in an even more shocking occurrence, stale midcard babyface Brian Pillman ran out and kicked Flair in the head, allowing Anderson to small package him for the pin. Anderson and Pillman started terrorizing Flair, until Flair had no choice but to complete the irony by going to longtime foe Sting for help against his longtime friend. Flair brought out a lineup of Sting-painted kids to beg him for help against Anderson and Pillman, and Sting reluctantly agreed, with reservations.

At this point, everyone could see what was coming. But that just made it all the better in the long run. Flair was "injured" before the show by Anderson & Pillman, so Sting started the match by himself. He lasted about 10 minutes before Flair dragged himself to the ring apron in street clothes, demanded the tag—then turned on Sting, as a 3-on-1 beatdown followed and the Four Horsemen had been reformed in style. WCW newcomer Chris Benoit was added as the fourth member soon after, and Flair was riding high again as *WCW Monday Nitro* made its debut and changed wrestling forever.

Flair would win another few World titles before all was said and done, and today has settled into semi-retirement, stopping by every now and then to save WCW, just like he always has before.

# ULTIMATE WARRIOR

One of the most amazing rises and rapid falls that the business has ever seen, the Warrior took the WWF by storm after his debut in 1987 and by 1989 had risen to World title contender and serious threat to Hulk Hogan's popularity. It wasn't meant to last.

Born Jim Hellwig in June 1957, the Warrior spent much of his early years pursuing a career bodybuilding and studying to be a chiropractor. After failing to win a bodybuilding competition in California in 1985, Warrior was ready to return to Atlanta to finish his degree. A phone call from Rick Bassman, operator of Gold's Gym in Venice Beach, changed his mind. Bassman was looking for four well-built young men to become a team of pro wrestlers called "Power Team USA" and move on to the big time. As mentioned, Sting and Hellwig survived the training process alone and moved to Memphis as "The Freedom Fighters" and later "The Blade Runners" before Sting was signed away by Bill Watts's UWF and the future Warrior was left out to dry.

Deciding to make the best out of the situation, Hellwig moved to Texas to find a new gimmick, and upon signing with Fritz Von Erich's World Class Championship Wrestling (WCCW) was given an Australian persona and dubbed "The Dingo Warrior," including the facepaint and armbands that would later define his character in the WWF. While completely

lacking in conventional wrestling ability, as he himself admitted on many occasions, Dingo Warrior swept through Texas in 1987 and took the fans by storm with his manic personality and weird charisma, winning the Texas heavyweight title and being prepped for a run against Texas favorite Kerry Von Erich. Before that could happen, however, the WWF took notice and grabbed him away, seeing the money they could make off him.

Keeping the basic Dingo Warrior mannerisms intact, he was now called The Ultimate Warrior and was allowed to turn the cartoonish facets of his personality up a few notches. The name was actually lifted from Bad News Allen (later Brown), who called himself "The Ultimate Warrior" as a nickname in Stampede Wrestling. Hellwig began dispatching jobbers with frightening efficiency and getting bigger pops for it each time. His finishing sequence—a simplistic press-slam and big splash—shouldn't have been effective in getting him over, and yet somehow it worked.

He steamrolled through a "who is the strongest" feud with Hercules Hernandez, and then crushed Honky Tonk Man to win the Intercontinental title in his first major spot on a PPV. He spent the rest of '88 making Honky Tonk into his plaything before the WWF decided to try something new with him.

The WWF had signed NWA mainstay and former bouncer "Ravishing" Rick Rude to a big-money deal the year previous, thinking that his chiseled look and playboy attitude would be enough to justify the investment. Rude, however, had heat with Hulk Hogan for reasons unknown and as such was not able to be put into the necessary feud with him in order to elevate Rude to the next level. As a result, Rude floundered in the midcard as something of a comedy figure, engaging in a hot, but drawn-out, feud with Jake Roberts over Roberts's wife. While the angle was solid, the matches were boring due to the incompatible styles of Rude and Roberts.

So the WWF gambled and had Rude attack Warrior at *Royal Rumble '89*, setting up a match between them at *Wrestlemania V*. Since Rude had no credibility, he had nothing to lose, and since Warrior was still new he had lots of time to be rebuilt if needed. The end result: Rude defeated Warrior in a shocking upset to capture the Intercontinental title, ending Warrior's reign at a little over 8 months. The fans, luckily for the WWF, did exactly the expected thing and rallied behind Warrior to destroy Rude in a rematch, which he did at *Summerslam '89* with the help of Rowdy Roddy Piper (who had just come out of retirement for the first time).

Warrior was then moved into a lackluster feud with Canadian strongman Dino Bravo over the belt, a feud that failed to draw money, but furthered the Warrior's push up the card by establishing him as the premier power wrestler in the WWF. He got into a feud with faltering Andre the Giant to attempt to get a rub off him, but the Giant's deteriorating health meant that the matches literally only lasted 30 seconds and ended with Warrior getting the pin off a clothesline. That didn't prove to be much help to Warrior's cause. Finally, with Hulk Hogan desiring time off, the WWF decided to gamble again and make Warrior the centerpiece of the promotion in 1990.

That decision would prove to be one of the biggest mistakes they would ever make.

Warrior was popular, there was no disputing that. In fact, he was *very* popular. But he had never been put in a position to draw serious money before, and further, he didn't have a marketable character as a top

draw. Hulk was very easy to relate to: American strength, saying your prayers, eating your vitamins, etc. Warrior preached a strange kind of abstract faith in oneself and him, using mythological allusions and very large words that completely went over the heads of most of the audience members. Sure, they liked to watch him destroy his opponents, but ask the average fan what Warrior actually stood for and why they liked him, and they drew a blank.

Further, people still liked Hulk Hogan. The assumption that the WWF had been making when setting up the Hogan-Warrior match was that people would automatically flock to the winner and forget the loser for the time being, and in fact the opposite happened. The people who supported the Warrior coming in still supported him after he defeated Hogan, but the people who supported Hogan also supported him still, and as a result Warrior was left with a

## WRESTLER SPOTLIGHT

## ULTIMATE WARRIOR

**BIGGEST CONTRIBUTION**
Tanking the WWF's main event drawing power.

**BEST MATCH**
Against Randy Savage at *Wrestlemania VII* (****3/4)

**BIGGEST MATCH**
His long-awaited dream match with Hogan at *Wrestlemania VI* drew a dream buyrate and sold out the 65,000 seat Skydome.

**BIGGEST RIVAL**
Randy "Macho Man" Savage

fanbase that was divided in half with Hogan's. This was a serious error on the WWF's part, and they soon made another one.

One of the biggest rules of making money in wrestling is to have your #1 babyface matched up against your #1 heel. Warrior was now the #1 babyface, but who was the #1 heel?

Perfect, although very over and very credible, failed to draw money against Hulk Hogan and was disqualified from the running, leaving former Warrior nemesis Rick Rude to get the shot. They retooled Rude from a playboy to a killer, giving him a marine-short haircut and a new attitude, ditching the opening spiel that accompanied his matches beforehand and the stalling that

**#1 Babyface**

VS.

**#1 Heel**

=

Earthquake? Perhaps, but he was still busy squashing jobbers in opening matches. Randy Savage? Locked into a feud with Dusty Rhodes because the WWF didn't think he could main event again. Ted Dibiase? Drawing pretty good money against Jake Roberts, and again the WWF didn't think he could main event. This left Mr. Perfect and Rick Rude.

occurred during them. They forgot one vital element, however: Putting Rude over other babyfaces. Despite Rude going months without winning a major match, he was immediately programmed into a feud with Warrior, and the fans didn't buy it one bit. A Warrior v. Rude cage match was the main event at *Summerslam*, and the heat was completely lacking as Warrior dispatched Rude with ease.

Warrior's popularity was becoming a definite concern now, as crowd noise often had to be inserted into his matches on TV to make his reaction seem louder, and his merchandise had to be handed out to ringside fans to provide the illusion of popularity. Around this time, house show business started getting so bad that shows were split into three: A, B, and C shows. "A" shows would run in the major markets and feature the top stars, and the "B" and "C" shows would be run on the same day in two different small markets, each featuring a variety of mid-level stars. For instance, while an "A" show would have a main event of Hulk Hogan v. Earthquake, a "B" show would feature Dusty Rhodes v. Ted Dibiase or indeed Ultimate Warrior v. Rick Rude for the WWF title.

Things got worse as Warrior was demoted to the "B" show circuit and put into six-man tag matches with

## SUPERSTAR STATS:

**Ultimate Warrior**
*Real name:* Jim Hellwig
*Height:* 6'6"
*Weight:* 275 lbs.
*Trademark move:* Gorilla Press
*Aliases:* The Dingo Warrior

the debuting Legion of Doom, taking on the three-man team of Demolition. Warrior was drawing less and less money, taking a back seat even to the Demolition-LOD feud, and finally the WWF decided to pull the plug on the Warrior experiment for good.

Warrior defended the title against Ted Dibiase on the last-ever *Main Event* special on NBC to laughably low ratings, and was attacked afterwards by "Macho King" Randy Savage, himself on his last legs as a draw at that point. The two were married for the winter and Warrior was signed to defend the title against Sgt. Slaughter at *Royal Rumble '91*. Before that match on the same show, Savage's manager Sherri Martell asked the Warrior for a title match with Savage, and Warrior refused. The enraged Savage attacked Warrior extensively during the match, and eventually cost him the match and the title. Warrior swore revenge and challenged Savage to the ever-popular retirement match for *Wrestlemania VII*.

And then, to the shock of everyone involved, it was like both men were suddenly hit by lightning and brought to life again. Savage wrestled like a man 5 years younger, and Warrior actually started giving coherent interviews leading up to the match. While the dull Hogan-Slaughter main event failed to excite anyone watching, Warrior-Savage was actually becoming perceived as one of the main reasons to watch the show.

And even more shocking, when the match finally happened, it was the best one of Warrior's career by far. An 18-minute classic featuring Warrior kicking out of 5 consecutive elbowdrops by Savage (with the thinking apparently being that Savage was retiring anyway, so killing his finisher wouldn't hurt in the long run) and rallying to score a hard-fought win. The post-match proceedings also proved interesting, as the now-retired

Savage was dumped by manager Sherri Martell, only to see Miss Elizabeth come out of the crowd and take an active role for the first time and chase Sherri off. Savage and Liz were "married" at the *Summerslam '91* PPV, in reality just rehashing their wedding vows from their original marriage years prior.

Following that big win, Warrior was put into a feud with the Undertaker. Undertaker had debuted a few months prior and was rapidly ascending the ladder to main event status. In an effort to keep either man from losing face in the feud, most of their matches were "body bag rules," where the winner had to stuff the loser into an actual body bag. Not exactly Olympic rules stuff, but it drew money, which was the important thing, and Undertaker came out of it still looking indestructible. Requiring assistance against Undertaker, Warrior went to Jake Roberts to show him "the dark side" and combat Undertaker that way. The week before *Summerslam*, Roberts turned on Warrior and left him for dead, turning heel in the process and revealing himself to be aligned with Undertaker the whole time.

At *Summerslam*, Warrior was in the tag team main event with Hulk Hogan against Sgt. Slaughter, Col. Mustafa, and Gen. Adnan, with the eventual plan being to build to a Warrior-Hogan rematch after the Warrior-Roberts feud was played out. Warrior, of course, was scheduled to return the job to Hogan. Warrior disagreed with this idea and the general demotion to the midcard, and following the match at *Summerslam* he ran back to the dressing room and never showed up for another show that year. Randy Savage was dragged out of his retirement to take Warrior's place in the Roberts feud and got on the biggest hot streak of his career as a result.

After being officially fired and spending months in exile in Arizona, enduring numerous "Warrior is dead" rumors, Warrior made a surprise return at

*Wrestlemania VIII* to save Hogan from an attack by Sid Justice and Papa Shango. With lighter hair, capped teeth, and new tights, Warrior then had to endure "It's a different person playing the character" rumors spread by people who believed that McMahon still wanted the name value without the ego problems. Sadly, the latter was still evident.

With Hogan retiring, Warrior was put into the obvious feud against Papa Shango. Shango, aka the Godfather, had a "voodoo master" gimmick, carrying a smoking skull on a stick to the ring and incanting various curses at his opponents. Nothing too out there, just flavor for the character. Warrior had a better idea, though: He felt the Shango character would provide a better challenge for the Warrior character if Shango had actual *magic powers*.

# "Growl...snort..."
## —Ultimate Warrior

And since Hogan was gone and the WWF desperately needed a top babyface to fill the void, they gave into his idea and before you knew it, Shango was using his "magic power" to cause Warrior to vomit on their nationally syndicated TV program. Soon after, Shango's "magic powers" caused an unexplained black substance to emanate from announcer Gene Okerlund's head and the boots of various jobbers. Sadly, Shango's powers couldn't make viewers buy tickets to see the eventual match. Shango's powers were severely downplayed and Warrior was moved up into another feud to try to boost the main events. This one would prove more successful.

Randy Savage, out of retirement as of 1992, had defeated Ric Flair to win the WWF title for the second time at *Wrestlemania VIII*, and offered his friend the Warrior a title shot at *Summerslam '92*. One problem: Ric Flair also wanted the title, and he began playing both men against each other by insinuating that one had paid him off to help against the other. The heat for this was enormous, as Warrior and Savage cut paranoid

promos against each other leading up to the show, which ended up selling out the 80,000 seat Manchester Stadium in London. It was another spectacular match for Warrior, ending with Ric Flair making his expected appearance—and turning on both men, giving Warrior a countout win while he pummelled Savage.

Interesting sidenote: The original result had Warrior turning heel and in fact joining with Flair to win the WWF title, but Warrior vetoed the heel turn and was denied the title as a result. The next step was a tag match with Warrior and Savage taking on Flair and WWF newcomer Razor Ramon at *Survivor Series*—but again, complications arose. Following the show, Vince wanted to demote Warrior yet again, this time in a feud with Big Bossman's arch-nemesis Nailz (Kevin Wacholz) in electric chair matches. Warrior didn't even wait for the PPV to flip out; he quit the WWF mere days before the show. Plan B was put into action, and Flair's manager Mr. Perfect turned face and joined Savage on an episode of *Primetime Wrestling* to take Warrior's place in the match.

Warrior was not to be heard from or seen on WWF TV for another three and a half years following that incident. Ironically, Nailz himself was fired by the WWF almost immediately after Warrior for demanding a contract renegotiation, thus showing that had Warrior stuck it out another two weeks, the whole situation may have been avoided entirely.

Finally, after years of living in Arizona and starting his own wrestling school, "Warrior University," both the WWF and Warrior himself were in bad enough financial shape that a deal had to be struck, and Warrior agreed to return to the WWF one more time starting at 1996's *Wrestlemania XII*. He squashed HHH in under a minute, then went on to feud with Jerry Lawler and Goldust before once again fighting with the WWF, this time over promotion of his wrestling school and comic book on WWF TV, and he was fired for no-showing several events a mere three months after joining. Outside of one un-notable stint in WCW in 1998, where he finally returned the job to Hulk Hogan but killed ratings in the process, Warrior has not been seen or heard from in the wrestling world, and his myth-like status fades daily.

# SHAWN MICHAELS

Formerly a part of Rock 'N' Roll Express ripoff the Rockers, Shawn turned on longtime partner Marty Jannetty in 1992 and launched a singles career that would turn him into a major star and influence the careers of wrestlers like him for years to come.

Born Michael Hickenbottom in June 1965, Shawn Michaels got his start at a very early age, wrestling his official debut match at 19 and training years before that. Shawn was a fixture of the smaller Texas promotions, and soon met up with Marty Oates, who wrestled as Marty Jannetty. Their team caught the eye of AWA promoters, who brought them into the fold in 1986 as the Midnight Rockers. The name was a tribute to their influences: The Midnight Express and the Rock 'N' Roll Express.

Initially undercard jobbers, soon the female-friendly duo started getting bigger face pops from the girls in the crowd, necessitating a push up the card. They were put in a program with tag champs Buddy Rose & Doug Somers, losing a series of title matches, including one notable TV match where all four men bled to extreme lengths, covering the ring with blood and finishing in a huge brawl for a double DQ. Finally, as 1987 began, the AWA relented and put the tag titles on the Midnight Rockers, making fans happy throughout the AWA.

Their reign would prove to be short, however, as the WWF brought them in for a tryout match midway through 1987, which meant dropping the titles to the evil

Russian team of Boris Zukhov and Soldat Ustinov. At this point, the WWF was essentially picking and choosing talent from the AWA at will, so it came as something of a surprise when the Midnight Rockers were sent back to the AWA without a WWF contract. The Rockers did a tour of the southern states while the AWA tried other tag champs, and ended up doing a mini-feud (as heels) with their idols the Rock 'N' Roll Express in Memphis.

After finishing this, they were brought back to the AWA with an expanded repertoire and personality, where they won the tag titles back, this time beating the Original Midnight Express. With the discovery of

steroids and weight training, however, the Rockers were now big enough that the WWF had interest again, and this time their tryout resulted in a WWF contract. The Rockers dropped the tag titles to Pat Tanaka and Paul Diamond and entered the WWF in early 1988, dropping the "Midnight" and simply going by "The Rockers."

The early tenure for them wasn't anything to brag about, mainly being used as "enhancement talent" for bigger teams, until the WWF decided to put them with the incoming Brainbusters (Arn Anderson & Tully Blanchard) and allow them to showcase their wrestling ability. The result was a series of spectacular matches, one of which aired on *Saturday Night's Main Event*, wowing the crowds, albeit in a fashion more to elevate the Brainbusters right away than to do anything with the Rockers. The losing streak continued for them, as they were squashed by the Bossman-Akeem team at *Wrestlemania V*. Both Shawn and Marty were reportedly partying all night before the event and the fact that they had as good a performance against the Towers as they did while hungover and stoned is a testament to their natural talent.

The Rockers floundered in the midcard for most of 1989, doing some spectacular jobs for the Powers of Pain and Demolition along the way, and increasing their fanbase with their high-risk offense and jaw-dropping bumps. As 1990 began, it was speculated that Shawn would be dropped altogether and Jannetty would be

given a singles push, but the WWF decided to stick it out with the team and try a program with the Orient Express (Pat Tanaka and Akio Sato, two more AWA refugees).

Given that the Express were actually smaller than the Rockers, there was finally a team that they could feasibly defeat, and they began doing so, winning over more fans in the process. They were given a real, actual feud midway through 1990, as Paul Roma turned on them and joined with Hercules Hernandez as "Power and Glory." A match was scheduled for *Summerslam '90*, but just before, Shawn suffered a serious knee injury and had to be "attacked" by the heels before the match so he would spend the whole match clutching his knee at ringside while Jannetty wrestled the entire match. It ended up as a squash for Power and Glory, but then something very odd happened.

By the summer of 1990, the WWF was making serious and drastic cutbacks in the midcard, and while the Rockers were a very young, very marketable team, the tag champion Hart Foundation was not. Specifically, aging Jim Neidhart was deemed expendable, and when Shawn returned from his knee injury, the Rockers were informed that they were getting the WWF tag team titles, in preparation to drop them to

Power and Glory. The match happened during a taping for *Saturday Night's Main Event*, and it was made into a 2-of-3 falls match for maximum value.

During the first fall, the bottom rope broke off on one side of the ring, meaning they had to wrestle the remainder of the match without using the ropes. The Rockers eventually won and were crowned the new champions. They defended in several matches against Power and Glory before the title change even aired, but the WWF suddenly changed their mind and decided to keep Neidhart around after all. Further, it was felt there was no need to take the tag titles off The Hart Foundation, so the title change was edited out of the broadcast when it aired. Local TV in Ft. Wayne, Indiana (site of the title change), had a message from

# WRESTLER SPOTLIGHT

# SHAWN MICHAELS

## BIGGEST CONTRIBUTION
Great matches in the ring, vicious politics out of the ring.

## BEST MATCH
Ladder match against Razor Ramon at *Wrestlemania X.* (*****)

## BIGGEST MATCH
Winning the WWF title from Bret Hart at *Wrestlemania XII.*

## BIGGEST RIVAL
Bret Hart

Jack Tunney stating that the decision was reversed due to the ropes coming loose, and no one else in the country was informed.

However, this seemed to give the floundering Rockers a huge shot in the arm, as they began stepping up their efforts in the ring, carrying more and more terrible wrestlers to great matches. They got the opening match at *Royal Rumble '91* against the retooled Orient Express (with Canadian Paul Diamond, replacing Akio Sato, playing the masked "Kato." As a note, whenever you see a masked Japanese guy in wrestling, that's usually because he's not Japanese). Anyway, the teams put on a blowaway performance. The Rockers also got the opening slot at *Wrestlemania VII*, shockingly enough defeating Bobby Heenan's new monster heel team of the Barbarian and Haku. The Rockers were truly hitting their prime as a team, even as they self-destructed behind the scenes.

To begin with, Marty Jannetty's minor drug usage in the '80s had slowly but surely blossomed into a full-blown addiction by the time the '90s started. Shawn Michaels was carrying the team by himself, and it was noticed by the WWF, who wanted to give one of them a singles push anyway. Shawn wrestled more and more singles matches against top-flight opponents (Ted Dibiase, Curt Hennig, and Ric Flair to name three) as dark matches for TV tapings, getting good response from the crowd each time out.

Finally, with Jannetty needing rehab to continue a normal life, a breakup angle was teased throughout the winter, with Shawn unhappy about Jannetty's performance in the ring, according to the story line. Jannetty made one last attempt to patch things up on Brutus Beefcake's "Barber Shop" interview segment, but after convincing Shawn to shake hands, Shawn did the seminal heel turn and superkicked his now ex-partner, then tossed him through a "plate-glass window," putting him out of the WWF and into a drug program. Shawn made his debut as the Heartbreak Kid at *Royal Rumble '92*, showcasing his new, arrogant personality as a heel.

After being paired up with Sherri Martell as a manager, Shawn began a slow but steady climb up the singles ranks. And speaking of climbing, when his series of matches with Intercontinental champion Bret Hart proved inconclusive, they imported a specialty match from Stampede Wrestling to solve the issue—the ladder match. Shawn and Bret actually had the first ladder match in the WWF on an episode of *Primetime Wrestling* in 1992, an awesome affair that saw Bret retain by the skin of his teeth.

Bret lost that title to the British Bulldog, and Shawn was finally rewarded for his years of service by going over the Bulldog and winning the Intercontinental title in October of 1992. Bret won the WWF title in the meantime, and they were actually given the main event slot for *Survivor Series 1992*, as Bret successfully defended against Shawn in an excellent match.

As 1992 drew to a close, Shawn no longer required the services of Sherri to get him through interviews, so the supposedly cleaned-up Marty Jannetty made a surprise reappearance one week and stole Sherri away from Shawn, challenging him to a title match at *Royal Rumble '93*. Marty showed up for that match obviously drunk, and lost the match, then was fired immediately afterward. Shawn defended the Intercontinental title against Tatanka at *Wrestlemania IX* successfully, then ran into the challenge of Jannetty again, as he was once again "clean and sober."

This time he convinced the WWF of his sobriety enough to actually be given the title, making a surprise reappearance on an episode of *Monday Night RAW* and upsetting Shawn with the help of

Mr. Perfect. In order to regain the title, Shawn felt he needed help, so he decided to hire a bodyguard. This twist in the story line would in fact change wrestling without anyone knowing it until years later.

Three weeks later at a house show, Shawn won the title back, with help from his new friend Diesel, played by WCW reject Kevin Nash. Nash had the advantage of being big, which got him his WWF contract. Michaels and Nash hit it off immediately in real life, becoming good friends. Michaels defended the title against Mr. Perfect at *Summerslam '93* in a match hyped incessantly by the WWF beforehand as the "greatest Intercontinental title match of all time," but it turned out to be merely average due to bad booking. In the fall of 1993, Shawn's contract was

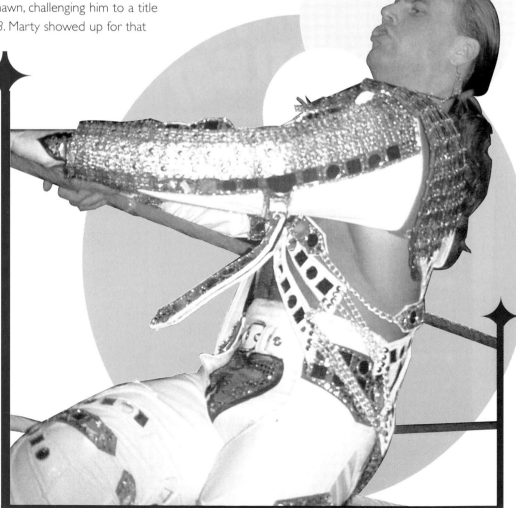

running out and he decided to bluff Vince McMahon by threatening a jump to WCW if he wasn't given a raise. Vince called it.

Shawn was suspended from the WWF, sent home, and stripped of his title. Razor Ramon won a battle royale and defeated Rick Martel to become the new champion, before finally Shawn gave in and came back to work, a little more humble and willing to cooperate. However, he brought with him the title belt that he never gave back to the WWF (in character, of course, not in real life) and noted that he never lost the title.

It was hate at first sight for Ramon and Michaels in the ring, as they battled over who was the "real" champion around the country in ladder matches. In real life, they were also hitting it off well, and soon Ramon, Michaels, Diesel, and the hanger-on, 1-2-3 Kid, were inseparable behind the scenes.

Michaels and Ramon made history at *Wrestlemania X*, taking their ladder match act to the bigtime and incorporating all of the best bits from their other ones around the country into one monster match that ran 18 minutes and featured some of the most amazing spots and bumps anyone in Madison Square Garden or watching at home had ever seen. It was a unanimous choice from fans everywhere as Match of the Year for 1994 and set the standard by which all other ladder matches are now judged. Ramon defeated Michaels to "unify" the real and fake Intercontinental titles, and Shawn was ready to jump to WCW, having fulfilled his contractual obligations to the WWF.

Hulk Hogan's sudden entrance into WCW (and the influx of big men who would leave the smaller Michaels in the midcard) caused Shawn to change his mind, however, and he surprised everyone by re-signing with the WWF for a long-term deal. Shawn took some time off to heal injuries, while the spotlight focused squarely on bodyguard Diesel. When Michaels returned to regular action, he and the rapidly rising Diesel defeated the Headshrinkers to win the WWF tag titles, a feat that Shawn never officially accomplished in his years with Jannetty as the Rockers. Diesel's star was on the rise and Shawn's was stagnant, so the WWF decided to split the team in the fall of

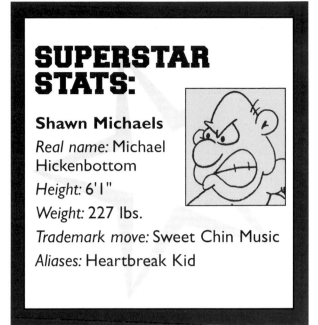

**SUPERSTAR STATS:**

**Shawn Michaels**
*Real name:* Michael Hickenbottom
*Height:* 6'1"
*Weight:* 227 lbs.
*Trademark move:* Sweet Chin Music
*Aliases:* Heartbreak Kid

1994 and take a huge chance. It would prove to pay off, but not in the way they expected.

Shawn and Diesel broke up, with Diesel going face and suddenly capturing the WWF World title by beating Bob Backlund in 8 seconds. With no real marketable main event for the upcoming *Wrestlemania XI*, the WWF decided to go the safe route and do Shawn Michaels v. Diesel for the title. To make that one work, they had to get Shawn into position as a serious contender. So he first won the 1995 *Royal Rumble* (an abbreviated 30 minute version) by drawing #1 and lasting the whole thing until he eliminated the British Bulldog for the win. Then, to establish a finisher that would work against big men, his finisher was changed from a side suplex to the now-familiar superkick. Next, he was put over the huge Adam Bomb and larger British Bulldog on WWF TV shows, giving the fans the impression that Shawn really could beat a big man without help.

Finally, he was given the returning Sid Vicious as a bodyguard, just because he needed someone cool in his corner. It not only worked to get him over as a contender, but suddenly the 7-foot Diesel was the *underdog* against Michaels going into the match, as everyone expected Shawn to walk out with the title after all the prep-work done on him by the WWF.

Shawn was also hearing increasing babyface pops thanks to his push and naturally emerging charisma, and by the time *Wrestlemania XI* rolled around, the crowd was 50/50 on who they wanted to win.

Well, Diesel still won because Shawn wasn't in the game plan as champion yet, but the WWF did recognize his growing popularity. The night after the show on *RAW*, Sid turned against Shawn and powerbombed him, turning Shawn face in the process. Shawn took some time off to sell the injury, and returned as the most popular babyface in the company.

He beat Jeff Jarrett to win his third Intercontinental title, and was supposed to defend that belt against Sid Vicious at *Summerslam '95*, but Sid was rapidly wearing out his welcome with the company and the match was changed to a ladder rematch against Razor Ramon, to ensure at least one great match on that show. And they delivered it, as Shawn retained the title in yet another awesome match with Ramon. It was now inevitable that Michaels would be moved onto bigger and better things. But…

One night in Syracuse, Shawn was at a local bar drinking with the British Bulldog and the 1-2-3 Kid. An argument ensued between the wrestlers and 3 (their story) or 12 (Shawn's story) men. The wrestlers attempted to leave, but the men from the bar flanked them, and isolated Shawn. Shawn was beaten unconscious and taken to a local hospital for treatment. Shawn suffered severe facial injuries as a result, and a concussion. Having been put into a feud with Shane "Dean" Douglas for the Intercontinental title, Shawn was scheduled to defend against (and lose to) Douglas at the *In Your House IV* PPV in Winnipeg, Manitoba.

Shawn showed up with two black eyes and an unsteady walk, and forfeited the title to Douglas. Douglas was pretty upset about this in real life, feeling that Michaels should have dropped the title in the ring to him. To make things worse for Douglas, he was then booked to drop the title to Michaels's friend Razor Ramon immediately after that, giving him a title reign of approximately 10 minutes. It should come as no surprise that Douglas left the WWF pretty soon following the whole thing.

Michaels returned to the ring in November of '95,

and the WWF decided to use his injury to do the greatest "shoot angle" ever seen. In this case, Michaels wrestled Owen Hart on *Monday Night RAW*, and at one point took an enzuigiri (kick to the head). He stood up to continue the match, then wobbled unsteadily and collapsed to the mat. The ref immediately stopped the match, and the crowd seemed unsure of what was going on. The announcers "broke character" to wonder about Michaels's health, and the show went to commercial. Shawn was admitted to a local hospital for treatment that night—thus fooling everyone. It was all planned from the start to build the necessary sympathy for him to make his big return at *Royal Rumble*, and it worked like a charm.

# "Shawn Michaels has left the building." —Shawn Michaels

Shawn took another month off and returned at *Royal Rumble '96*, winning the match by superkicking Diesel out of the ring. The plan for Shawn was no big secret: Bret Hart had won the WWF title from Diesel at *Survivor Series '95* to stop the financial bleeding that the WWF was going through, and Shawn Michaels v. Bret Hart was carved in stone for *Wrestlemania XII*. Bret was largely considered a lame duck champion, someone to hold the fort until Shawn could be moved into that spot.

It was made into an Iron Man match—a 60-minute match where the person with the most pinfalls at the end of 60 minutes gets the win—to add intrigue. Complications arose, however, as neither man wanted to be the first one to lose a fall to the other, so the match was booked to go 0-0 through the entire 60 minutes, with Shawn winning in "overtime" with two superkicks to capture his first World title. Bret wan't too happy about that.

Shawn was now the undisputed #1 guy in the company, and started getting matched up against bigger men to prove that a smaller man could hold the title. He carried Diesel to the best match of his career at the *Good Friends, Better Enemies* PPV, did a short series with the British Bulldog that bombed, then got into a feud with Vader. The outcome of that one was supposed to be Shawn losing the title at *Summerslam*, but a soon-to-be familiar trend began as Shawn refused to job and ended up winning instead. Shawn, despite his flamboyant personality and great matches, wasn't drawing money as a babyface.

Shawn had yet another awesome match, this one with Mankind at *Mind Games* in September, in another match where Shawn was booked to lose the title before last-minute booking changes gave him a DQ win instead. Finally, the fan sentiment against Michaels was becoming too pronounced to ignore, as the male half of the audience was actively booing his "pretty boy" image and sappy association with mentor Jose Lothario. Vince finally pulled the trigger and decided to change the title, and put it on Vader.

But again Shawn refused to job, and, with the backing of the rest of the so-called "Clique" (Shawn, Diesel, Ramon, and the 1-2-3 Kid), threw a temper tantrum until it was at least changed to someone he wanted to lose to—in this case, Sid Vicious. A bogus story about an ankle injury suffered by Vader was invented, and Sid got the title shot instead, winning the belt at *Survivor Series '96* to a huge babyface pop.

Sid, however, was an even bigger failure as champion than Shawn was, so with *Royal Rumble '97* happening in Shawn's hometown of San Antonio, they decided to put the title back on Shawn. Oddly enough, the quasi-heel that Shawn had been playing since losing the title suddenly vanished and Shawn was a full babyface again, with the fans apparently having forgiven him already now that Jose Lothario was out of the equation. Vince wanted Shawn to drop the title back to Sid Vicious to set up a Sid v. Undertaker main event

for *Wrestlemania XIII*, however, and that didn't sit well with Michaels.

Shawn invented a story about knee surgery and addiction to painkillers, and gave a tearful interview on a special Thursday *RAW* where he talked about "losing his smile," and surrendered the WWF title back to the WWF. This meant he quite conveniently didn't have to "return the favor" (lose) to Bret Hart at *Wrestlemania XIII* as payback for the show from the year before. The *Wrestlemania* card was reshuffled hastily, and it was a poorer show as a result. Shawn, for his part, returned a month later with no ill effects of his "knee injury" and won the WWF tag team titles with Steve Austin.

Tensions were building between him and Bret Hart, however, as they got into a heated fight backstage over an offhand comment made by Shawn about a possible affair with Tammy "Sunny" Sytch. Shawn was supposed to face Bret Hart at *King of the Ring*, but it was felt there was too much heat between them to prevent someone acting unprofessionally, so that match was scrapped and Shawn began a gradual heel turn to use the growing sentiment against his antics to the WWF's advantage.

When that heel turn finally happened, the results would shake the wrestling world to its foundations and propel the WWF back into the #1 spot—a spot it had lost to WCW. That heel turn begat D-Generation X, and led to a title match with Bret Hart—in Montreal.

To be continued…

# KEVIN NASH

Enduring a series of silly gimmicks in his early years, Kevin Nash left for the WWF in 1993 and hit upon gold in the Diesel character, winning the WWF title in 1995 and nearly bankrupting the promotion in the process.

Born July 1958, Kevin Nash spent his college years at the University of Tennessee playing basketball thanks to his huge size. After a failed pro career, he was noticed by a desperate Turner organization in 1990 and converted into a wrestler. He was given a mohawk and a fellow rookie for a partner, and their team was dubbed "The Master Blasters." Nash was called "Steele." This was truly inspiring stuff, but amazingly didn't last for more than a few weeks before his partner, "Iron," was fired. Nash was kept around because he was big. Despite the addition of a new partner, Al Greene ("Blade"), the team ultimately failed after two months in the sport.

WCW kept trying, however. You've gotta give them credit for that.

Next up, Ted Turner had recently purchased the rights to the MGM catalogue of movies, including *The Wizard of Oz*. To promote showings on WTBS, it was decided to give a wrestler a gimmick based on the movie, and Nash was the lucky winner. With his hair grown back in, it was now dyed white, along with his beard. Given a lime green pair of tights and an elaborate 15-minute entrance complete with characters from the movie and a monkey, The Great and Mighty Oz debuted in June of 1991 and was on the shelf by August.

Feeling that it had to be the gimmick that was the problem, WCW repackaged Nash again.

This time he was given a tuxedo and an Italian accent, and dubbed "Vinnie Vegas," a high-rolling gambler who dropped his opponent face-first on the top turnbuckle as his finisher ("Snake Eyes," a move he still pulls out today on occasion). That one didn't fare too well, either, but at least fans were buying him as Vinnie Vegas, so he stuck to that role for a while. He kicked around WCW as a jobber for most of 1992, partnering occasionally with Diamond Dallas Page and Big Sky (Tyler Mane, last seen playing Sabertooth in the *X-Men* movie) before Bill Watts dumped him for financial reasons in late 1992.

That should have done it for Nash's career as a wrestler, but luckily for him the WWF was in need of a big wrestler to play a bodyguard for Shawn Michaels. No actual wrestling was to be involved, which was even more of a bonus for Nash, who had very limited skills. He made his debut in Shawn's corner at a house show in June of 1993, assisting Shawn in beating Marty Jannetty to regain the Intercontinental title for a second time. Initially unnamed, he was dubbed "Diesel" within a few weeks of his debut and given a distinctive look, with black gloves and leather pants. His career picked up where it left off in WCW—doing nothing of note and not getting over. Diesel was in even more trouble when Shawn got into a contract dispute late in 1993 and was suspended, leaving him to actually—gasp—wrestle! He took part in the 1993 *Survivor Series* in the opening match, making a quick exit via Randy Savage's flying elbow, and seemed to be in career limbo without Michaels. Luckily, Shawn returned and Diesel returned to his post as bodyguard.

But then...

Diesel was put into the 1994 *Royal Rumble* as a warm body to fill time, and the bookers figured that since he was big, he might as well eliminate some smaller guys. So he tossed out 7 guys in a row at one point—and the crowd was suddenly chanting his name. This was an interesting development for someone who had never actually been over before, so the WWF

# SUPERSTAR STATS:

**Kevin Nash**

*Real name:* Kevin Nash

*Height:* 7'1"

*Weight:* 367 lbs.

*Trademark move:* The Jackknife Powerbomb

*Aliases:* Commissioner Nash, Steele, Oz, Vinnie Vegas, Diesel, Big Daddy Cool, Big Sexy

decided to take another step with him.

They let him talk for the first time during one of Shawn's "Heartbreak Hotel" interview segments, and he dubbed himself "Big Daddy Cool" for the first time. He also started raising his gloved fist into the air as a trademark mannerism, and the fans started copying. He challenged Intercontinental champion Razor Ramon (who was hot off beating Shawn Michaels at *Wrestlemania X* in the ladder match) and they met for the title on an episode of *WWF Superstars*. Astonishingly, Diesel won the title on his first try, with an assist from Shawn.

What was really going on was that the Clique was gaining power, and with all three men being friends behind the scenes, Ramon and Michaels desperately wanted to get Diesel over too, and were willing to put him over themselves in order to accomplish that. Diesel also established his finisher—the jackknife powerbomb—in that match, putting the final touch on the character that would carry him to his greatest fame.

He got his first taste of the main event at the lackluster *King of the Ring '94* PPV, which, to be fair, was plagued with inattentiveness by the WWF bookers due to the steroid trials going on at the time. At that show, Diesel challenged WWF champion Bret Hart (in an effort to give him opponents who could make him look like a legitimate wrestler) and almost won the match before interference from Bret's second Jim Neidhart caused a DQ. He and Shawn, becoming more popular with the fans by the day, defeated the Headshrinkers at a house show in Indianapolis a few weeks later to win the WWF tag team titles, giving Diesel both titles at once.

He lost the Intercontinental title back to Razor Ramon at *Summerslam '94* due to botched interference from partner Shawn Michaels, sewing the seeds of dissent in the team. By this point, Diesel's popularity was eclipsing Shawn's due to the inherent cool factor that Kevin Nash was bringing to the character, despite doing nothing more strenuous than standing on the ring apron and posing most of the time.

Vince McMahon, always a mark for big men, decided to abort his experiment with Bob Backlund as the WWF World Champion only a week into his title reign, and try Diesel as his #1 babyface. To pull it off, the tensions between Shawn Michaels and Diesel came to a head at *Survivor Series '94*, where Shawn accidentally superkicked Diesel one time too many and got chased back to the dressing room for his troubles.

Shawn voluntarily forfeited his half of the tag titles (he did that sort of thing quite often), and it was announced that Diesel would get the first shot at Bob Backlund for convoluted reasons involving the former tag champs not having any obligations for the MSG show due to their breakup. The reasoning proved to be unimportant, as Diesel

squashed Backlund in 8 seconds to win the title and kick off the era of Diesel Power.

Well, it was all well and good to enjoy popularity while doing essentially nothing, but could he draw now that he was in the top spot? Continuing the trend started earlier in 1994, Diesel was matched up with Bret Hart at *Royal Rumble '95* in hopes of getting a good match out of him and convincing the fans that Diesel was "for real" as champion. The match was very good, but a multitude of run-ins ruined the effect and gave the match a non-finish. The WWF went with the obvious main event for Diesel at *Wrestlemania XI*, pitting Diesel against former friend Shawn Michaels. Diesel won the match, but it still didn't serve to elevate

# "I'm a bad mother trucker."

## —Kevin Nash

Diesel to the next level, and in fact Shawn's gutsy performance moved *him* up the ladder. A rematch was signed for the first ever *In Your House* mini-PPV for the next month, but Sid Vicious accidentally injured Shawn in an angle shot the night after *Wrestlemania* and Sid took Shawn's place in the title match.

This was yet another example of the WWF's misguided policy of pushing big men when business wasn't doing well. In this case, *Wrestlemania XI* had a very disappointing buyrate, even with the media circus surrounding the Lawrence Taylor v. Bam Bam Bigelow main event, so Vince went back to the big men in hopes of boosting business. The Diesel v. Sid title match was pretty awful, featuring a 5 minute chinlock from Sid before Diesel won by DQ. The show didn't draw very well, but despite the fans growing demand for Shawn Michaels as the #1 babyface, they went back to Diesel v. Sid again for the *King of the Ring* PPV a month later, in the form of a tag match involving the two men.

## WRESTLER SPOTLIGHT KEVIN NASH

### BIGGEST CONTRIBUTION
Made lazy wrestling vogue and had dismal buyrates and house show revenues in '95.

### BEST MATCH
Against Shawn Michaels in 1996 (****3/4).

### BIGGEST MATCH
Against Shawn Michaels at *Wrestlemania XI*, his only *Wrestlemania* main event appearance.

### BIGGEST RIVALS
Equally heated rivalries between Bret Hart and Shawn Michaels

Again, the show bombed and the main event was terrible, and the show quickly gained the reputation as being one of the worst shows in WWF history. The King of the Ring tournament itself was won by another big, slow wrestler: Mabel, a 450-pound lovable rapper turned 450-pound evil King by winning the tournament. The crowd turned hostile at having Mabel win the tournament, and refused to play along with the WWF's main event plans for him.

Yet another Sid v. Diesel main event headlined *In Your House II,* and that show died a quick death, too. It also featured Mabel attacking Diesel to set up the main event for *Summerslam '95*, with an audible groan from the crowd being heard when they realized that this would be the next big program. The WWF was now losing serious amounts of money and was in very real danger of bankruptcy if something didn't happen to level off the losses. Diesel hadn't sold out a house show since he won the title, and *Summerslam* was another financial disaster, failing to break the 1.0 buyrate mark despite huge advertising. The increasingly desperate WWF was forced to try something they didn't normally resort to: Cheap bait-and-switch tactics.

At the *In Your House III* show, WWF champ Diesel & Intercontinental champ Shawn Michaels challenged the tag champions Owen Hart & Yokozuna in a match where whoever was pinned lost their title. It was heavily advertised as a "guaranteed title change." However, instead of actually switching a title, the WWF did an angle where Owen Hart didn't show up and was replaced by British Bulldog for the match. Owen ended up running in and getting pinned, apparently making Shawn & Diesel the tag champions. However, the next night on *RAW*, it was announced that no title change had actually taken place. This caused an instant backlash from loyal WWF fans, and now the writing was on the wall for Diesel.

The WWF made one last try at having him as the #1 guy in the company by turning British Bulldog on him in a tag match a month previous to set up *In Your House IV*: Diesel v. British Bulldog. The match was not only horrible, proving that only Shawn Michaels & Bret Hart were capable of getting anything out of Diesel in the ring, but the show did one of the lowest buyrates in wrestling history. Once the cameras went off the air, Vince McMahon (doing commentary for the show) threw down his headset in disgust and frustration and basically told Diesel on the spot that he was done as champion.

Diesel's contract was nearing its end, and now former employer WCW was showing interest again, so Diesel stepped up his effort to increase his worth. Diesel lost the WWF title in a foregone conclusion to Bret Hart at *Survivor Series '95*, which proved to be another good match in their series. Diesel turned heel after that loss while remaining a babyface, thus becoming wrestling's first real "tweener," someone who straddles the fence between heel and face. A feud with Undertaker was began as Diesel started a newer, edgier personality change and regained much of the lost fanbase who didn't buy into his corporate makeover in 1994. Diesel dropped a decent match to Undertaker at *Wrestlemania XII*, and signed a contract with WCW shortly after. He did a farewell job to Shawn Michaels the next month, wrestling the best match of his career in a match notable for ending when Shawn hit Diesel with Mad Dog Vachon's artificial leg for the win.

He showed up in WCW a few weeks later, and nothing would ever be the same as a result.

# SCOTT HALL

Now plagued with demons, Hall took the WWF by storm in 1993 as Razor Ramon, capturing an eventual 4 Intercontinental titles and challenging for the World title a few times.

The world first said hello to the bad guy in October 1958, when Scott Hall was born. He made his debut in the world of wrestling in 1984 in Kansas City, as part of a tag team called American Starship with fellow big man Danny Spivey. With names like Coyote and Eagle, how could it not be a success?

## WRESTLER SPOTLIGHT

### SCOTT HALL

**BIGGEST CONTRIBUTION**
Ladder matches.

**BEST MATCH**
Against Shawn Michaels in 1996 (****3/4).

**BIGGEST MATCH**
Shawn Michaels at *Wrestlemania X* (*****).

**BIGGEST RIVALS**
Shawn Michaels in the WWF and the nWo after he helped create it in the WCW.

Well, it wasn't, but Spivey was big enough and a dead ringer for the departing Barry Windham to boot, so the WWF grabbed him away in 1985 and left Hall to embark upon a solo career as Magnum Scott Hall, in an effort to capitalize on the success of Magnum TA in the NWA. Hall began in the AWA, and made an immediate impact with his size by partnering with Curt Hennig to win the AWA World tag titles in 1985. Hall's size and speed meant that he was in demand as a solo act elsewhere, and so he ended up drifting from Florida as "Gator" Scott Hall to the NWA as "Big" Scott Hall, not doing much of note. In Florida, he met and befriended Page Falkenberg, who would help him later on.

Hall drifted from promotion to promotion, making a name for himself with his size and natural talent, but not much more. The main criticism around him was his bland personality and lack of the killer instinct that only comes from playing a heel. His early-'80s porn star look, with feathered brown hair and a bushy moustache, didn't help his cause, either. In 1989, the NWA tried him again, but that proved to be a short-lived stay before cutbacks ended his career there again.

In 1991, Page Falkenberg, better known as Diamond Dallas Page, had come into the renamed WCW as a manager for the Fabulous Freebirds, but with the Freebirds going in a different direction, Page needed a different person to manage. He showed up at the first *Superbrawl* PPV to cut an interview and introduce his newest charge: A huge behemoth with jet black hair, Don Johnson stubble, and an arrogant attitude named The Diamond Studd. The Studd had his own personal women rip his tearaway pants off, and he would intimidate his opponents by flicking his ever-present toothpick at them.

Sound familiar? It didn't to hardcore fans at the time, who had no idea who the guy was. Finally, someone realized that Scott Hall was missing from the wrestling scene, and put two and two together long enough to deduce that he had finally found his calling as a wrestler with the help of some desperately needed cosmetic changes. He also found another desperately needed innovation: The Diamond Death Drop, a crucifix powerbomb that looked as devastating as the name suggests.

Best of all, WCW actually had the foresight to feed him skinny jobbers to squash, so that his size would be played up to the maximum and his finisher would look as awesome

as possible. Unfortunately for Hall, politics intervened as WCW played musical VPs at the end of 1991, and none of them quite knew what to do with the character before his contract expired in 1992.

The WWF didn't have that problem at all.

They signed him to a big money deal almost the minute his WCW deal expired, and made a few further cosmetic changes to the Diamond Studd gimmick: The Diamond motif was changed to razors, the tough-guy accent was turned into a bad imitation of a Cuban accent straight out of *Scarface*, and he was turned from ladies' man into drug dealer. Say hello to the bad guy: Razor Ramon. His finisher was renamed from the Diamond Death Drop to the much wittier Razor's Edge, and it remained equally as over as in WCW. To really rub WCW's loss in their face, the WWF pushed Ramon to the moon, making him Ric Flair's right-hand man when he made his debut in the summer of 1992 and having him cost Randy Savage the WWF title to Ric Flair. Ramon and Flair lost to Mr. Perfect and Savage at *Survivor Series '92*, but Ramon was so over as a heel that the WWF continued pushing him hard. He challenged Bret Hart for the WWF title at *Royal Rumble '93*, unsuccessfully, and embarked on a losing streak that would eventually take him to the next level.

He was upset by Bob Backlund at *Wrestlemania IX*, and soon after on an episode of *RAW*, he would meet up with the biggest challenge of his career: The Kid.

The Kid hadn't exactly been a threat to that point. He had been signed out of the indy promotions in Minnesota as a hot prospect, but smart fans weren't thrilled with the WWF's treatment of him at first. He debuted on *RAW* as the Cannonball Kid, and was quickly disposed of by Doink the Clown. The next week, he returned, this time as the Kamikaze Kid, and again had the same luck, getting crushed by Mr. Hughes. Finally, he gave it one more go, this time just as The Kid, and was well on his way to the same fate at the hands of Razor Ramon—when he suddenly hit a fluke moonsault and got the pin. Ramon was in shock as The Kid celebrated.

The next week, he officially picked his permanent name in the WWF to commemorate that fateful three-count: The 1-2-3 Kid. You would, of course, know him better today as X-Pac. Ramon challenged The Kid to a $10,000 rematch, and again was killing him before The Kid simply grabbed the money and ran away.

Ted Dibiase, nearing retirement at that point, found the whole thing very amusing and offered to hire Ramon as his maid in order to defray the costs involved in not winning a match in months. Ramon didn't take too well to that, and actually helped The Kid win a match against Dibiase in retaliation. Ramon was now a babyface, and he got the honor of retiring Ted Dibiase at *Summerslam '93*, beating him clean to get the rub. Ramon, who remained essentially the same character without the drug dealer undertones, was now extremely popular thanks to his anti-hero characteristics, and the WWF pressed their advantage.

When Shawn Michaels tried his contract ploy in 1993 and was stripped of the Intercontinental title as a result, the title was put up for grabs in a battle royale on *RAW*, with the last two men fighting for the belt the week following. Ramon and Rick Martel were the last two men, and Ramon defeated him to win the title the next week. When Shawn Michaels returned shortly thereafter still claiming to be Intercontinental champion because he never lost the belt, a feud over the title was elementary.

A team captained by Ramon emerged victorious at *Survivor Series '93*, but Ramon himself was eliminated due to interference from Mike "IRS" Rotundo, setting up a mini-feud to hold him over until Shawn could be

properly worked into the story. To further what little story line there was, IRS repossessed Ramon's gold chains to make up for "tax cheating." Engaging stuff, no?

Ramon and IRS had the inevitable match at *Royal Rumble '94*, with Shawn seemingly costing Ramon the win before justice prevailed and a second referee

## "Say hello—to the bad guy!"
### —Scott Hall

restarted the match. Ramon retained his title to set up the showdown with Michaels over who the "real" champion was. They did a series of ladder matches at house shows leading up to their big match at *Wrestlemania X*, with the general concensus being that the ladder matches were pretty good, and nothing more.

It turned out that they were just doing what Savage and Steamboat had done 7 years previously—they were practicing the match in bits and pieces to prepare for *Wrestlemania*. When it came, both men pulled out all the stops, doing things and taking sick bumps that no one else had ever seen on PPV before. After 19 minutes of brutalizing each other (and their own bodies) with the ladder, Shawn got tripped up in the ropes and Ramon was able to climb the ladder and retrieve both the real and fake versions of the title to "unify" the Intercontinental belt.

It was voted Match of the Year for 1994 in a landslide by nearly every publication to write about wrestling, and is generally considered one of the greatest matches of the '90s. Razor Ramon was an instant sensation as a result, guaranteeing him a top card spot for as long as he wanted one. Shawn was assumed to be leaving the WWF following that, but in fact the Clique was just solidifying their power.

$10,000 Rematch

Ramon had a surprisingly short title reign, dropping the belt to fellow "New Generation" star Diesel on an episode of *WWF Superstars* and setting up a feud between them to culminate at *Summerslam '94*. On the way there, Ramon made it to the finals of the unremarkable *King of the Ring '94*, losing out to Owen Hart. This led to several very good matches featuring Ramon & Bret Hart v. Owen Hart & Jim Neidhart around the country. The main goal for Ramon was obviously the Intercontinental title, however, and he was given football great Walter Payton as a cornerman to help bolster interest in the rematch with Diesel at *Summerslam*. An errant superkick from Shawn Michaels proved to make the difference, as Ramon regained the title from a stunned Diesel.

Ramon had essentially hit his peak as a babyface draw at that point, but was kept from moving downward by the influence of the Clique. Ramon and new buddy the 1-2-3 Kid took on tag champions Shawn & Diesel on one of the early episodes of the *WWF Action Zone* on USA, and with the four friends all willing to do whatever it took to make each other look good, the end result was an awesome tag match, still talked about to this day by those who saw it. Diesel & Shawn retained there, while sewing the seeds of dissent in their team. That split came at *Survivor Series '94*, as another missed superkick caused Diesel to chase Shawn back to the dressing room, and gave Ramon an improbable 5-on-1 comeback victory.

Ramon's new program was with bland heel Jeff Jarrett (that's J-E-double-F, J-A-double-R-E-double-T), who was apparently using the WWF to further his singing career, if that makes sense. They did a long series of house show matches, all with the same finish: Jarrett wins by countout, calls

Ramon a chicken, and they start the match again with Ramon winning to retain. They had another one of those matches at *Royal Rumble '95*, with a twist: This time, Jarrett had a new manager known as the Roadie (Road Dogg Jesse James) who beat up Ramon's knee enough that Ramon was counted out.

When he was called back in by Jarrett this time, his knee couldn't hold up, and Jarrett took advantage and reversed a Razor's Edge for the pin and the title. Ramon continued feuding with Jarrett, winning a rematch at *Wrestlemania XI* by DQ, then beating both Jarrett and Roadie in a handicap match at the first *In Your House* PPV. It was supposed to be a tag match with Ramon and the 1-2-3 Kid, but the Kid was having injury and alcohol problems and missed the show. Ramon actually regained the Intercontinental title from Jarrett at a house show in Quebec, but dropped it back the next night. Those switches were simply done to reward Quebec fans for their years of devotion.

At the *In Your House* show, Ramon was saved from a Jarrett attack by his "longtime friend" and "Caribbean legend," Savio Vega, thus pushing the Kid out of the sidekick role and setting up his later heel turn. Ramon got injured shortly after and had to skip the *King of the Ring '95* show, and Vega took his place and made it to the finals, a fitting conclusion to one of the worst WWF shows ever. Vega lost out to Mabel (of Men on a Mission—Mabel and Mo), setting up a tag match with Ramon & Vega v. Men on a Mission at *In Your House II*. Ramon & Vega lost that one, and Ramon's career was on a definite downswing again.

Shawn Michaels had won his third Intercontinental title on that same show, and was scheduled to defend against Sid Vicious at *Summerslam '95*, but due to the generally ugly looking match setup to that point, the WWF decided to swap Ramon into the match in Sid's place and make it a ladder match for fun. Once again, the match was voted Match of the Year as Ramon returned the favor to Shawn after another brutal exhibition of ladder spots.

On that same show, WWF newcomer Dean Douglas made rude comments about the match on his blackboard, prompting an attack from the exhausted Ramon. Voila, insta-feud! They met at *In Your House III*, with Douglas scoring the upset win on a roll-up thanks to mistimed interference from Ramon's increasingly estranged friend, the 1-2-3 Kid.

At *In Your House IV* in October, Ramon and The Kid took on the WWF tag champs, the Smoking Gunns (Billy and Bart), in an effort to get back on the same page as a team. The Kid selfishly attempted to get the win for himself, and ended up getting pinned once he got too fancy on a roll-up attempt. He, of course, blamed Ramon, and soon after turned on him in a Ramon v. Vicious match where he was acting as special referee.

But first, on that same show, Dean Douglas was supposed to beat Shawn Michaels for the Intercontinental title, but Michaels was injured and had to forfeit the title to Douglas. Dean was busy celebrating when he was informed that he would have to defend immediately against—Razor Ramon. Douglas dropped the title to Ramon (Ramon's record fourth) in an unnotable match, and he still blames the Clique to this day for perpetrating those sorts of politics against him.

Ramon was moved into another pair of programs. First of all, the one with the treacherous 1-2-3 Kid, who had joined up with Ted Dibiase's Corporation and now had Sid Vicious as his backup. Ramon and new partner Marty Jannetty met Sid & Kid at *In Your House V*, with Ramon pinning Sid for the win. In the audience at that time was newcomer Goldust, who portrayed a gay wrestler and was the son of wrestling legend Dusty Rhodes. Goldust then began sending love letters to Ramon to win him over.

This was clearly a weirder direction than wrestling had ever gone down before, and Ramon was chosen as the lucky recipient because his contract was expiring

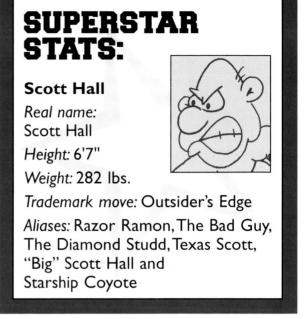

## SUPERSTAR STATS:

**Scott Hall**

*Real name:* Scott Hall

*Height:* 6'7"

*Weight:* 282 lbs.

*Trademark move:* Outsider's Edge

*Aliases:* Razor Ramon, The Bad Guy, The Diamond Studd, Texas Scott, "Big" Scott Hall and Starship Coyote

and his previously well-hidden problems with drugs and alcohol were now coming to the forefront more rapidly as the Clique gained more power. Ramon dropped the Intercontinental title to Goldust at *Royal Rumble '96* after several weeks of bizarre and disturbing propositions (which were later revealed to be only mind games), but Goldust needed the help of the 1-2-3 Kid to beat him. With Ramon now openly talking to WCW and agreeing to a deal once his current one was up, the WWF decided to go for the full humiliation package before he left.

Ramon was put in a "crybaby" match with the 1-2-3 Kid at *In Your House VI*, where the loser would be powdered and diapered. Ramon won that one and proceeded to strap a diaper on The Kid and give him a baby bottle, but Ramon's demons were coming after him again. This time, he was forced to take two months off and go into rehab due to his decreasing ability to function like a normal person between matches. His spot in a street fight with Goldust at *Wrestlemania XII* was given to Roddy Piper, and Ramon signed a deal with WCW once he was sober enough to. He closed out his WWF career in quiet fashion, losing clean to Vader at *Good Friends, Better Enemies* before departing for WCW.

And once he got there, everything changed.

# BRET "HITMAN" HART

Son of wrestling legend Stu Hart, Bret was an underachiever in wrestling before breaking out in 1991 as a singles star, escaping the shadow of his teammate, brother-in-law Jim Neidhart.

Born into the huge Hart family in July 1957, Bret was never interested in pursuing the pro-wrestling lifestyle, despite the overwhelming influence of his brothers and father. He was a champion wrestler in high school, and did some occasional refereeing for his father's Stampede Wrestling, but his career goal was to be a director, to which end he entered the Mount Royal College of Film. However, when that didn't work out, he had a spot waiting for him in wrestling, and he proved to be a natural. Despite his untraditional

look and physique, he proved to be the most popular and talented of all the Harts, winning the North American title six times from '80-'83 and having some shockingly violent matches with Bad News Allen, including the first-ever ladder match in wrestling.

When the WWF bought out Stampede in the early '80s, Bret made the jump to them, along with brother-in-law and family friend Jim Neidhart. Bret began as a jobber with very unfashionable black tights, and lacking in personality and style. Seeing the potential in him, the WWF teamed him with Neidhart and gave a manager to talk for him, in the form of Memphis import Jimmy Hart, and dubbed the trio The Hart Foundation. The focus on the team in the early days was Jim Neidhart's act as a crazed psychotic, and Bret provided the solid wrestling foundation to carry the team.

They were entered in the wrestler-football player battle royale at *Wrestlemania II*, and ended up as the last two men eliminated, both by Andre the Giant. Bret's technical skills were starting to turn some important heads by this point, as he was given the nickname "Excellence of Execution" by announcer and WWF honcho Gorilla Monsoon, and a push was soon to follow as Bret rapidly adjusted to the more fast-paced and entertainment-based style of the WWF. The tights changed to the more familiar pink-and-black colors, and he added his trademark wraparound shades for that true "Hitman" look.

The Harts spent much of 1986 challenging the British Bulldogs for the tag titles, never being considered a serious threat. They also had a mini-feud going with the Killer Bees (Jim Brunzell and Brian Blair) over the #1 contender spot, which was generally won by the Bees. Oddly enough, the Harts got most of the title shots out of the deal. With the total deterioration of Dynamite Kid as 1986 drew to a close, the WWF wanted to go with a heel tag-team champion to replace the British Bulldogs for a long run, and the Hart Foundation were given that chance.

With the help of crooked referee Danny Davis, the Harts stole the tag titles from the Bulldogs and became the #1 team in the promotion. Davis joined them as an unofficial member and general lackey, teaming up with them for a six-man match at *Wrestlemania III* against the Bulldogs and Tito Santana. Davis got the fluke pin

on Davey Boy Smith to win the match, and the Harts ended up with huge heel heat because of it.

The Hart Foundation shocked its critics and fans alike by holding onto the tag titles for nine months, gaining credibility to a degree that most didn't think would have been possible before they won the titles. During this time Bret was rapidly developing a personality, another unheard of feat during his early WWF tenure. The Hart Foundation helped to elevate the Young Stallions, ex-jobbers Paul Roma and Jim Powers, into a tag title feud with them by dropping a non-title match to them, then narrowly retaining the titles on *Saturday Night's Main Event* in the rematch. The provocation? The Young Stallions "stole" Jimmy Hart's "Crank it Up" theme song for themselves.

During this period, Bret Hart's rep as a singles wrestler was given a sudden boost as well. The Harts had been doing some flunkying for the Honky Tonk Man, including beating up Randy Savage in the attack that led to the formation of the Megapowers. This attack, however, led to a match between Savage and Bret on *SNME*, easily the best one of Bret's WWF career and on a high-profile show no less. This began building something of an "underground" following for Bret, who had always been regarded as the weak link in the team before that point. Now, Bret was clearly becoming the focus of the team and Neidhart was simply the hired muscle.

The Hart Foundation was actually becoming too popular to be heels due to their increasingly cool attitude and aura, but they weren't popular enough to overtake the Can-Am Connection of Rick Martel and Tom Zenk for the #1 babyface slot yet, so the WWF decided to put the titles on the Can-Ams in October of 1987. There's a funny story behind that:

Despite Rick and Tom's image as squeaky-clean best friends on-screen, behind the scenes they hated each other and were constantly plotting against one another. The proverbial last straw came when Zenk and Martel were both renegotiating their contracts behind each other's backs, with each thinking themselves to be the star of the team. Martel ended up getting the most money due to his longevity in the business, and Zenk indignantly quit the next day. It was the kind of bizarre

## WRESTLER SPOTLIGHT

# BRET "HITMAN" HART

### BIGGEST CONTRIBUTION
Redefined main eventers as wrestlers rather than bodybuilders.

### BEST MATCH
Out of many great ones, his cage match with brother Owen at *Summerslam '94* stands out (*****).

### BIGGEST MATCH
Winning the WWF World title from Yokozuna at *Wrestlemania X* and thus proving Vince wrong about Lex Luger's drawing power.

### BIGGEST RIVALS
Shawn Michaels was his biggest in the ring, Vince McMahon was his biggest outside of it.

relationship that only wrestling can produce. Zenk was quickly and easily replaced with journeyman WWF wrestler Tito Santana and they beat the Hart Foundation (with Neidhart submitting to a Boston Crab to protect Bret Hart's heat) for the tag titles two weeks after forming the new team. The fans hated this replacement duo known as Strike Force, and were bitter about the Harts losing the titles during their peak. Strike Force was disposed of by Demolition soon after.

Bret Hart's face turn continued at the first-ever *Royal Rumble* in January '88, as he set the first longevity record at 25 minutes after drawing entry #2. The official turn came at *Wrestlemania IV*, as he was entered in the battle royale that kicked off the show. It came down to Bret, Bad News Brown (aka his old nemesis Bad News Allen from Stampede), and the Junkyard Dog. Bret and Brown formed a heel alliance to eliminate JYD, but since there's no honor among heels, Brown turned on Hart and won the thing himself.

This had the effect of both turning Bret face and getting him away from Jim Neidhart long enough to start a singles push for him. Bret and Brown's only major match occurred at the special "WrestleFest" card in Milwaukee in 1988, where Brown outsmarted Hart and got the win. But the seeds were planted in the WWF's mind for a Bret singles push, and he kept getting the occasional singles match to hone his skills in that area.

Meanwhile, the Hart Foundation was turned into a tag team again, and this time they fired Jimmy Hart as their manager. Hart retaliated by siding with the Fabulous Rougeau Brothers instead, and then upped the ante by selling one half of the Hart Foundation's WWF contract to the Rougeaus, which essentially gave the heels control of the Harts' bookings, in story line terms, for a few weeks.

Jimmy Hart caused the Harts to lose their tag title match at *Summerslam '88*, and the whole situation built to a Hart Foundation & "Hacksaw" Jim Duggan v. The Rougeaus & Dino Bravo tag match at the *Royal Rumble '89*. The Harts won that one in two straight falls in a 2-of-3 falls match, then beat Honky Tonk Man & Greg Valentine at *Wrestlemania V*. The Hart Foundation spent most of 1989 in total career limbo, losing as many matches as they won and not doing anything of note aside from being "senior team on the totem pole" to act as a measuring stick for new contenders to the titles.

Bret Hart did several singles matches for WWF's home videos during this period, including an excellent draw with Ted Dibiase, to fill the time. The Harts lost a non-title match at *Summerslam '89* to new champions Tully Blanchard & Arn Anderson, before they once again were split up in time for *Survivor Series*. Bret Hart was put on Jim Duggan's team and jobbed to Randy Savage in short order, but the pop his entrance got was not ignored.

The Hart Foundation squashed the Bolsheviks (Nikolai Volkoff and Boris Zuhkov) in 8 seconds at *Wrestlemania VI,* and made it known that they wanted a shot at Demolition for the tag titles. In response, Demolition added a third member to their ranks: Crush. In reality, Ax (Bill Eadie) was aging and suffering from a heart problem and the WWF didn't have the confidence (or medical insurance) in him to send him out on the road every night and risk a heart attack mid-match. The Smash and Crush duo were actually superior to the original Ax and Smash one in some ways, but Crush's lack of experience and credibility with the fans weighed them down in the end. The title match came at *Summerslam '90,* and it was there that fans were given a double-whammy:

The Hart Foundation not only swept Demolition in a 2-of-3 falls match, but they did so with the help of the Legion of Doom (Hawk and Animal), the team that Demolition had been patterned after by the WWF in an attempt to cash in on their success. Fans had been calling for a "dream match" between LOD and Demolition for years, but now that both teams were in the WWF it was actually going to happen. It turned out to be a total squash for the LOD, of course, but that's another story.

Following *Summerslam,* the WWF was in financial disarray and began handing out the pink slips. Wisely deciding that Jim Neidhart was no longer worth the money he was being paid, he was fired in October and the Harts lost the tag titles to the Rockers in the infamous "phantom title reign" match detailed in the Shawn Michaels section. The belts were returned when the WWF changed their minds and Bret's singles push

was delayed yet again.

Bret drew #1 in the 1991 *Royal Rumble* to showcase him for the fans on his own, and impressed a great deal of them. In fact, Bret was now more over in his minimal singles appearances than much of the midcard was in their regular ones, so as 1991 began, the WWF finally pulled the trigger on the Bret Hart singles push. The Hart Foundation lost the tag titles to the Nasty Boys (Jerry Saggs and Brian Knobs) at *Wrestlemania VII,* and Neidhart was fired soon after. Bret Hart did a double-countout with Ted Dibiase on *Saturday Night's Main Event* in April as a dry run, and he was still very over with the fans. So they went to the next stage with him.

At *Summerslam '91,* Bret defeated Mr. Perfect to win his first major singles title, winning the Intercontinental title by blocking a legdrop and hooking his new finisher: The Sharpshooter. Bret had been taught the move by Mexican star Konnan during the time when Konnan was portraying "Max Moon" in the WWF, and the move quickly became the premier submission move in the WWF. Bret's reign was an instant sensation, as he quickly became one of the most popular stars in the WWF without Neidhart to anchor him down.

# SUPERSTAR STATS:

**Bret "The Hitman" Hart**

*Real name:* Bret Hart

*Height:* 6'0"

*Weight:* 235 lbs.

*Trademark move:* The Sharpshooter

*Aliases:* The Hitman, Excellence of Execution

With Hart on the rise, WCW was making overtures to him by January of 1992 for when his contract expired. In fact, WWF was so nervous about losing their star, they took the title off him and put it on The Mountie (Jacques Rougeau) at a house show two days prior to the *Royal Rumble* (where Bret was set to defend the title against the Mountie again), just in case Bret "tried" something on PPV like Honky Tonk Man attempted on live TV almost four years earlier to the day. The WWF claimed that Bret had the flu and thus his game was off that night, because in reality, Mountie was little more than a comedy jobber by that point. With Bret at home, "convalescing" from the flu, Roddy Piper got the shot at the Mountie instead at the PPV, and won the title easily.

After signing Bret to a new long-term deal, just in case, this set up a face v. face confrontation between Piper and Bret at *Wrestlemania VIII*, and Bret regained the title from Piper in a very good match. It also had the effect of using Piper's stardom to elevate Hart yet again. And elevate him they soon would, because Bret was becoming a phenomenon in his own right: A wrestler who got over not on gimmicks or interviews or soap opera, but on wrestling. He went out and gave it his all and the fans loved him for it. Bret was a throwback to a prior era thanks to the work ethic instilled by his father, Stu Hart, and it paid off as Bret kept climbing the ranks. Ultimately, that same philosophy would destroy his life, but that's later on.

Bret did another face v. face match, this time against brother-in-law Davey Boy Smith at *Summerslam '92* in Smith's home country of England. In front of more than 80,000 people at Wembley Stadium, Smith blocked a sunset flip and pinned Hart to win the Intercontinental title. But bigger things were in store for Bret.

After puttering around the midcard for a few months, Bret was suddenly informed, out of nowhere while doing a TV taping in Saskatchewan, that the entire direction of the WWF was going to be changing, and that aging stars like Hulk Hogan and Ric Flair were going to be phased out, and Bret was going to be phased in. He was put over WWF champion Ric Flair that very night, and was now the WWF champion to the shock of millions. Hart immediately began defending against every contender who wanted a shot, night after night, quickly earning a rep as the most hard-working champion the WWF had seen in some time. He beat Razor Ramon at *Royal Rumble '93*, and would have gone over Yokozuna at *Wrestlemania IX* had the Hulk Hogan situation not interjected itself, leaving Bret to job the title in a shortened match with only the hope of a rematch down the road with Hogan. None ever came.

By way of consolation, Bret was given the King of the Ring tournament win in June of '93, beating Razor Ramon, Mr. Perfect, and finally Bam Bam Bigelow to take the crown. However, following that win, announcer Jerry "The King" Lawler, taking exception to someone other than him being

"King," attacked Hart and stole his crown. Lawler verbally tormented Bret on *Monday Night RAW* for weeks following, taking cheapshot after cheapshot at him until finally a match was set for *Summerslam '93* between the two. Lawler initially attempted to duck out of the match, claiming a "broken leg" and sending Doink the Clown to take his place.

After Bret dispatched Doink, Lawler himself was forced into the match by WWF President Jack Tunney, and was beaten senseless by Hart to the delight of the fans. However, Bret refused to release the Sharpshooter and got disqualified, making Lawler the undisputed King. A gigantic pull-apart brawl with the entire Hart family storming the ring resulted, and a rematch was on the horizon.

It was supposed to be at *Survivor Series '93*, with Bret and brothers Keith, Bruce, and Owen taking on Lawler and his three masked "Knights" (Barry Horowitz, Greg Valentine, and Jeff Gaylord), but complications arose.

Mere weeks before that show, a 13-year old Memphis girl accused Lawler of raping her, and Lawler was indicted on the charge. His name was cleared, but not soon enough to make the show, and Shawn Michaels took his place. The match was nothing special, featuring the Harts systematically taking out all of the Knights before Shawn ran away, but Shawn did get one pinfall in: On Owen Hart, who accidentally bumped into Bret and got rolled up by Shawn. Owen had been working in the WWF for years before this, kept mostly on the payroll thanks to the influence of his brother, and now Bret wanted to do something bigger with Owen.

Owen accused Bret of being jealous because Owen had more natural talent than Bret did; he also called Bret selfish for not sharing his success. Bret insisted for weeks that he didn't want to fight his own younger brother, finally convincing Owen to reconcile and team with him to challenge the Quebecers for the tag titles at *Royal Rumble '94*. However, Bret's knee was injured during that match, and when he went for the Sharpshooter it gave way and the match was stopped and awarded to the Quebecers. A frustrated Owen, who felt that Bret should have tagged him in, snapped

and attacked his brother, doing further damage to the leg and setting up a feud between the brothers. Later in the night, however, something very interesting happened to Bret's career.

Vince McMahon was, if nothing else, stubborn. It generally took a lot to convince him of the error in his ways, and 1993 was no different in that regard. He had turfed Hulk Hogan out of the promotion in June of 1993, but for different reasons than everyone else thought at the time. The general feeling among fans was that Hogan's act and formula was stale and in need of an update, while McMahon felt that the problem lay in Hogan himself and the formula could still draw money. It could also be argued that he just wanted to show up Hogan and prove that the WWF could survive without him.

Either way, the "new" Hulk Hogan was appointed to be Lex Luger. Luger had been signed away from WCW in 1991 for McMahon's vanity project: The World Bodybuilding Federation. When that fell flat, surprising no one, the WWF talked Luger into becoming a wrestler again, giving him the "Narcissist" persona as a gimmick, and turning him into a top-level heel. Luger's essential boredom with the wrestling business prevented him from a full effort toward the character, and it failed to get over.

So a repackaging was in order, as WWF champion Yokozuna (who weighed upwards of 500 pounds) challenged anyone to bodyslam him on the fourth of July aboard the U.S.S. Intrepid. The winner would get a shot at his title at *Summerslam*. The assumption was that the very hot Crush (repackaged as a solo act after the death of Demolition some months earlier) was the guy for the job, but he failed to slam the champion. Finally, Lex Luger emerged from a helicopter (previous gimmick forgotten), slammed the champion, and did everything to cement himself as a supporter of the good ol' U.S. of A. The intention was to create Hulk Hogan II, the result was Jim Duggan II.

Fans appreciated the xenophobic sentiment, but didn't buy Luger, who spent his entire career blowing the big match, as a legitimate threat to Yokozuna. So the WWF started the biggest push in the history of professional wrestling (and that's not hyperbole).

Millions of dollars were spent advertising and marketing Luger, including an actual touring bus that Luger travelled around the country in called The Lex Express.

Luger did autograph sessions, speeches, personal appearances, talk shows, you name it. And when *Summerslam* rolled around—he still wasn't *over*. Okay, yes, he was over, but he wasn't *over*. People didn't put their money down just to see him, and given the insane budget that his promotional push had been given building up to the show, everyone in the building would have had to pay their money specifically for Luger alone in order to justify the cost.

So the WWF decided to delay the title win until *Wrestlemania X* and had Luger win the match by countout, which might have given them more time, but it also made Luger look like a stiff who couldn't win the big one. He obviously needed a new evil foreigner to feud with, but given the touchy political climate, the WWF was running out of choices. So they had Luger feud with Ludvig Borga, the evil Finnish environmentalist who was nicknamed the "Helsinki Hellraiser." For some strange reason, this didn't draw money, and as 1994 began, the fans were becoming noticeably upset with the continued Luger push toward the title and the ignoring of Bret Hart. So the WWF decided a little experiment was in order, and that's where we come back to Bret…

Both Luger and Bret were entered in the *Royal Rumble* match itself, and drew high numbers. After eliminating the competition, it was down to those two, but the WWF didn't want to eliminate one of them as a title contender for *Wrestlemania*, so they had both men hit the floor simultaneously, making the match a draw and producing "co-winners"—something that would happen again in 2000 when The Rock and The Big Show hit the floor at about the same time. The fan sentiment was clearly with Bret Hart, however, and that was all the WWF needed to hear.

*Wrestlemania X* was set up with the unique

stipulation that a coin toss would decide who got the first shot at Yokozuna; then whoever won that match would face the other person at the end of the night for the championship. Luger won the toss, so he was to face Yokozuna first; the winner would meet Bret Hart for the title in the main event.

To ensure fairness, Bret Hart had to face brother Owen as "suitable competition" before that main event so both competitors for the title match would have already wrestled once. The week before that show, the WWF tried to swerve online fans by doing a (never used) TV taping segment where Luger "stole" the WWF title belt from Yokozuna and paraded around with it—a segment that was intended to make people think of the Ultimate Warrior-Honky Tonk Man situation from 1988 that foreshadowed Warrior's title win. Further, Lex got drunk in a bar the night before the show and accidentally let a New York newspaper columnist know that he was going to win the title from Yokozuna, which put that result front-and-center in the paper the morning of the show.

The night began with Bret Hart losing to brother Owen in a shocking upset (and a ***** match) as Owen reversed a victory roll for the pin. The big swerve of the night then came, as Luger lost the title match to Yokozuna by DQ, setting up Bret v. Yokozuna for the title in a rematch of *Wrestlemania IX*, which was the plan all along. This was the WWF's way of apologizing to Bret for the treatment of him, as Bret regained his title when Yokozuna missed a buttdrop and was pinned. Lex Luger, whose heat had all but vanished, was demoted to the midcard and left for WCW in 1995.

Bret spent much of 1994 fighting brother Owen, although behind the scenes they were closer than ever thanks to having the chance to work together every day. Bret won every rematch after *Wrestlemania*, stopping to defend against Diesel at *King of the Ring '94*

along the way, leading up to the last match between the brothers: A cage match at *Summerslam '94*. Bret won that one after about 40 minutes of intense action, producing the second ***** match between them that year, a match that was still overshadowed by the Michaels-Ramon ladder match at *Wrestlemania X* at year-end awards time.

Bret's final challenge for the title came in the unlikely form of Mr. Bob Backlund. Bob, who at 45 years old was making a most unexpected comeback, had "snapped" during a televised title match with Bret Hart earlier in the year and became a raving psychopath. This was in stark contrast to the white-bread, "Howdy Doody" image portrayed by Backlund for decades before the match. He began attacking random WWF officials and wrestlers, locking them all in his crossface-chicken wing submission move and openly claiming that he had never lost the WWF title to the Iron Sheik ten years prior.

Backlund finally got another shot at Bret at *Survivor Series '94*, in a submission match. To win, you had to make your opponent's cornerman throw in the towel, literally. Bret was represented by the British Bulldog, and Backlund by Owen Hart. At one point in the match, Backlund caught Bret in the crossface, but Bulldog had been knocked unconscious in a skirmish with Owen and was unable to throw in the towel to save Bret.

that match by DQ at *Summerslam*, but then got stuck in a feud with the pirate Jean-Pierre Lafitte and had to get a good match out of him, too. He was growing more disenchanted with the WWF's insistance on making him sit by the sidelines while Diesel tanked the promotion as champion, and he started becoming vocal about it. The WWF finally capitulated and put the title back on him at *Survivor Series '95*, with intentions of an eventual Bret v. Shawn match at *Wrestlemania*.

Owen suddenly had a change of heart, begging and pleading with Stu Hart (sitting at ringside with wife Helen) to spare Bret further agony and throw in the towel on his behalf. While Stu knew what Owen was up to, Helen wasn't so wise to her son's ways, and, after enough (fake) tears and pleading from Owen, she grabbed the towel and threw it in, making Bob Backlund the new WWF champion. Owen, of course, immediately hollered with joy and ran away, having cost Bret the title.

After drawing with new WWF champion Diesel at *Royal Rumble '95*, Bret's career became bogged down with helping to elevate midcarders and generally having his potential wasted. He easily dispatched Bob Backlund in an "I Quit" match at *Wrestlemania XI,* then got put back into a feud with Jerry Lawler, this time a less-than-inspired one. Lawler first brought in Japanese star Hakushi (Jinsei Shinzaki) to go after Bret. Bret defeated him at the first *In Your House* show, but was then goaded into a match with Lawler himself, which he lost thanks to Hakushi's interference. Bret destroyed Lawler at *King of the Ring '95* in a "Kiss My Foot" match, and Lawler was indeed forced to kiss Bret's foot.

Bret was becoming less than thrilled with the WWF's treatment of him, and that continued as Lawler then recruited his dentist, Isaac Yankem (known today as Kane) to go after Bret. Yankem was played by Glen Jacobs, a rookie recruited straight out of Smoky Mountain Wrestling due to his size and speed. Bret won

Bret wasn't happy about being a champion solely so that Shawn could beat him in six months, but he was still the champion. Bret defended the title against the British Bulldog in a gruesomely bloody match at *In Your House V* (although the company line was that Bret's blood was "accidental," as though anyone ever accidentally cut their forehead open), and then defeated the Undertaker by DQ at *Royal Rumble '96* when Diesel prevented a pinfall for the challenger. This made Bret look even weaker (he would have lost without Diesel's interference), and led to a Bret v. Diesel cage match at *In Your House VI*. Again, Bret's standing was diminished when the finish saw Undertaker screw Diesel out of the win and essentially hand the title to Bret.

Bret's stay at the top of the WWF limped to its end as Bret jobbed to Shawn Michaels at *Wrestlemania XII* and lost the WWF title. He cut a bitter promo on the WWF TV shows following that loss, refusing to put Michaels over and essentially saying, "I'll be back." Then he took some time off to mull over whether the WWF was where he wanted to spend the rest of his career, or if WCW might be worth a shot.

The decision he made would send shockwaves through the wrestling industry, and probably not in the way you think.

# UNDERTAKER

WCW just thought they had an agile big man in "Mean" Mark Callous and weren't terribly concerned when he left for the WWF in 1990. The WWF, however, knew otherwise...

Born Mark Callaway in March 1962, Undertaker first came into the wrestling business in the southern states in 1989, dubbed either Master of Pain or The Punisher depending on which area he was working at the time. Despite his size, the WWF wouldn't give him a look, so he settled for signing a short-term deal with

WCW in 1990. Intended only as a quick fix to a quick problem, Callaway was brought in to work a few dates with Danny Spivey as part of the Skyscrapers team.

Sid Vicious had suffered a punctured lung in a match against the Steiner Brothers and needed a replacement, and Callaway had the size to take that spot. The makeshift team was viewed as a joke by WCW fans, however, and was split up when Spivey left WCW for Japan. Callaway (now dubbed "Mean" Mark Callous) had demonstrated remarkable speed and skill for a man his size, specifically his flying clothesline and amazing ropewalk, where he would hold onto his opponent's wrist and literally walk along the top rope before launching himself off at him.

With manager Paul E. Dangerously to talk for him, he was pushed into a U.S. title match with Lex Luger at

*Great American Bash '90*, and despite showing tremendous effort, he was booked to lose the match and was cut from the roster with the changeover to the Ole Anderson regime for monetary reasons. The WWF immediately snapped him up.

Seeing the potential in Callaway, the WWF decided to go for broke with him, and essentially create the largest larger-than-life character ever—a living superhero with limitless powers and a different set of rules than the rest. The result was one of the darkest and gloomiest villains seen in wrestling to that point—The Undertaker.

Given no real backstory, Undertaker made his WWF debut at *Survivor Series '90*, managed by Brother Love (Bruce Pritchard) and awing the crowd with his cold demeanor and deliberate walk to the ring. He was the much-debated "mystery member" of Ted Dibiase's team for the series, and he quickly demolished Koko B. Ware and team captain Dusty Rhodes, but was counted out while chasing Dusty back to the dressing room.

Undertaker was given a brief name change to "Kane, The Undertaker," but that was dropped after a couple of weeks. Brother Love, the ridiculously over-the-top televangelist spoof, was deemed wrong for managing Undertaker, so he "sold the contract" to newly imported manager William Moody, fresh off a long start as a nemesis of the Von Erich family in Texas as Percy Pringle. He was given a black dye-job and renamed "Paul Bearer."

KERRY VON ERICH

More backstory was also added to the Undertaker's character, as Bearer always carried a mysterious urn around with him that gave Undertaker his powers. Most guesses by the announcers had the urn containing the ashes of Undertaker's dead parents, a plot point that would later be explained when Undertaker's estranged brother Kane was introduced in 1997. In 1990, however, all anyone knew was that Bearer had an urn, and Undertaker was really attached to it.

Undertaker shot up the ranks in record time, as he endeared himself to the WWF creative team by doing

whatever was asked of him and never, ever, breaking character. Even in "real life" he would maintain the façade of being a member of the undead. As Undertaker's character advanced, he went from being a big scary guy to a big scary supernaturally powerful guy, and eventually a sort of living zombie who didn't feel pain and only ever had three words to say: Rest in peace.

Undertaker made his *Wrestlemania* debut at the seventh show, crushing Jimmy Snuka in short order and getting a noticeable face pop as a result. The fans were clearly into this guy, because he was violating the primary rule of being a "classic WWF heel": Instead of making threats and then backing down, he simply targeted someone, then beat them without selling anything. No fuss, no muss. The more efficiently he dispatched his opponents, the more popular he became.

In order to curb this popularity, he was pushed into the B-Show main events against the Ultimate Warrior in "body bag matches," where the loser would get stuffed into a body bag. This led to a short-lived practice whereby Undertaker would stuff his opponent into a body bag after beating them. Undertaker more than held his own in these Warrior matches, and the WWF's confidence in the character was high.

When Jake Roberts turned heel in mid-1991, Undertaker began hanging around with him as an undead flunky in order to firmly establish Undertaker as evil. The fans kept cheering him, however, and the WWF was at the point where they couldn't use traditional heel tactics because it would compromise the character. Why would Undertaker fear anyone, for instance, if he was already dead?

At *Survivor Series '91*, Undertaker won his first WWF World title, beating Hulk Hogan with his tombstone piledriver (and a little help from Ric Flair), and got a large face reaction from it. His title reign only lasted a week, however, as Hogan regained it after tossing ashes from the urn in Undertaker's face and getting the pin. However, the controversy that arose from Hogan's tactics caused the title to be vacated, and it was put up for grabs at the *Royal Rumble '92* and won by Ric Flair. Finally, the cheers were simply too much to ignore, and in early 1992, Undertaker stopped an attack by Jake Roberts on the innocent Miss Elizabeth, and turned face just like that.

With no real change in his actions or motivations, the character was now established as a babyface thanks to the dedication to the act brought by Mark Callaway. Undertaker crushed former ally Jake Roberts at *Wrestlemania VIII,* completely burying him (figuratively speaking, of course) as Roberts was on his way out. The WWF decided to go in a standard direction for a big man like Undertaker following this, programming him with other big men. Unfortunately, most of them were uncarriable.

The first such feud was against Kamala, who played the character of an Afircan Tribesman. Their match at *Summerslam '92* featured a double DQ, and this led to the first casket match in the WWF, at *Survivor Series '92.* Undertaker won that one easily, and seemed to be back on track for the WWF title again. But at *Royal Rumble '93,* where he was the favorite to win the match and gain the title shot at *Wrestlemania,* he was eliminated by the debuting Giant Gonzalez.

Gonzalez, who was more than 7 feet tall, dwarfed Undertaker who stood at 6' 10", and would have made for an intriguing opponent had he not already been established as one of the worst wrestlers in the history of the entire sport by his stint in WCW. Undertaker and Gonzalez met at *Wrestlemania IX* in a match that summed up the general awfulness of that whole card, as Gonzalez was disqualified for using an ether-soaked rag on Undertaker. Even worse for Undertaker, Gonzalez' manager Harvey Wippleman *stole the urn,* thus robbing Undertaker of his powers temporarily. By this point, the WWF was getting quite silly with the whole Undertaker deal and it was showing. Undertaker beat Gonzalez at *Summerslam '93,* and he hasn't been seen in the Big Two since then.

Undertaker was in the main event of *Survivor Series '93,* as a part of Lex Luger's All-American team, facing off against the Foreign Fanatics (a team that included two Americans) and it was there that he would battle to a double-countout with WWF champion Yokozuna and make everyone think that there was no way they could avoid putting the title back on him that time.

## WRESTLER SPOTLIGHT

## UNDERTAKER

### BIGGEST CONTRIBUTION

The gimmick to end all gimmicks.

### BEST MATCH
Against Mankind at *King of the Ring '98.*

### BIGGEST MATCH
Scoring a mostly clean win over Hulk Hogan to win the WWF World title at *Survivor Series '91.*

### BIGGEST RIVALS
Had feuds with many, including the likes of Hulk Hogan, the members of The Corporation, Mankind, and Kane.

Everyone couldn't have been more wrong.

At *Royal Rumble '94,* Yokozuna defended the WWF title against Undertaker in a casket match. If you're an afitionado of bad wrestling, you've probably heard of this one before. The goal of a casket match is to shove your opponent into a casket to win—so there are no DQs or countouts. The WWF bookers took full advantage of this, booking no less than 10 guys to come in and pound on Undertaker to help Yokozuna. The urn was rendered powerless when the lid came off and thick green smoke poured out of it as the announcers speculated that the Undertaker's powers were draining as a result. Finally, they rolled Undertaker into the casket to give Yokozuna the win, and carted The Undertaker back to the dressing room.

## SUPERSTAR STATS:

**Undertaker**

*Real name:*
Mark Calloway
*Height:* 6'10"
*Weight:* 328 lbs.
*Trademark move:* Tombstone
Piledriver and The Last Ride
*Aliases:* Texas Red, Mean Mark
Callous, Master of Pain, Punisher,
Punisher Dice Morgan

On the way there, however, Undertaker appeared on the video wall near the entrance (presumably still inside the casket) and delivered a long soliloquy about how he wouldn't rest in peace, at which point, the lights dimmed and Marty Jannetty (dressed as Undertaker) was raised from the entranceway on a wire and lifted to the rafters in a crucifix pose amidst low-grade thunder and lightning effects.

This was generally regarded at the time as the low point of the year, despite only being one month into 1994. Most people felt that it couldn't possibly be topped, even with 11 months left to go and Vince distracted by a steroid trial. And again, they couldn't have been more wrong.

The idea in Undertaker disappearing like that was to give him a few months off to heal some injuries and spend time with his new wife. In his absence, the WWF decided to go high-concept with the gimmick. Ted Dibiase, who had recently become a manager, started doing vignettes from a graveyard, promising to personally bring Undertaker back from the dead like he had done in 1990 when he first brought him into the WWF. And indeed, soon enough, he reintroduced—the Undertaker. This version was, in fact, played by Callaway's friend Brian Lee, who was on loan from Jim

Cornette's Smokey Mountain Wrestling. He was also six inches shorter than the real Undertaker, but you couldn't tell that without having them side-by-side.

Well, apparently the fans *could*. Almost no one bought the fake Undertaker (or "Underfaker" as he was dubbed by online fans), and fan reaction to this idea became downright hostile within weeks of his introduction. Despite the blowoff being planned for much later in the year, it was quickly (and with little fanfare) moved up to *Summerslam '94* following a series of goofy vignettes with Leslie Neilson searching for Undertaker. None of it made sense, which would probably explain the lack of fan concern for who even won the match. Undertaker beat Underfaker in a horrible match with no heat at *Summerslam*, as Undertaker debuted his new purple-themed costume and began moving away from the original character.

He finished off Yokozuna once and for all at *Survivor Series '94* in a casket match, and moved into yet another dead-end feud to continue his fight with Ted Dibiase. He beat IRS at *Royal Rumble '95*, only to see the urn stolen yet again in a formula that was already cliché. The urn was given to Corporation member Kama (aka The Godfather), who melted it down into a gold chain. Undertaker continued plowing through the Corporation, beating King Kong Bundy at *Wrestlemania XI* in another painfully bad match. It got worse for him, as he was upset by Kama to trigger a feud that no one wanted to see at *King of the Ring '95*. This led to a rematch at *Summerslam '95* (a casket match, of course) which Undertaker won. His career was clearly going nowhere, due to the WWF's reluctance to move him back into the main event and compromise Diesel's already waning popularity.

New WWF booker Bill Watts re-energized Undertaker somewhat by having King Mabel do a huge gang attack on him, but Undertaker suffered an accidental fracture of his orbital bone (eye socket) as a result, which was then written into the story line by having him wear a protective facemask when he returned. That return came at *Survivor Series '95*, as Undertaker's team faced Mabel's team. Undertaker singlehandedly went through Jerry Lawler, Hunter Hearst Helmsley, and Isaac Yankem before Mabel chose to run away from the match. The suffering thus continued for wrestling fans, as Undertaker beat Mabel in a casket match at *In Your House V* to end that feud.

However, Diesel had now turned heel, so Undertaker was free to move back into the main event picture again, and in this case feud with Diesel himself. Diesel cost Undertaker the WWF title in a match with Bret Hart at *Royal Rumble '96*, so Undertaker cost Diesel the title at *In Your House VI*. And since Diesel was on his way to WCW, the inevitable match at *Wrestlemania XII* between the two ended overwhelmingly in Undertaker's favor. The character was in desperate need of something to shake it up, and the night after *Wrestlemania*, it happened.

"It" was WWF newcomer Mick Foley, 100 pounds lighter than today and on his first gimmick in the WWF: Mankind. Mankind attacked Undertaker and laid him out with his mandible claw— an unheard-of thing. The first match between the two happened at *King of the Ring '96*, and it was there that Mankind shocked the crowd by getting a clean pin on Undertaker after Paul Bearer "accidentally" hit Undertaker with the urn.

A rematch was set for *Summerslam '96*, in a "Boiler Room Brawl," where the winner was the first one to fight out of the boiler room, make it to the ring, and take the urn from Paul Bearer. Undertaker accomplished the first part, but when he tried the second, his longtime manager turned on him, knocking him out with the urn and presenting it to Mankind instead.

Mankind got yet another win over Undertaker at the *Buried Alive* PPV, in a match where the loser was the first to be literally buried alive in a grave. With the help of Terry Gordy (who was playing the masked Executioner), Mankind rolled him in the grave and buried him for the win. This would mark the official end of the undead zombie interpretation of the Undertaker. Although the lightning bolt and the hand rising from the grave to end the PPV was probably a bit heavy-handed on the WWF's part.

The final recreation of the character happened at *Survivor Series '96*, as he shed his "grey and purple mortician" undertaker costume entirely in favor of a new leather-themed outfit that had no connection to the former undead nature of the Undertaker character. He began doing his own interviews to establish himself as a separate entity from Paul Bearer. Mankind was defeated at *Survivor Series*, and the Executioner was executed at *It's Time*. With his new, vulnerable persona, Undertaker dropped a match to Vader at *Royal Rumble '97* to try to make Vader into a monster, but it didn't work. Finally, after years of waiting, Undertaker defeated Sid Vicious at *Wrestlemania 13* to recapture the WWF World title. In one final effort to humanize the character, estranged manager Paul Bearer began making claims of a lost Undertaker family member, who was eventually revealed as Kane.

After losing the WWF title to Bret Hart at Summerslam '97, Undertaker's career began a downward turn, which the WWF attempted to compensate for by tinkering further with the gimmick (leading to the Ministry of Darkness and "American Bad Ass" phases), but aside from two excellent matches with Shawn Michaels to close out 1997 and one very memorable one with Mankind at *King of the Ring '98*, the character appears to have run its course as a groundbreaker and has settled into being just another gimmick.

# AWA

In the days before Extreme Championship Wrestling was half-heartedly declared by followers of the business to constitute the third part of the "Big Three," there really was a Big Three, and the race was very close indeed. Up until the mid-'80s, the players in the game that was wrestling were upstart Vince McMahon Jr.'s WWF, Jim Crockett Jr.'s steadfast WCW/Mid-Atlantic territory, and the reliable workhorse that was Verne Gagne's American Wrestling Association. With a long and storied history equaling that of Crockett and McMahon's promotions, Verne Gagne seemingly had everything needed to follow Vince Jr. into the 21st century: A national TV deal, a loyal fanbase, talented workers, and, most important, the services of the wrestler who was rapidly becoming the buzzword in Hollywood and wrestling in general—Hulk Hogan.

By 1991, Verne was reduced to running spot shows in Minnesota for 150 people, and eventually filing for bankruptcy at the beginning of 1991 and making false claims about the monetary worth of his tape collection to avoid losing every cent that he had. Amazingly, the

seeds of Verne's destruction had been sown 8 years earlier, and in the end he had no one to blame but himself for the demise of the third-largest wrestling promotion in America.

As is the case with most things in wrestling from before 1980, the AWA was founded as a result of a dispute over who exactly the NWA World champion was. The National Wrestling Alliance, from its official formation in 1948, had become the single most powerful entity in professional wrestling, unifying several of the top promoters across the country with a common champion to promote.

However, as with any gathering of power (and hence ego) as large as this, complications and cracks in the unity eventually started showing through. The first major one occurred in July 1957, as Eduardo Carpentier defeated Lou Thesz for the NWA title in a 2-of-3 falls match. However, since one of the falls was a DQ, a dispute arose among the promoters as to whether or

*The Buzzword in Hollywood. . .*

**HULK HOGAN**

not Carpentier should rightly be recognized as the champion. The NWA's official decision was that the title was to be returned to Thesz, and indeed that occurred shortly after.

However, several "renegade" promoters, led by Wally Karbo of Nebraska, continued to recognize Carpentier as the NWA World champion, and in fact sanctioned passing the title from Carpentier to former NWA Junior champion Verne Gagne in August 1958. With one group of promoters recognizing Gagne as NWA champion and the other recognizing Thesz, it became apparent that some sort of unification match was needed—but it never came.

By 1960, after unsuccessfully lobbying the NWA for a match between Verne Gagne and the NWA World champion to rejoin the titles, Wally Karbo (with Gagne holding the true power behind the scenes) split off from the NWA and formed the American Wrestling Association. As a last-ditch "peace offering" (in reality a cynical political ploy), the newly formed AWA recognized current NWA World champion Pat O'Connor as their first champion, and gave him 90 days to defend that "title" against #1 contender Verne Gagne or be stripped of it.

And as you might expect, the NWA ignored this challenge, and Verne Gagne was awarded the AWA World title in August of 1960, a title change that the NWA further ignored, and as a result, there were now two officially recognized World champions for the first time since the formation of the NWA: The NWA and AWA versions. And most of the time, that AWA version was around the waist of Verne Gagne.

The period of the late '60s until 1980 saw only two people wearing the AWA title: Verne Gagne and Nick Bockwinkel. Wally Karbo maintained his presence in the NWA despite representing another promotion and recognizing a different champion, and the AWA continued its national expansion, although staying mainly in the mid-west and Winnipeg, as Gagne defended his title in NWA mainstay cities against former NWA champions. And for the better part of those 10 years, not much else happened of note in the AWA: Bockwinkel's title victory over Verne Gagne in 1975 was the first one in 7 years, and he would proceed to hold the title until 1980.

The AWA established itself as a solid, if unspectacular, alternative to the NWA and the growing WWWF, featuring an emphasis on the mat wrestling of Gagne over the showmanship of the WWWF. By 1980, however, it was becoming rapidly more obvious that the wrestling world was changing. Whereas the '70s had actually seen matches between the World champions (with WWWF champion Bob Backlund meeting AWA champion Nick Bockwinkel on at least one occasion), the more competitive TV decade, which was dawning, ended the cooperation between the promoters, almost for good. And no one did more to encourage the end of that cooperation than Vince McMahon Jr. Especially since Verne Gagne had something that Vince wanted very, very badly: Hulk Hogan.

The essential problem was this: Gagne was stubborn. He believed in "sports" over "entertainment," as was evidenced by his matches in the '70s featuring extended wrestling holds and counters that would span 40 or 60 minutes. Verne, however, was not sold on the more circus-like atmosphere of the WWF, and felt that his way of thinking, the traditional athletic competition of wrestling, was the way to keep making money, since it had always made him money before. He felt that aging stars like Mad Dog Vachon, The Crusher, Baron Von Rashke, and even Nick Bockwinkel could continue to be used effectively in the upper card, while the new breed of power wrestler such as Ken Patera, Scott Hall, and even top draw Hulk Hogan, were more of a side attraction to be used to build to Bockwinkel's title defenses.

Verne's ego was another problem: He won the AWA title from Bockwinkel in 1980 (his ninth total), despite his obviously advanced age and deteriorated physique, and actually retired for the first time, still as champion, in 1981. This sort of inexcusable ego-stroking led to a major break in the lineage of the title, with Bockwinkel being awarded the championship following Gagne's retirement. Even worse, Verne insisted on pushing his untalented son Greg beyond the boundaries of all sanity.

Despite showing no remarkable flair inside the ring, or head for the business outside the ring, Greg Gagne was turned into one of the biggest attractions in the AWA from his debut in the late '70s until his retirement in 1989. Verne even tried several times to put the World title on Greg in the mid-'80s, with several promoters nearly quitting in protest to prevent the move. But still, Verne was convinced that Greg, not Hogan, was the babyface of the future for his company.

The match that summed up the growing problems of the company occurred April 24, 1983, as Nick Bockwinkel defended the World title against Hulk Hogan at "Super Sunday," the AWA's first real true "supercard." Hogan pinned Bockwinkel to win the title, but the result was disputed, as Bockwinkel had been thrown over the top rope earlier in the match and thus AWA President Stanley Blackburn reversed the decision on the spot and gave the belt back to Bockwinkel. The arena nearly erupted into a riot as a result. That same hackneyed "Dusty Finish" had been used by the AWA several times in the past to reverse an unwanted title change, but the more youthful and exuberant crowd brought to the arena by the lure of Hulk Hogan was unwilling to accept a ridiculous finish such as that, indeed one that Gagne had been doing with Hogan and Bockwinkel for months leading up to that match.

This was becoming the era of the cartoonish babyface who won the big match cleanly, something that Gagne's old-school mentality couldn't properly grasp.

And it cost him, big.

Hulk Hogan, after basically being told that the World title was not coming his way, left for the World Wrestling Federation by the fall of 1983, and never looked back. Vince McMahon put his World title on Hogan almost immediately after Hogan's entrance into the WWF, and as a result of years of clean pinfall victories for Hogan over his challengers, gave the upstart WWF title the kind of credibility that Bob Backlund could never bring to it. The war between the Big Three suddenly looked very different, with the WWF on top of the world, Jim Crockett struggling to find his identity, and Verne Gagne vainly trying the same tricks that worked in 1975 in an effort to maintain his suddenly shrinking fanbase and talent base against the onslaught of the MTV generation.

In an effort to win back the fans who were increasingly migrating to the more "cool" WWF product, Verne entered into an agreement with the NWA, which pretty much marked the first time in more than a decade that the two groups were willing to work together in any significant fashion. The end result was *Superclash* in Chicago, putting 21,000 people in a baseball stadium to witness both the NWA and AWA titles being defended on the same show. It was a novel idea that drew some pretty good attention from the general wrestling fanbase, but the NWA stars on the show clearly eclipsed the AWA ones, and as a result, the tentative agreement fell apart fairly quickly.

Verne also entered into another cross-promotional agreement, this one with Shohei Baba's All Japan Pro Wrestling. However, this one would prove much more costly to Verne. The AWA World title was rapidly losing prestige due to ridiculous backstage political maneuvering (such as Otto Wanz reportedly paying Gagne $50,000 in exchange for a title reign) and Nick Bockwinkel's generally stale act. As a show of good will, the AWA title was put onto top Japanese draw Tommy "Jumbo" Tsuruta in 1984, which was completely the wrong move to make in order to win back fans in the more important United States.

Further, Verne had the idea of making bland Rick Martel into his top babyface, and so he put the title on him during a tour of Japan. His reception upon returning to the States with the title was lukewarm at best. Finally, needing a dominant heel to carry the promotion while he found someone to fill his babyface role, the title was moved to the unstable and undependable Stan Hansen, killing Rick Martel's credibility in the process due to a humiliating submission loss, and Gagne decided to stop and regroup.

This would prove to be the beginning of the end for the promotion.

In 1986, Verne decided to try Nick Bockwinkel as a babyface champion, and turned Bockwinkel by using a confrontation with Larry Zbyszko as the catalyst. Gagne asked Hansen to job the title to Bockwinkel in June of 1986. Hansen, a longtime employee of Baba's AJPW, considered himself to be Baba's champion first and Gagne's second, and so asked Baba for his okay on the title change. It was not given, so Hansen simply took the title back to Japan with him on the next tour and defended it there against challengers of All Japan's choosing. The AWA stripped Hansen of the title and awarded it to Bockwinkel, with the no-show being the official reasoning, and Hansen was to be effectively blackballed from the U.S. for four years as a result.

By 1987, things were looking somewhat up for Gagne. He was developing young talent in Curt Hennig (son of longtime AWA associate Larry Hennig), along with the Midnight Rockers (Shawn Michaels and Marty Jannetty), a team discovered in Texas. Curt Hennig was first established as a top babyface, then turned heel to prevent him from eclipsing Greg's popularity. He was

given the AWA World title in April 1987, and Nick Bockwinkel retired soon after at the hands of Larry Zbyszko. Hennig proved to be by far the most marketable and popular heel champion that the AWA had seen in years, and he enjoyed a long reign that was only interrupted when the biggest threat to Gagne emerged: The talent raids by the WWF. Indeed, the AWA was rapidly becoming Vince McMahon's personal wrestler shopping center. From 1986-1991, Vince took, practically at will, every major (and minor) star developed or signed by Gagne until finally entire title reigns were being dictated by the whims of the WWF and how soon they were likely to sign away the champions at a given time. Curt Hennig left in 1988, The Rockers followed soon after, along with Ron Garvin, Rick Martel, Sherri Martell, Boris Zhukov, Baron Von Rashke, Bobby Heenan, Ken Patera, and anyone else that the WWF felt like signing away to a big money deal. Even long time AWA star Buddy Rose was claimed, for no conceivable reason other than to rub it in Verne's face.

By the midpoint of 1988, Gagne was left with only his loyalist supporters within the promotion, a World champion ready to depart for the competition, dwindling attendance, and a TV deal that needed new shows every week. He strayed into the world of the ridiculous gimmicks, creating Nord the Barbarian (from Norwegia), various cartoonish Russian figures, and a series of teen-idol heartthrob wannabes to replace the departed Rockers, but nothing clicked for the more old-school clientele that he was catering to. So now becoming increasingly desperate and running out of money, Verne once again made a cross-promotional deal.

In May of 1988, the AWA World title was put on longtime contender and AWA sympathizer Jerry Lawler, who just happened to own the Memphis-based CWA and all its talent. Lawler began challenging anyone from any promotion, and his first test came in the form of Terry Taylor, who was working for Fritz Von Erich's World Class Championship Wrestling at the time. And thus was formed a three-way alliance between the AWA, CWA, and WCCW. Lawler began a heated feud with WCCW World champion Kerry Von Erich over who was the "real" champion (never mind that both titles were considered to be bush league by most of the casual fans at that point), and the payoff was the AWA's first ever pay-per-view, *Superclash III* in Chicago. The titles were to be unified there into one, with the AWA and WCCW thus becoming a single entity in the process.

And then everything went completely wrong.

To start, the building held thousands, and even with months of hype and promotion, the paid attendance ended up being a little over 1,000 people. So the event was already a huge money-loser from the start. The buyrate wasn't terribly impressive, doing about one-fourth of the business that the NWA and WWF were doing at the time. And the backstage planning sessions were plagued with political squabbling between the major promoters, none of whom wanted to end up looking the least bit bad when all was said and done.

In the end, Jerry Lawler was awarded the decision over Kerry Von Erich due to blood loss, a bogus cop-out booking decision if there ever was one. But for a week or so, at least, there was peace and harmony as Lawler began defending the so-called "Unified World title"—mainly in Memphis.

Two problems became apparent. First: Now that Lawler had what he wanted, he seemed reluctant to fulfill the dates set forth by the AWA. Second: World Class was rapidly running out of time and money, and needed the funds from the PPV to stay alive. Third (and most important): Verne lied about the revenues from the show, keeping most of them for himself, and ended up stiffing the promoters who had contributed talent to his big show.

In early 1989, everything hit the fan, as Lawler refused to defend the title in AWA territories from that point on until his share of the PPV revenue was paid. It was never paid to him, so the CWA pulled out of the deal altogether. As a result, the AWA stripped Lawler of the AWA title, leaving him as the World Class champion, and leaving the AWA with no champion. Then World Class quickly declared that they were no longer financially solvent, leaving Lawler to bail them out and merge the CWA and WCCW into the USWA, thus turning the Unified World title into a meaningless hunk of tin in the span of a month. This was a new record for self-destruction, even by wrestling's lofty standards. Lawler wouldn't even give the AWA title belt back, leaving Gagne the task of having a new one made and using the TV title in the interim.

The AWA panicked and put the title on the one guy who had stuck with them through all the chaos: Larry Zbyszko. Back from a brief stint in the NWA, Larry won the AWA World title in a battle royale over Tom Zenk, which was just about the worst possible way they could have passed the title on to a new champion. Larry had no credibility and the crowd continued to dwindle. Desperate for some new talent, they turned longtime jobbers

Wayne Bloom and Mike Enos into the new #1 tag team, the Destruction Crew, and even loaned them out to the NWA under masks as the Minnesota Wrecking Crew II in exchange for cash, but the WWF machine stepped in again: Pat Tanaka, Paul Diamond, the Destruction Crew, Kokina Maximus, and even the announce team fled to the WWF, and the signs were pointing to the end faster than wrestling pundits could point fingers.

By 1990, the situation was unsalvageable. Larry Zbyszko dropped and regained the title from Mr. Saito in an effort to build interest, but none was there. They were finally going to put the title on Sgt. Slaughter, who was at least known in the mainstream, but then the WWF signed him, too, and that fell apart. Left with a TV deal with ESPN and no talent, Verne allowed junior announcer Eric Bischoff into the production end of things, and the AWA's last gasp for life came about: *The Team Challenge Series*. The TV shows became completely focused on three teams fighting each other in a series of gimmick matches for points, and the team with the most points would be declared the winner after some undefined time period. The results were chaos, with no one keeping track of the results to any great degree, and crowds were finally so embarrassingly small that the only feasible way to keep from going broke was to film everything in a closed studio with no fans.

In late 1990, in a fitting end to the Series and the AWA, longtime jobber Jake Milliman won a "turkey on a pole" match to claim the victory for his team on the last original episode aired of AWA wrestling on ESPN. World champion Larry Zbyszko, left with no dates to work, signed with WCW immediately following this, leaving the title belt behind him as an afterthought.

No replacement was ever crowned, and in early 1991, with no contracted wrestlers left, no more TV deal, and no more money, Verne Gagne filed for bankruptcy and folded the AWA after 30 years of existence.

Perhaps it's fitting that a promotion as quiet and unassuming as the AWA would go out with a whimper rather than a bang, leaving no more ripples in its wake than a few disgruntled stars leaving for rival promotions, but many people did mourn the loss of the only true competition for Titan and Turner, and indeed that was considered the greater loss. Although Verne Gagne's promotional methods were stale and outdated by the time of expansion in 1983, he did provide a necessary counterpoint to the circus that was the WWF and the mismanaged hellhole that was the NWA, replete with Dusty Rhodes and Ole Anderson's inept booking strategies. The nepotism displayed by Verne was no worse than anything seen in just about any promotion in the history of wrestling, yet sadly that seems to have become his greatest legacy as a promoter.

Indeed, as WCW enters the next century making many of the same mistakes that Gagne did, one has to wonder if the same fate can possibly befall them, as it did the AWA years before. The same arguments were made back then: Verne has too much money, and too much support from ESPN, to let his promotion slide into bankruptcy. Most felt that he'd pull it out, somehow, even as the promotion lay on its deathbed like a cancer victim. That's what's saddest about the passing of the AWA: Many people did care for it deeply and enjoyed the straightforward, less-is-more philosophy it put forth—a throwback to the days when steroid-monster quasi-athletes weren't necessary to make money in the business.

The AWA truly lived in interesting times, but in the end, it just wasn't interesting enough to keep up with them.

# 6
# THE MONDAY NIGHT WARS, 1996–PRESENT

O nce Eric Bischoff was able to convince Turner executives that Nitro was the way to pull the promotion out of the doldrums, the war was on. Signing newer and younger WWF stars away like Scott Hall and Kevin Nash proved that they meant business, and the WWF's response was less than inspiring. However, no one foresaw the sudden rise of WWF writer Vince Russo to the levels he would hit, revitalizing the WWF with the new "Attitude" that the infamous Montreal screwjob began, and the Steve Austin–Vince McMahon feud furthered. Eventually, the WWF returned to its former glory, crushing WCW to the point where the promotion was currently in dire financial straits by late 2000.

# ERIC BISCHOFF
## AND THE nWo

Lawn-mower, coffee boy, junior announcer—not exactly the credentials of a proven winner in the wrestling business. But Eric had a dream—and friends in high places.

As covered in the AWA section, Eric Bischoff got his start working out of Verne Gagne's AWA promotion as a junior announcer, and before that he made his start in the business by fetching coffee and mowing lawns for Gagne. With the loss of announcer Rod Trongard to the WWF near the end of the AWA, however, Gagne's promotion was in need of a new announcer and so Bischoff got his first shot there. Despite his basic lack of knowledge about the business, he proved to be a fast learner thanks to help from friend and heel manager Diamond Dallas Page, and soon had advanced into doing production and some booking.

By 1990, with the AWA on its deathbed, WCW signed away Page, and once DDP had established himself within the company, he convinced the higher-ups to bring in his friend Bischoff as an announcer. Eric Bischoff made his announcing debut at *Great American Bash '91*, roundly considered one of the worst PPVs of all time. One has nothing to do with the other, but it might have been considered an omen. Eric was solidly on the lower tier of announcers, mainly doing locker room interviews like Kevin Kelly does for the WWF today. And then came the nWo.

## WRESTLER SPOTLIGHT

## ERIC BISCHOFF

**CONTRIBUTION TO THE ERA**
The nWo and Monday *Nitro*.

**QUOTE**
"I love each and every one of you!"

Wooed from the WWF by the growing WCW, Scott Hall and Kevin Nash were expected to make a minor midcard impact, but instead shocked everyone by changing wrestling forever.

In 1996, both Diesel and Razor Ramon were about to leave the WWF, each for entirely different reasons. The WWF was eager to unload Diesel after a horrible 1995 with him as champion and establish a "new era" without the association Diesel brought with him. With Ramon, his drug and alcohol problems were hindering his performance in the ring, and he was essentially let go without a fight because of that.

WCW signed both men at the same time to roughly equal deals, and Ramon and Diesel made their farewell appearance on WWF PPV at *Good Friends, Better Enemies* in July. Before they left, however, they had one more notable appearance to make in Madison Square Garden, where they would unknowingly sow the seeds of WCW's own doom before they even went there. But that comes later.

On Memorial Day, 1996, WCW *Nitro* was featuring a non-descript match between two jobbers, when out of the audience came Scott Hall, wearing street clothes. He cleared the ring of both wrestlers and grabbed the house mike, as the live crowd sat in shock. The gist of his statement: If WCW wanted a war, they had one.

The angle itself was based on Japan's "Ishigun" story line of the '80s, when Riki Choshu's younger faction invaded Antonio Inoki's older New Japan Pro Wrestling and "took over," triggering a huge war. Eric Bischoff figured that the story could be adapted to fit American wrestling, and decided to use Scott Hall as his test case. The angle's effectiveness was based on a notion put forth by Jim Cornette years earlier: The only thing wrestling fans truly believed anymore was that WCW and the WWF hated each other. So if Scott Hall suddenly wandered out, in Razor Ramon character, and challenged WCW to a war, then by god they'd believe it. And did they ever.

See, the average fan wasn't aware of Hall and Nash's departure from the WWF because Vince McMahon's policy had always been to bury departing people and never mention them again once they were gone. So people just assumed they were MIA and didn't think anything of it until both showed up in WCW one day. There was nothing to suggest that they *weren't* affiliated with the WWF anymore, so people assumed that they were.

Hall began terrorizing the announcers out of nowhere, making veiled threats to a "takeover" and generally being a huge bully. One week, he promised a big surprise—and unveiled Kevin Nash. Neither man had even been named yet by the promotion, but already they were generating tremendous heel heat and were dubbed "The Outsiders," for obvious reasons. At the *Great American Bash* PPV, they showed up and challenged WCW to a six-man match at the next PPV, where they would unveil the mysterious third member. Eric Bischoff accepted the challenge on behalf of WCW (and officially got both men to state for the record that they were not employed by the WWF) before taking a sudden powerbomb through a nearby table, courtesy of Kevin Nash. The war was on.

Hall and Nash launched attack after attack on

WCW stars leading up to the show, which would feature the Outsiders and a partner taking on Randy Savage, Sting, and Lex Luger, and speculation ran rampant about who the third man would be. In reality, there were three choices:

1) Bret Hart, who was pondering a decision to jump from the WWF at that point.
2) Sting, Lex Luger, or another WCW midcarder who could use the heel turn to boost their fortunes.
3) The guy it turned out to be.

After much wavering back and forth, Bret Hart signed a contract with the WWF, eliminating him from the running. Feeling that either Sting or Luger would be a huge letdown, Bischoff went with choice #3.

The match started three-on-two with Hall and Nash finally getting named as such, until Lex Luger was knocked unconscious at one point and taken out on a stretcher. This was meant to build suspense as to whether he was the third man or not. It proceeded two-on-two with Sting & Savage v. The Outsiders, until the babyfaces gained the advantage. Suddenly, the tide turned again and The Outsiders began beating down Randy Savage with the ref knocked out. Out of the dressing room to make the save came— Hulk Hogan!

Except this time he didn't make the save, and instead shocked the world by dropping the big leg on Randy Savage and covering him for a bogus pin to win the match. The ring started filling up with garbage and Hogan gave a famous interview afterwards where he told the fans to "stick it" because of the way they had turned on him.

See, when we last left Hogan, he was fighting the cartoonish Dungeon of Doom and defending the honor of America against them or something like that. The fans, however, actually started booing Hogan's tired act, and once WCW had established that they weren't just saying "Boo-Urns" and had given away all the free merchandise they could afford in order to make Hogan look popular, it was decided something drastic was needed. So Hogan was basically told that he was turning heel, with promises of another World title reign if he cooperated. Hogan agreed and made the change at *Bash at the Beach*.

The next night on *Nitro*, he debuted a new look for himself, dressed in black with a bizarre painted-on beard, and dubbed himself "Hollywood" Hogan as an update for the '90s on the character. Announcer Larry Zbyszko called them the "New World Order," building on an offhand remark made by Hogan during his big speech, and the trio started attacking everyone in sight. One notable attack saw Kevin Nash tossing Rey Mysterio Jr. into a trailer like a lawn dart.

The group was truly revolutionary, changing the rules of how heels act and wrestle. Whereas most heels in WCW would traditionally beg off from their opponents and cower in fear, the nWo stood their ground and ended up looking better than the babyfaces. They dressed all in black with cool "nWo" logos, which in turn skyrocketed sales of nWo merchandise.

They had hand-signals that all the fans could do (taken as an homage to the "Kliq Sign" invented by

Shawn Michaels in the WWF as a secret wink to the real clique) and a catchphrase fans could sing along with: "Too Sweet!" In short, they were the coolest bunch of guys to come along in ages, and the WWF had absolutely nothing good to counter them with. The upstart WCW *Nitro* started winning the ratings battle, and didn't look back for 82 weeks.

The WWF had no recourse but to try and detract from WCW's credibility. The first such attempt was "Billionaire Ted's Wrasslin' War-Room" in early 1996, featuring actors playing the roles of "The Huckster" and the "Nacho Man" in a desperate and mean-spirited parody of WCW's top stars. The fact that the WWF had pushed those same stars for years doing the same stuff they were still doing in WCW didn't occur to them, and the strategy backfired by making Hogan and Savage look like even bigger stars as a result. Then, the WWF filed a lawsuit directly against WCW for using Hall and Nash in a way that used mannerisms "invented" by the WWF and thus tricking fans into thinking they were WWF stars. WCW counter-sued, and the matter dragged on until 2000 before WWF settled out of court for an undisclosed amount of money.

Finally, and most bizarrely, the WWF had announcer Jim Ross say that Diesel and Razor Ramon were returning to the WWF. Cynical fans weren't buying it, so the WWF stepped up their campaign by announcing that Jim Ross would bring them back to a live episode of *RAW* in September. WCW made sure that Hall and Nash were on in the beginning of *Nitro* to show viewers at home that indeed they were still there and still under contract. And in the end, Jim Ross cut a bitter promo against the WWF and the business in

general, and produced Rick Bogner, an indy wrestler who was playing an obvious ripoff of Razor Ramon. This completely sunk the fan's trust in the WWF at the time, and it took nearly a year to rebuild it.

But back to the nWo…

With three men already joining, speculation was running wild as to who else would join. And indeed the fourth man showed up one week, as Ted Dibiase was seen sitting in the audience, fresh off leaving the WWF. And where Dibiase was, Virgil was sure to follow, and indeed he debuted as "Vincent," the head of security, soon after. The name was a play on Vince McMahon, just as Virgil had been a play on Dusty Rhodes.

The 1-2-3 Kid had been released by the WWF after weeks of whining on his part about his spot in the promotion and his desire to go to WCW, and he showed up next

as the sixth man, dubbed Syxx as a result. The inevitable occurred at *Hog Wild '96*, as Hulk Hogan defeated the Giant (aka The Big Show) to win the WCW World title for a second time, and the nWo proceeded to spraypaint the belt with their logo—a condition the belt stayed in for two years following. The Giant joined the nWo with no real explanation a week later.

The momentum was building for the nWo now, and they challenged WCW (the angle was that the nWo were a separate organization, see) to a Wargames match at *Fall Brawl*, with Hogan, Hall, Nash, and a mystery man taking on Ric Flair, Arn Anderson, Sting, and Lex Luger. It was originally going to be the Four Horsemen, but Sting and Luger replaced Chris Benoit & Mongo MacMichael to hopefully draw a better buyrate. In that match, WCW's biggest feud for the next year was established, as the nWo seemingly had Sting turn to their side the week before, only to have it revealed here that it was an imposter. The real Sting cleaned house on the fake one and the rest of the nWo, but then left the match and left his team hung out to dry for not trusting him. He began growing his hair out and sitting in the rafters, brooding.

At *Halloween Havoc '96*, Hollywood Hogan defended his title against Randy Savage in a stall-filled main event that saw massive interference leading to Hogan retaining—only to be shocked by the appearance of Rowdy Roddy Piper once the match was over. Piper challenged Hogan to a match at *Starrcade*, which was exactly the sort of big-money match that WCW needed to

solidify their new position as the #1 company in wrestling. On the same show, the Outsiders won the WCW World tag titles from Harlem Heat (Booker T and Stevie Ray, a title that they would hold for more than a year following).

Meanwhile, the nWo kept expanding.

They announced a "membership drive" in December, offering anyone in WCW a chance to join the nWo and thus avoid further beatings. Accepting were Marcus Alexander Bagwell (later called "Buff" Bagwell), Michael Wallstreet, Big Bubba, and Scott Norton. They even went international, as Masa Chono and Great Muta formed nWo Japan as a part of WCW's partnership with New Japan Pro Wrestling. And then an even bigger development happened.

Hulk Hogan was dragging his feet on signing the match with Piper for *Starrcade*, and Piper finally brought WCW Vice President Eric Bischoff out for some answers as to why it was taking so long. When no answer was forthcoming, Piper accused Bischoff of lying to him—and Bischoff suddenly revealed that he had been a member of the nWo all along!

A mass beatdown on Piper followed, and Hogan finally granted the match at *Starrcade*. It was only after Piper won that it was revealed to be non-title. The nWo's marketing stepped up a notch around this time, as they began producing striking, black-and-white, post-modern ads for themselves selling T-shirts, a method that almost amounted to militaristic propaganda at times. This was becoming heavy stuff for a bunch of wrestlers. The ratings continued to climb unabated until January.

The first real cracks in the armor of the nWo marketing machine were revealed when they

## nWo

**CONTRIBUTION TO THE ERA**

Defined the "cool heel" and introduced the concept of merchandising for heels. Made more money for WCW than they could spend.

**BEST MATCH**

Didn't compete as a team often enough to judge.

**BIGGEST MATCH**

Obviously the six-man that introduced Hulk Hogan as the third man in the group.

**QUOTE**

"When you're nWo, you're nWo 4 Life"

got "their own PPV," *nWo Souled Out* in January of 1997. A weird, black-lit set and sporadic camera tricks made for a depressing three-hour show featuring the nWo humiliating WCW wrestlers all night, ending with the Giant (who had left the nWo) getting a DQ win over Hollywood Hogan in the main event. The buyrate was extremely disappointing and proved what wrestling experts already knew: The nWo *needed* a strong WCW to oppose them and make for a better show. WCW didn't pay attention, however.

Roddy Piper got another shot at Hogan at *Superbrawl VII*, and this time the title was on the line. Meanwhile, a standoffish Sting was hanging out in the rafters with Randy Savage, who had been beaten up one time too many by the nWo and wanted nothing more to do with the whole war. Savage, however, chose to come down to ringside for the Hogan-Piper match, presumably to help Piper.

The fact that he was dressed exactly like Hogan should have tipped everyone off that something else was up, and indeed Savage turned on Piper and joined the nWo that night, helping Hogan retain the title. *Uncensored '97* saw the induction of former

basketball star and media personality Dennis Rodman into the nWo, as they won a weird three-way, 12-man tag-team match to claim the right to challenge for any title at any time. Sting finally took action following that match, rappelling from the rafters and destroying everyone with a baseball bat. The big Hogan-Sting match seemed imminent, but WCW, to their credit, held off on it, hoping to build it up more.

WCW would score their highest buyrate (1.01) to that point with *Bash at the Beach '97*, featuring Hulk Hogan and Dennis Rodman against Lex Luger and the Giant, and with the ratings gap between *Nitro* and *RAW* increasing all the time, they decided to go for the kill in August. *Nitro* scored its biggest rating ever that month, as Lex Luger made Hulk Hogan submit to the Torture Rack and won the WCW World title for the second time, triggering a huge celebration and scoring an unheard-of 5.0 rating for the show. Hogan regained the title at the *Road Wild* PPV six days later in a horrible match with tons of interference, but the ratings record had been set.

The nWo angle continued in cruise control for the next few months, with Curt Hennig turning on the Four Horsemen to join the team in September and everyone pretty much knowing by now that Sting v. Hogan was going to headline *Starrcade '97*, potentially the biggest drawing show in the history of WCW. There seemed to be no way now for things to go wrong— and yet they did.

*Starrcade '97* was a tremendous success, drawing more than 20,000 people to Washington, D.C., for the show and doing the largest buyrate (1.8) that WCW ever has done and probably ever will. Sting defeated Hogan after a "fast" three-count by crooked ref Nick Patrick and a reversal of the decision by temporary referee Bret Hart. Despite the ludicrous overbooking for what should have been a straightforward victory for Sting, most people were forgiving on the show and praised it. The *Nitro* show was hitting its rating peak around this time and making more money for WCW than ever before, and everyone was getting rich off the whole deal.

So then, it should come as no surprise that the WWF overtook them in the ratings battle only 4 months after this.

Why? Consider the main people involved in the nWo angle: Hulk Hogan, Kevin Nash, and Scott Hall. Putting those three together on top is begging for self-destruction, and it came in spades in December.

For instance, take as an example an *nWo Nitro*. The nWo was popular, yes, but the people running WCW interpreted this popularity as "We like these people" rather than the "We like to hate these people" popularity that logic would dictate it was. There's a world of difference, because the second one requires strong babyfaces to counter the heels, and none were in evidence in WCW at that time.

WCW was then given a 2-hour timeslot on TBS for another live wrestling show, to be called *Thunder*. The idea being toyed with by Bischoff and his crew was to give *Nitro* exclusively to the nWo and have WCW "retreat" to *Thunder*, then run two separate "promotions" under the Turner banner. Fine idea in theory, but when they ran a test show of *nWo Nitro* the week before *Starrcade*, the ratings dropped. Huge.

Most of this could be attributed to arrogantly using 30 minutes of head-to-head airtime to show the new set being built, but *RAW* ran 20-minute interviews all the time without hurting their viewership. In fact, *RAW*, which had been trailing by more than a point for months, came within less than a point of winning that segment of the ratings battle, something which people at the time thought would never happen again. The idea of doing *nWo Nitro* was quickly scrapped, but a small amount of permanent damage had been done.

The next factor was the booking. The nWo *always* won, and when they didn't win, the finish was generally everyone running into the ring and the show ending without a definite conclusion. The most arrogant use of this tactic by WCW occurred on the *Nitro* immediately following *Starrcade '97*, a show that featured a rematch of the Sting-Hogan World title match. After the announcers spent much of the previous few shows crowing about how *Nitro* always stayed on the air until the conclusion of the main event, this show featured the show going off the air before its usual ending time with no finish for the match evident. The tease there was that the viewer would have to watch the new *Thunder* show to see what the finish was.

This particular tactic annoyed a significant number of viewers, many of whom made angry phone calls to TNT's offices following the show to voice their anger at WCW. More often than not, however, rather than resorting to that "cliffhanger" approach, WCW would simply have as many people as possible run into the match to produce the illusion of story line advancement when in fact the story wasn't advancing at all. After more than a year with no conclusive victory by the babyface WCW, fans completely lost patience with the "good guys" and simply began regarding those who sided with WCW as losers, and only nWo members as worthwhile of their time.

So, of course, everyone suddenly wanted to join the nWo. This is the third factor that led to WCW's downfall, because while the WWF was busy with a tightly focused Steve Austin v. Vince McMahon feud, WCW was busy catering to 7 or 8 different egos at once. Dissension was teased all the time in early 1998, but it was teased every week and rarely led anywhere. Hulk Hogan and Randy Savage fought off and on in the early part of 1998, most notably in a cage match at *Uncensored* with no finish, but they generally reunited by the end of the show.

Finally, after staggering through the first half of 1998 without a direction, WCW finally pulled the trigger on the nWo split and created nWo Wolfpac. The name was an homage to the trio of Kevin Nash, Scott Hall, and Syxx. Syxx himself had suffered a serious neck injury and was fired via FedEx by WCW while recovering, and his arrival on WWF *RAW* in April signaled the turning point in the ratings war. The Wolfpac consisted of Kevin Nash, Randy Savage, Konnan, Curt Hennig—and pretty soon top babyfaces Sting and Lex Luger. To distinguish themselves, they switched from the traditional black-and-white colors to red-and-black.

The remaining "classic" nWoers were renamed nWo Hollywood and they retained the white color scheme.

Two problems immediately became apparent: 1) Those WCW stars who were babyfaces but chose not to join the nWo in some fashion were now effectively left out of the biggest angle in the promotion. WCW as a whole was now left looking like total losers, as nWo effectively had control of the entire promotion. 2) Splitting into factions only delays the inevitable: At some point, one group is going to have to be beaten by the other and someone has to win. This never happens. Things were complicated further when Bill Goldberg burst onto the scene and immediately muscled his way into the main event without ever wearing either nWo shirt, thus annoying a lot of people who spent months playing politics for their position, only to lose it to a guy who was being pushed because he was over. Hogan immediately took charge of the situation and made sure that the Wolfpac was buried and his nWo was emphasized, then generously offered to job the World title to Goldberg in exchange for being the one to break his incredible winning streak later on.

The nWo started falling apart completely in the summer of 1998 with Goldberg taking the spotlight, as he systematically destroyed all the Wolfpac members until they were a non-force, then did the same to the nWo Hollywood members. By the time Ultimate Warrior made his return to wrestling in the fall of 1998, the nWo was practically a non-issue except for a group of second-stringers generally referred to as the "nWo B-Team." Hogan announced his "retirement" in November of 1998 to escape the growing ratings gap between the WWF and WCW and to avoid the blame, leaving Scott Steiner to lead a weak team of jobbers as the nWo. People pretty much wrote off the nWo for good once Scott Hall fought Kevin Nash at *Halloween Havoc '98* and later once Nash won the World title from Goldberg as a free agent.

Those hopes proved to be premature, however. In an ill-advised ratings stunt two weeks after *Starrcade '98*, Kevin Nash conned Bill Goldberg out of a title rematch and took on Hulk Hogan instead, only to suddenly and voluntarily lie down for the so-called Fingerpoke of Doom and turn the World title over to Hogan. A new nWo then formed around Hogan, one that would be "elite" and consist of Hogan, Nash, Scott Hall, Scott Steiner, Buff Bagwell, and Lex Luger. They were clearly heels and had a clear opponent in Bill Goldberg. To signify the union of both nWos, they called themselves the Wolfpac and wore red, black, and white. Surely, this one couldn't fail.

Well, that lasted about three weeks before Hall was back in rehab, Bagwell was a babyface again, Hogan was doing his own thing in a feud with Ric Flair, and the rest just stopped wearing nWo merchandise altogether. So what happened that time? The problem is pretty easy here: The group was supposed to be "elite," but the straggling "nWo B-Team" was never split from the group and left for dead, leaving the group as a whole looking watered down. Everyone thought that this time the group was done, for sure.

Nope.

In December of 1999, the Vince Russo regime revived the nWo yet again as nWo 2000, this time with Bret Hart, Jeff Jarrett, and the Outsiders. That one lasted all of a month before it was down to Jeff Jarrett on his own. The group finally appears to be dead for good, but one never knows in a business that is notorious for being the snake that consumes its own tail.

# "MONTREAL"

Okay, now let's jump back over to the WWF side of things for a moment.

Having established that the nWo contributed heavily to WCW's meteoric rise, the question remains: How did the WWF counter? How did they go from drawing ratings in the low 2.0s to ruling the cable world in the span of a year?

Well, if you ask most knowledgeable fans, the response will be one word: Montreal. What does a city in Quebec have to do with the revitalization of the WWF? Here's a story for you…

When we last left Bret Hart, it was mid-1996 and he had lost the main event of *Wrestlemania XII* to rival Shawn Michaels, and his WWF title in the process. Bret felt somewhat cheated by the experience, thinking that the WWF was favoring Michaels over him for political reasons. So he started entertaining offers from Eric Bischoff and WCW, offers that made him the biggest potential "free agent" signing in wrestling history.

Make no mistake, Bret Hart was now a very hot property, and it would have been a major crowing point for WCW if they had managed to "steal" Kevin Nash, Scott Hall, *and* Bret Hart within a span of six months. It was no big secret that Vince McMahon was in bad financial shape following the Kevin Nash WWF title experiment, and to lose Bret Hart to rival WCW would be a blow to the ego too big to recover from. So he sucked up his pride and, instead of competing directly with Ted Turner's pocketbook, offered Bret an equal monetary deal, but spread out over 20 years, with Bret retiring and joining the front office when the deal was over. In October of 1996, Bret accepted, and Vince promised him the slot as the #1 babyface in the company again, and all was well.

That lasted all of one week.

By November, with Bret under contract, Vince was already asking Bret to turn heel. Vince's reasoning: As a face, Bret's opponents were limited to essentially Vader or Mankind, while as a heel Bret could draw good money against Undertaker, Shawn Michaels, or Steve Austin. Given that explanation, Bret agreed and helped to come up with the "Canadian Hero" gimmick for his feud with Steve Austin. To that end, Bret began cultivating a "whiner" image, losing the Royal Rumble due to shenanigans from Steve Austin and complaining about it incessantly afterward.

Bret was given a one-day WWF title reign, his fourth, when original choice Steve Austin was injured during the "Final Four" match and couldn't finish. Bret and Austin had a gruesome, intense match at *Wrestlemania 13* where Bret officially turned heel and Austin officially turned face and, from there,

Bret launched the "Canadian Hero" gimmick that he had planned. Bret and Austin went to war on *Monday Night RAW* for the next four months, a feud that served to make Austin look like a convincing badass and Bret like a crybaby. Bret found himself becoming more and more uncomfortable with this portrayal after years of being the "hero" of the story, and Shawn Michaels was now tweaking him every chance he could, trying to provoke a reaction out of him backstage at every opportunity.

By August, Bret was so over as a heel that the WWF had no choice but to put the title back on him, and they did so at *Summerslam '97*, as Bret defeated Undertaker for the title in a match where Shawn Michaels was the special referee. Bret was becoming increasingly paranoid about Michaels upstaging him in instances exactly like this, as Michaels hit Undertaker with a chair by accident to cost him the title, thus shifting the heat from the feud onto Shawn v. Undertaker. Bret was then left in the cold, fighting the midcard Patriot for the title while Shawn and Undertaker headlined the next two PPVs. Bret's momentum as lead heel was now evaporating at the hands of Michaels, and then McMahon dropped the bomb on him.

In September of 1997, Vince approached Bret and told him that the WWF's financial situation was now worse than when Bret had signed the contract, and he would need to defer some of the money promised him. Bret was wary but trusted McMahon. By October, McMahon's story had now changed and he wanted to nearly halve Bret's pay and reimburse him later. Bret refused for obvious reasons, and then a few days later, McMahon simply told him outright that the WWF could no longer afford the contract and would be intentionally breaching it. Bret was encouraged to go visit Eric Bischoff and make whatever deal he wanted, with the blessing of the WWF.

In essence, Vince had gotten an extra year out of Bret at a reduced rate, and now he wanted to rid himself of him and use Shawn Michaels as the #1 heel. Shawn had defeated Bret's brother-in-law and partner Davey Boy Smith in England one month prior to win the European title, puzzling many people. The title was generally considered to have been created solely as a trophy of sorts for Smith, and to actually change the title, and in Smith's home country no less, seemed to have no explanation short of removing the Hart family from the WWF scene.

The plan was now clearly for Shawn to get the title from Bret (they were scheduled to meet at *Survivor Series '97*), but with an increasingly arrogant Michaels now publicly stating that he wouldn't job to anyone else in the promotion, Bret's paranoia was seeming more real by the day. The show was in Montreal, Quebec, Canada.

The legal hassles began immediately. Bret's contract had a "creative control"

that would weaken his position even further before jobbing him to Steve Austin (which was going to happen to whoever was champion by *Wrestlemania*, short of Pope John Paul

II himself becoming a wrestler and winning the title, so no big deal there). Bret tearfully bid the WWF good-bye and accepted the WCW offer, for about $3 million per year.

And that was that.

clause in it that essentially gave him reasonable control over his character for 30 days before his termination, should he leave the promotion. That meant that the WWF couldn't just tell him to lose to anyone, he had to agree to it. And the last person on earth he would lose to at that point was Shawn Michaels. Vince attempted a compromise: Lose to Michaels in Montreal, regain it a month later, leave the WWF as champion and give it up on *RAW* before you go. Bret responded by noting that he had no guarantee that Michaels would agree to job the title back to him.

Everyone was brought together in a meeting and Shawn broke down in tears and promised to return the favor to Bret after *Survivor Series*. Bret was skeptical, and that was proven to be a good instinct, because a few days following, Michaels was up to his old tricks again, taking potshots at Bret's family in on-screen interviews despite an agreement between them not to do that.

Bret was now becoming more torn, as Bischoff made him a huge money offer as the deadline for his decision was approaching. Bret called Vince asking for some sort of reassurance for his position in the company to convince him to stay, but Vince presented a scenario for Bret's last three months in the company

Oh, wait, sorry, they still had to get the title off Bret. McMahon was insistent on Bret jobbing to Shawn in Montreal. Bret issued a counteroffer—he would job the title to anyone in the entire company from Vader down to the Brooklyn Brawler anywhere in the United States in the two weeks leading up to the show, and what they did with the title from there was the WWF's business. Vince made a counter-counter-offer: Job to Michaels, in Montreal, or they would sue. Bret made a counter-counter-counter-offer involving kissing his nether regions, and an argument ensued that lasted well over a day. Finally, after hours of yelling and legal threats, they agreed to a DQ finish for the show and Bret would surrender the title on *RAW* the next night.

Well, that's what Bret thought he agreed to. Vince had something entirely different in mind.

And then the news of Bret's departure broke over the Internet and the Canadian media, and the reaction was immediate: Shock and disbelief. WWF Canada tried to lie and cover the situation up, but the truth came out soon enough. A good chunk of the wrestling fanbase now knew that the *Survivor Series* would be

Bret's farewell match. The WWF played up the "last Shawn v. Bret match ever" aspect to get more buys for the show, and by then, the public sniping from both sides was becoming more bitter by the minute.

Vince McMahon made a public statement, the famous "WWF Attitude" speech, where he insisted that the intelligence of the fans not be insulted and that his characters were shades of grey, rather than black-or-white "good guys" and "bad guys." The speech was intended to spin the situation to make it sound like Bret was leaving because of the content and direction of the WWF. Bret Hart went on TSN's *Off the Record* talk show and admitted that he had given his 30-day notice, but didn't say much more. Bret did a house show in Toronto, and another in Detroit, two opportunities for the WWF to get him to drop the WWF title before *Survivor Series*, neither of which was taken. They wanted the title on the line to give the Shawn-Bret feud maximum impact.

If Bret's paranoia had been bad before, he was positively suspicious now. Other wrestlers began giving him ominous warnings about the "old days," back when Lou Thesz used to have to handle himself in real-life fight situations when a situation with a promoter turned ugly. Bret couldn't quite bring himself to admit the possibility, but just to be on the safe side, he went to the referee for the match—Earl Hebner—and asked for his personal word of honor that he would not screw Bret over and double-cross him. Earl made that

promise, going so far as to swear on his kids' lives that he wouldn't double-cross Hart. Bret's fear was that if Vince couldn't convince Bret to lose the title in a worked match, it would turn into a real one and he'd get the title off him that way.

The WWF braintrust and Shawn Michaels had a secret meeting that day, 24 hours before the *Survivor Series*, and all emerged looking unhappy with what had been discussed. Bret was never informed of the meeting. At *Survivor Series*, Bret and Shawn were put in opposite sides of the dressing room with armed guards. Thankfully, they weren't needed, as both acted like professionals in discussing the match. Bret had no idea what the finish would be, thinking only in vague terms of a DQ. Shawn has since sworn up and down that he didn't know what the finish would be, most believe him to be lying. By a weird quirk of fate, the camera crew for the documentary *Wrestling with Shadows* just happened to be backstage filming at the time, so that everything that went down was captured on film for posterity.

Bret and Shawn had a very good match that night, giving the fans a wild brawl for about 13 minutes before moving into the ring for the actual match. Vince McMahon, the usual announcer for the WWF PPVs, was strangely absent from his position that night, a position to which he has never returned since. Shawn made sure to disgrace the Canadian flag to solidify himself as a heel for the Canadian crowd.

As they fought back into the ring, Vince himself made his way to ringside to watch, and many other WWF personnel joined him. Security began moving into position. Had Bret noticed these things, he might have saved himself, but he didn't. As the match neared what Bret thought was the scheduled finish, a disqualification, referee Hebner was bumped and knocked unconscious. Shawn put Bret in his own finisher—the Sharpshooter. Then everything went weird.

At that point, a second referee, Mike Chioda, was supposed to come in and take over, followed by the other Hart Foundation members (Owen and Bulldog in this case), who would cause the DQ loss for Bret.

Instead, Earl Hebner miraculously recovered and jumped back into position. Backstage, Chioda and the Harts immediately panicked, realizing what was about to happen. They were

prevented from going anywhere by security, however.

Bret Hart was in a submission move, his own move, and Earl Hebner was now in position to check for the submission. None came, but Vince McMahon, suddenly moving from his position at ringside, jabbed the timekeeper in the ribs and yelled at him to "Ring the bell, ring the fucking bell" as Earl called for the submission. Bret continued the match for a few seconds, unaware of what had just happened, and reversed the move as planned. But the bell had rung and Shawn's music was playing, and now it sunk in.

He had been double-crossed. Or, to use Bret's words, screwed.

Shawn was hastily given the title belt and herded to the dressing room, and Earl Hebner followed and was put into a taxi bound for the hotel at top speed to escape Bret if need be. Bret, attempting to maintain his dignity, spit on Vince McMahon, drew the "WCW" letters in the air with his finger, and then lost all semblance of temper and smashed several ringside monitors and furniture.

Back in the dressing room, Vince apologized, and Bret punched his lights out with one shot to the face. The general feeling in the locker room was that they wanted to do exactly the same thing, but Vince was out cold so they didn't have to. The WWF locker room came the closest it ever has to completely rebelling against McMahon that night, with many wrestlers vowing not to work *RAW* the next day in Ottawa. In the end, cooler heads prevailed, and only Owen Hart, British Bulldog, and Mankind missed the show in protest.

Mankind was only barely important enough to the company at the time to skip the show and avoid being fired outright. Things looked bleak Monday night and the WWF put on a dreary show that annoyed the already upset Canadian crowd even further. People speculated that this was rock bottom for the WWF, and that WCW would now crush them for good.

Then the ratings came in the next day, and those people's eyes nearly bugged out of their head in surprise. The ratings were up a full point from the week before due to the controversy and intrigue of the *Survivor Series*. Everyone assumed that they would drop again soon enough, but they didn't, because the WWF was putting on a strong product at that point, and all they had needed was a jumpstart to get some extra viewers hooked on it. Shawn Michaels, who had

promised Bret the night before that he had no part in the screwjob, had also guaranteed that he would never in a million years accept the WWF title under those circumstances, and would never in a million years trash Bret after the fact. And on that fateful show, Shawn proceeded to formally accept the WWF title and trash Bret after the fact. Bret Hart was now, as far as the WWF was concerned, dead and buried.

But what of Vince McMahon? Smarter fans had always held a grudge against him for turning wrestling from a pseudo-sport into a huge circus of the absurd, and this just gave them more cannon fodder. The average fan just thought he was an announcer, but with the recent "coming out" Vince did as owner of the WWF for a segment where Steve Austin gave him the Stone Cold Stunner, even the casual fans now knew his real role. And they didn't like him one bit for screwing Bret over. So after 4 years of character rehabilitation following a federal indictment for steroid distribution, Vince McMahon decided to flush Mr. Nice Guy away and go for the biggest money he'd ever shot for.

He did an interview (with his black eye now heavily made up so as to call attention to it) on *RAW* laying out "his side" of the Bret story, which was deliberately scripted to make him sound like a manipulative liar, and gave the world his famous catchphrase for the Montreal incident: "Bret screwed Bret," said Vince. The fans didn't buy it one bit, and began booing him upon even his entrance into the arena. He wouldn't have had it any other way.

Vince McMahon the mild-mannered play-by-play announcer was dead. Mr. McMahon the evil owner was born. Whereas Bret was bound for three years of misuse, injuries, and political problems with the nWo, Vince came out about a billion dollars ahead on the whole deal when his character met up with Steve Austin again in December of 1997 and kicked off the biggest-drawing feud in the history of wrestling.

You have to wonder exactly how much of it was planned that way by Vince.

No one likes being told who to cheer for, least of all the WWF's fanbase, but when that happened in 1996, the backlash changed The Rock's career in ways that no one couldhave predicted.

# THE ROCK

Born Dwayne Johnson, son of WWF star Rocky Johnson and grandson of former WWWF Peter Maivia, it was pretty much inevitable that the Rock would end up as a wrestler if for no reason other than genetics. After a successful run in college football with the Miami Hurricanes, Dwayne moved to Memphis for his first run as a pro wrestler, and his first gimmick certainly didn't bode well: Flex Kavana, a sort of Rick Rude ripoff. But a bad first gimmick didn't stop Hulk Hogan, and the Rock was no exception. He moved to the WWF while still a rookie—and got another bad gimmick.

Hoping to play off WWF fans' memories of Rocky Johnson and Peter Maivia, Dwayne Johnson became Rocky Maivia and dedicated his matches to his family. Trouble was, the WWF's policy was to whitewash the past so

that newer fans wouldn't remember it, and thus his family history meant nothing to the majority of the people he was attempting to win over. After weeks of vignettes, he made his debut at *Survivor Series '96* in MSG, winning the match for his team and getting a decent pop, despite a goofy hairstyle and early '80s babyface personality.

The WWF seasoned him in the undercard for the next few weeks, before suddenly and unexpectedly putting him over Intercontinental champion HHH for the title on live TV, thinking that they had a sure thing. As it turned out, it took a little longer than they thought to cash in on it.

Rocky defeated HHH in a rematch at the *Final Four* PPV in February of '97, but since HHH didn't have any heat to begin with that didn't do much for Rocky. In fact, the more the WWF seemed to push him as a squeaky-

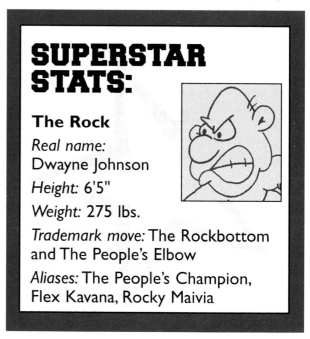

## SUPERSTAR STATS:

**The Rock**

*Real name:* Dwayne Johnson

*Height:* 6'5"

*Weight:* 275 lbs.

*Trademark move:* The Rockbottom and The People's Elbow

*Aliases:* The People's Champion, Flex Kavana, Rocky Maivia

clean babyface, the more the fans resented it, until they started becoming openly hostile toward the young Maivia. Hoping to find a way to benefit, the WWF got Rocky involved in the developing story line between Marc Mero and Sable, as they prepared to split the popular couple and turn Mero heel. The idea was to have Mero eventually accuse Rocky of going after Sable himself, turn heel on him, and win the Intercontinental title at *Wrestlemania 13* to take the pressure off the kid for a while.

But there was one problem: Mero blew his knee out two weeks before the show, so badly in fact that he was out for the rest of the year. Left with no challenger, Rocky instead got to retain his title by beating the Sultan, a jobber with an evil Arabian gimmick. (The Sultan is currently known as Rikishi.) However, the crowd wasn't buying this title defense as a legitimate use of their time, and took it out on Rocky, chanting "Rocky Sucks" loud enough to be heard clearly by those watching on TV. Rocky suffered through another few weeks of "Rocky Sucks" chants at TV shows and house shows, and signs reading "Die, Rocky, Die," until finally the WWF was taking such heat over their choice of Intercontinental champion that they simply jobbed Rocky to Owen Hart on an episode of *RAW*, to get the title off him before his career was damaged permanently.

Rocky put other WWF stars over for the next few weeks while they tried to figure out what to do with him, but fate intervened and he suffered a serious knee injury in a match with Mankind, necessitating surgery and more than three months off. He returned in August and turned on Chainz of the DOA (which also included Skull and 8-Ball); then he joined the Louis Farrakhan parody group known as the Nation of Domination in the process and playing up his black heritage.

The fans picked up right where they left off, chanting "Rocky Sucks" at him with incredible enthusiasm now that it was the acceptable thing to do. Rocky responded by coming up with comic book muscle poses to annoy the fans and a tendency to refer to himself in the third person. This, combined with a new mat-based wrestling style born from necessity (he could no longer do high-flying moves with a bad knee) turned him from a "rookie sensation" into a pain-in-the-ass heel, and that's when the WWF knew they could cash in.

Rocky's bizarre form of popularity grew as the fans hated him more and more with every match and Rocky's character grew more arrogant by the week, insisting on being called the Rock now and slowly taking the spotlight away from the Nation's leader, Faarooq. This was setting up an obvious Rocky-Faarooq feud, but the WWF considered the aging Faarooq to be small potatoes at that point compared to the insane amounts of heat and money Rocky had the potential to draw for them. So the night after *Survivor*

# WRESTLER SPOTLIGHT

## THE ROCK

### BIGGEST CONTRIBUTION
Buckets of money drawn, T-shirts sold, and catchphrases that even the non-wrestling fan could use.

### BEST MATCH
Against HHH at *Judgment Day*, a 60-minute Iron Man match that showed that an old-school style could still be used in the modern wrestling world (****3/4).

### BIGGEST MATCH
Winning the WWF title for the first time at *Survivor Series '98* and capping off the McMahon family story line.

### BIGGEST RIVAL
All the major modern players, such as HHH, Mankind, and "Stone Cold" Steve Austin.

### QUOTE
"If ya SMEELLLLLLLLLL what the Rock is cooking?!"

Austin began playing mindgames with Rocky to the delight of the fans, humiliating him at every turn and generally making him out to be not even a threat to his title. At the *D-Generation X* PPV, when they met for the title, Austin survived the onslaught of the whole Nation and pinned the Rock with little trouble to retain his title. And that was that.

Almost.

The next night on *RAW*, Vince McMahon, who had only recently been revealed as the owner of the WWF, declared that the unconscious ref in the title match meant that Rocky deserved a rematch that night. Austin refused, and chose to simply give the title to Rocky rather than defend against him. In reality, Austin was unwilling to job the title in the ring for fear of damaging his character at a point when he was the hottest of his entire career.

*Series '97*, in front of an already pissed-off Canadian crowd, Rocky stepped up as the next challenger to Steve Austin's Intercontiental title. The crowd responded with a groan, but this feud would prove to turn the WWF's fortunes around for good.

Rocky went on his merry way as the champion again as 1998 began, this time having even less credibility as champion, but enjoying a higher position on the card, deservedly so. He was put into a feud with Ken Shamrock and found new and interesting ways to lose the match but keep the title

each time out. At *Royal Rumble '98*, he lost a clean decision to Shamrock—but planted brass knuckles on him after the fall to gain a reversed decision. At *No Way Out* in February, he lost a clean decision to Shamrock—in a tag match.

At *Wrestlemania XIV*, he lost a clean decision to Shamrock— but Shamrock refused to let go of his anklelock finisher and was DQ'd after the fact. The

WWF changed things up a bit by having Faarooq get kicked out of the Nation after *Wrestlemania* and beat the Rock in a six-man match at *Unforgiven* in April, but Rocky disposed of Faarooq in the long-awaited showdown between them at *Over the Edge* in May. Finally, Shamrock got a clean, one-on-one submission victory at *King of the Ring*—but it was in the tournament, so the title wasn't on the line. In the story line, however, he considered that payback enough, and moved on, as did the Rock.

What the Rock moved on to was a feud with the "new" D-Generation X, which consisted of HHH, X-Pac, and the New Age Outlaws (Bad Ass Billy Gunn and Road Dogg Jesse James). The plan was to match HHH up against the Rock in a feud that would elevate both men. DX had been heels during the Shawn Michaels–HHH era of the team, but skits done by them harassing WCW had turned them babyface. A feud against the most hated guy in the WWF would obviously turn them all the way to the good side of the force, and it did that in spades. HHH was suddenly enjoying more heat than he ever had, as a babyface no less, and a HHH v. Rock 2-of-3 falls match was set for *Fully Loaded '98* in July.

The match ended up as a 30 minute draw to set

up a bigger ladder match at *Summerslam*, and Rock went into full-blown "evil villain" overdrive, including a creepy interview segment a week before the show where he and the Nation cornered HHH's manager Chyna and implied an attempted rape of her. The match itself settled things, however, as HHH beat Rocky to within an inch of his life with the ladder and eventually got help from Chyna to climb to the top and grab the title, ending the Rock's 8-month reign as champ.

However, now something weird was happening. During that match, Rocky was giving as good as he was getting, and the fans noticed it. They already popped for his "People's Elbow" move—*the* most electrifying move in sports entertainment—and at certain points in the match they would actually chant "Rocky," without the "sucks" suffix. The next night on *RAW*, the Rock declared that he was now setting his sights on the WWF title—and the fans approved. The Rock was put in a three-way, #1 contender match with Ken Shamrock and Mankind at *Breakdown*, and was very clearly the fan favorite.

He didn't act like a babyface, but he got a huge reaction in that direction anyway. He won that match, but never got a title shot. The next month, the Nation dumped him from its ranks, and Rock lost to former friend Mark Henry at *Judgment Day* to try to help elevate him up the card along with Rock, a feat that proved impossible even for Rocky. On that same show, a WWF title match between Kane and Undertaker proved inconclusive, setting up a tournament for the title at *Survivor Series '98*—and Rock was entered and was clearly the favorite going in.

Vince McMahon (the evil character, not the actual owner) had other ideas going into the show, however, declaring that since Rocky was the "People's Champion," and Vince hated the people, therefore he hated Rocky. Can't argue with that logic. After losing, and then regaining a week later, his spot in the tournament, Rock was set to begin the biggest night of his career. Rocky went through the Bossman in three seconds, then defeated ex-rival Ken Shamrock for the first time that year, then beat the Undertaker by DQ to set up a tournament final against Mankind, who was Vince's newest surrogate son.

This was actually the culmination of a month-long story line involving the McMahon family. Vince's son, Shane, had been the announcer for *Sunday Night Heat*, but hadn't really played up the family angle to any degree. However, in October of 1998, Vince had finally gone through with his often-promised threat to fire Steve Austin for being a bad employee, bringing Shane into the mix as a result. The next night on *RAW*, Austin stalked Vince and captured him, mentally torturing him for the entire show before bringing him to the ring and firing a fake gun at his head, then shoving a contract into his pocket and leaving.

That contract was revealed to be a new deal for Austin to reinstate him, and it was further revealed that it had been given to him by Shane McMahon. Shane was upset because Vince had spent years running the WWF while ignoring him, and Vince responded by busting him all the way down to referee. The McMahons were quite the happy family. Shane then made his father's life miserable for the next four weeks, costing various members of Vince's stable of heel wrestlers victories (including one that put the Rock back into the tournament at *Survivor Series*).

At *Survivor Series* itself, however, during the Steve Austin–Mankind semi-final match, Shane McMahon ran in to take over as referee—and turned on Austin, revealing himself to be a McMahon to the bone. That put Mankind in the finals, and put Shane back at his father's side.

The Rock and Mankind, having no real preparation time beforehand, improvised most of the match as they went along and did fairly well at it. After exchanging their finishers with neither man getting the win off them, Rocky suddenly shared a glance with the McMahons, then put Mankind in the Sharpshooter, as Vince called for the bell to ring in a tribute to the Montreal incident and one final shot at Bret Hart. The Rock was now the WWF champion, and Vince's corporate stooge, and once again a heel.

To solidify this status, a Rock v. Steve Austin match was set for *RAW* the next night, and it did record

"elite nWo" on *Nitro*) and with the help of Steve Austin, this time he won the title. Rock regained it in a brutal rematch at *Royal Rumble* after handcuffing Mankind and smashing a chair into his head more than 20 times.

Mankind regained it again in the "empty arena" match that aired during the Super Bowl halftime show on USA. They did a "last man standing" match at *St. Valentine's Day Massacre* in February of 1999, which had an inconclusive ending. Finally, they finished their series with a ladder match on *RAW*, which ended with interference from new WWF acquisition Paul Wight (aka the Big Show) as he chokeslammed Mankind off the ladder and allowed Rock to regain the title for a third time.

Rock went on to *Wrestlemania XV* to defend against the unstoppable force of Steve Austin, and lost the title. By now, the fans had developed a new way to interact with the Rock to irritate him, besides the favored "Rocky Sucks" chant: They would wait for him to start an interview, and then finish his sentences for

ratings. Austin won by DQ and moved onto a feud with the Undertaker, while Rock was scheduled to defend against Mankind in a rematch at the PPV named after Rocky himself—*Rock Bottom*. Rock lost that one clean, but a goofy technicality kept Mankind from winning the title. Mankind got another shot at the title on *RAW* in January (up against the formation of the

him. The Rock would get flustered and insist that "it wasn't sing along with the champ night," but pretty soon the fans little game took a strange twist, as they began to enjoy finishing those sentences. Rocky would call someone a "Roody-Poo…" and the fans would finish with "…Candy Ass." At first Rocky would yell at the fans for doing that, but pretty soon he stopped yelling at them and just let them do it. And pretty soon after that, Rocky's interviews were making him the most popular heel around, and when that happened it was time to turn him babyface, for real this time.

Rocky was attacked by his former corporate friends and became the #2 babyface in the company after Austin. He was put back into a feud with HHH, this time closer to the main event and this time featuring HHH as the heel, and they had an inconclusive series of matches before HHH finally won out to earn a title shot at Austin. Rock was spun off into a feud with Billy Gunn that went nowhere, but did give the world a new catchphrase for the Rock. In an interview leading to the match, Rock talked about how Billy had met God a few days prior, but God kept calling him "Bob" instead of Billy. When "Billy" went to correct him, God had noted that *"It doesn't matter what your name is!"* and suddenly every wrestling fan in America was spouting that line.

Rock squashed Billy Gunn at *Summerslam* and moved back into the World title picture. But at the same time, he took an interesting sideroad. Undertaker and Big Show had won the tag titles at *Summerslam '99,* and Rock didn't particularly like either one. They challenged him to a

match for their titles on *RAW,* if Rock could find a partner. The problem was that Rocky had pissed off everyone in the locker room, so there didn't appear to be anyone left who would team with him. It ended up being old enemy Mankind who answered the call, and despite Mick's insistence of stealing Rock's mannerisms in a weird form of hero worship, the makeshift team hit a double People's Elbow on Big Show to win the WWF tag titles.

The Rock wasn't thrilled with his dorky partner, but played along for the most part. He began verbally abusing Mankind on several occasions, as the team lost and regained the tag belts to Undertaker & Big Show. The angle hit new highs (or lows) of surreal as Mankind & Rock improvised a 20-minute segment one week on *RAW* called "This Is Your Life, Rocky," with Mankind attempting to cheer up a dejected Rock by bringing out notable people from his past in a segment that went on and on, and finished without an ending. It drew an 8.4 rating, however, making it the most watched wrestling segment in the history of cable TV.

Mankind was becoming increasingly agitated with Rock's ignoring of his good intentions, and a heel turn seemed on the way, but before it could happen, WWF writer Vince Russo left for WCW, and the entire story line was scrapped completely, with only references to the Rock N Sock Connection made now and then as a way to lighten the moment from that point on.

Back to the main point: Rocky tried several times to unseat new champion HHH on *Smackdown*, but was turned on by the special referee on two occasions: First by Shawn Michaels, then by British Bulldog. He disposed of the Bulldog at *No Mercy* in October to end that little feud quickly enough, and popped back into the World title scene again. He lost out at *Survivor Series* in a three way, as Big Show prevailed over he and HHH to win the title. Steve Austin left the WWF to have major neck surgery done at this point, and now the #1 babyface spot was Rock's for the taking.

Rocky won the *Royal Rumble* in January 2000 to earn the title shot at *Wrestlemania* by throwing Big Show out, but controversy cropped up over whether his own feet had hit the ground before the Show's did. A match was scheduled between them at *No Way Out* to settle the issue, where Shane McMahon returned after a hiatus, turned on the Rock, and gave Big Show the title shot at *Wrestlemania* with a pinfall victory. Rock won a place in the title match back by beating Big Show with the help of Vince McMahon, and the main event was set for *Wrestlemania 2000*: Rock v. HHH v. Big Show v. Mick Foley, each with a McMahon in their corner. Rock had Vince.

Not for long, however, as the match came down to HHH v. Rock. Most people assumed that Rock winning there was a formality due to 15 years of tradition (babyfaces always go over

at *Wrestlemania*), but Vince turned on the Rock (he never said "thank you" for Vince getting him the belt in the first place, see) and HHH became the first heel to walk out of *Wrestlemania* with the title intact. That booking decision went over with the fans like a lead balloon, so at *Backlash* the next month, a HHH v. Rock singles match was signed, and there Rocky finally beat his longtime rival and won the WWF title for a fourth time, with the help of Steve Austin.

Rock lost the title back to HHH at *Judgment Day* in an Iron Man match, then regained it again at *King of the Ring* in a six-man featuring Rock, Kane, and Undertaker v. HHH, Vince, and Shane McMahon, with stipulations that whoever scored the pinfall was the WWF champion. Rock pinned Vince and had the title for a fifth time. He defended successfully against Chris Benoit at *Fully Loaded*, then against HHH & Olympic hero Kurt Angle at *Summerslam*.

Rocky is by the far the biggest star in the business today, and with more years of money drawn will likely earn a spot as one of the biggest stars of all time. Not bad for a guy who started out as Flex Kavana—if you *smell* what the Rock is cooking.

From a neglected midcarder to a Shawn Michaels lackey to the biggest drawing heel ever, no one could have predicted the incredible rise of "The Game," HHH.

Born Paul Levesque, HHH trained in Killer Kowalski's school at a young age, which is also where he met future love interest Joanie Laurer, better known as Chyna. Considered a hot prospect when he made his pro debut in 1992, WCW snapped him up and signed him to a short-term deal to develop him as a wrestler. Their first crack at it wasn't a huge success by any means—Terry Taylor came up with the gimmick of "Terra Ryzin" and stuck him out there doing a wildman gimmick.

That one went over about as well as you'd expect, so later in 1994 they repackaged him as a protégé of Lord Steven Regal and gave him his real name—Paul Levesque—with an extra "Jean" added on the front for an aristocratic air. Jean-Paul Levesque was put into a feud with TV champion Larry Zbyszko, and while it didn't go anywhere, he did learn some valuable lessons on stalling from the master.

Levesque made his PPV debut at *Starrcade '94*, facing fellow wunderkind Alex Wright in a singles match that was given 10 minutes too much and no attention from the announcers or the booking team. Wright won an unexceptional match and another repackaging was in order for Jean-Paul. This time he was going to be booked as a partner of Lord Steven Regal and made into a tag-team wrestler. His developmental deal ran out at that point, and the WWF made him a smaller money offer, but it was strictly as a singles wrestler. Levesque decided to take a chance and go with the WWF's offer.

About that time, as Vince McMahon was escaping the steroid trials of 1994, he was attempting to buy a house in Greenwich, in the richer part of town. However, as a wrestling

## SUPERSTAR STATS:

### HHH

*Real name:* Paul Levesque

*Height:* 6'4"

*Weight:* 246 lbs.

*Trademark move:* The Pedigree

*Aliases:* The Game, Terra Ryzin', Jean-Paul Levesque, Hunter Hearst Helmsley

"unremarkable." He beat Bob Holly in his PPV debut at *Summerslam '95*, and got into the inevitable "blueblood snob gets a taste of down home common sense" feud with pig farmer Henry Godwinn, leading to a showdown in a "hogpen match" at *In Your House V* in December. That particular feud has its own bizarre bit of irony, because Vince (a Greenwich snob) considered rival Ted Turner to be an uneducated hillbilly, only to watch as Turner outsmarted him and outspent him at every turn. HHH won that feud, and moved onto an even more exciting one—against Duke Droese, the scrappy garbageman turned wrestler!

A loss to Droese in the pregame show of *Royal Rumble '96* gave HHH the #1 spot in the *Rumble*, and he actually lasted more than 40 minutes before being ousted. He beat Droese in a rematch at *In Your House VI*, and he had some very important friends he was about to use to his advantage.

promoter, the other members of the neighborhood looked down upon him and (in Vince's eyes) considered him an undesirable. Given Vince's tendencies to use the WWF as his personal venting ground, it should come as no surprise that newcomer Paul Levesque was turned into American blueblood Hunter Hearst Helmsley, complete with stuffy mannerisms, snotty disposition, and formal bowing at every opportunity.

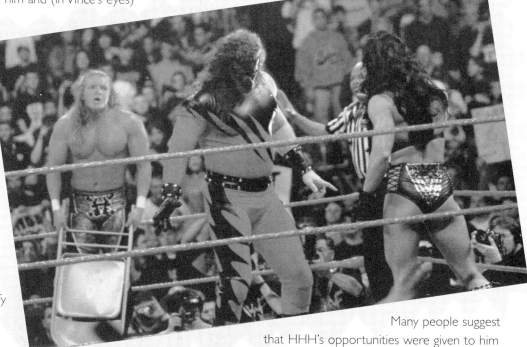

Not quite the same image he has today, is it? That's also why his finisher is called a "Pedigree"—because of the character he used to portray.

Helmsley's initial run could best be described as

Many people suggest that HHH's opportunities were given to him because of his association with the Clique. By 1996, in fact, HHH was the fifth member of that prestigious group and was best friends with Shawn Michaels. Unfortunately for him, that didn't prevent him from being squashed in 30 seconds by the returning Ultimate Warrior at *Wrestlemania XII*, but HHH was promised a fair trade: If he did that job, he would get to win the *King of the Ring* tournament in June. Whether it was because of legitimate interest in pushing HHH on the WWF's part or simply because of his connections isn't really known, and it doesn't matter anyway, because circumstances prevented his big win and royally screwed up his whole year.

Kevin Nash and Scott Hall were of course bound for WCW in the early part of 1996. Before they left,

# WRESTLER SPOTLIGHT

## HHH

### BIGGEST CONTRIBUTION
Yin to the Rock's Yang, HHH elevated himself up to the main event and redefined the heel act for the year 2000.

### BEST MATCH
Against Cactus Jack at *Royal Rumble 2000*, a horrifically intense and bloody brawl (*****).

### BIGGEST MATCH
Beating Vince McMahon at *Armageddon*, the match that changed him from a pretender to a legitimate World champion.

### BIGGEST RIVALS
The Rock and Mankind

### QUOTE
"Because I am that damn good!"

they were doing a series of farewell jobs (to other members of the Clique, of course) to put WWF guys over. In their last date at MSG for the WWF, Kevin Nash put Shawn Michaels over in a cage match, and Scott Hall put HHH over in a regular singles match. 1-2-3 Kid had the night off. At the conclusion of the cage match, HHH and Hall both rushed into the ring—where the Clique engaged in a big group hug and bid farewell to the MSG crowd.

This was a major, major no-no. Heels and faces did not engage in group hugs in the biggest market in the U.S. Someone was gonna pay. But who? Well, Shawn was the WWF champion, so that wasn't gonna happen. Hall and Nash were already in WCW by then, so that wasn't gonna happen. 1-2-3 Kid was practically fired as it was, so no dice there. That left HHH to play scapegoat, as his friends essentially did the wrestling equivalent of dinner at an expensive restaurant and running out to leave him with the check. And pay he did.

First of all, that *King of the Ring* plan? Forget it. Instead, HHH ended up jobbing to 40-year-old Jake Roberts in the first round. Then, he was benched for the next three PPVs and made to job to Roberts on house shows in the interim. He returned to PPV in October and jobbed to Steve Austin in the opening match; then he jobbed at *Survivor Series,* to Marc Mero. Finally, after 6 months of punishment during which all of HHH's heat was completely demolished, they decided to rebuild him, away from the influence of the Clique.

Marc Mero had won the tournament for the Intercontinental title in October, beating Faarooq in the finals. After that match, he dedicated the win to his mentor, Mr. Perfect, who had supposedly helped him in training for the tournament along the way. Mr. P had been a busy bee around this time, truth be told. See, HHH's gimmick during most of 1996 was that he'd have a supermodel sitting at ringside to cheer him on, in hopes of giving him some cheap heat. This was also meant to reinforce his snob image.

But in September, Mr. Perfect started showing up at ringside and escorting the various ladies away from the action, and back to the dressing room. This obviously distracted HHH enough to lose the match,

on more than one occasion. Things seemed to be coming to a head in December, as HHH started openly confronting Perfect about his actions, until a match seemed to be inevitable.

Behind the scenes, Perfect had been collecting a Lloyds of London insurance payout for his back injury since 1994, giving him millions of dollars in the bank. However, by 1996, the insurance company's definition of "career ending injury" apparently didn't include "walking around and interfering in matches." They accused Perfect of defrauding them and cut off payment, forcing him back into the ring to make money again. His first match back was against HHH…but at the beginning of the *RAW* that the match was scheduled for, HHH attacked Perfect, injuring him badly enough to knock him out of action before his return match.

HHH angrily stormed the ring and demanded Perfect come out for his match anyway, knowing full well (as heels do) that he couldn't come out due to the injury caused by HHH. Perfect emerged, but offered a new deal: HHH could fight Perfect's student, Marc Mero. HHH agreed, but only if the Intercontinental title was on the line. Mero looked to have the match won and his title retained, when Perfect suddenly turned on him, siding with HHH. HHH won the title, and in their victory speech, Perfect explained that he was just trying to get HHH's mind off the women and onto the match by stealing them.

This was probably the best angle Perfect had been involved in since 1992, and gave HHH tons of heat again, so of course WCW went and signed Perfect to a deal as a wrestler and left the WWF hanging in the wind.

HHH was boring again, but he was slowly losing

aspects of his snobbish character. The bowing was still there, so was the clothing and the use of "Ode To Joy" as his music, but he at least talked like a normal person now and did standard heelish things. The WWF felt he needed a new manager, however, and a feud with Goldust provided that opportunity. HHH defended his title against Goldust at *Royal Rumble*, debuting his new bodyguard—Mr. Hughes.

HHH lost the title in a hastily booked match with Rocky Maivia on the special *Thursday RAW* in February, then they had their rematch on the *Final Four* PPV. Goldust and his manager Marlena (today known as Terri Runnells) came out to interfere and give Maivia the win, but from out of the crowd popped a mysterious, muscle-bound woman, who proceeded to choke out Marlena before getting hauled away by security. This happened a couple of more times before the woman, Chyna, simply started accompanying HHH to ringside and looking imposing. The fans didn't like her. They booed.

And now, finally, HHH stood for "Hunter Has Heat." Not much, not main eventer heat, but it was there, and it was noticeable. The WWF pounced while they could, restarting HHH from the undercard but scrapping his personality entirely and making him into a generic heel with a badass female bodyguard. Chyna interfered constantly in Hunter's matches, and he got more and more over as a result. He was given his *King of the Ring* title a year late, beating Mankind in the finals (with Chyna's help, of course). He faced Mankind again at the *Canadian Stampede* PPV in July, and it was a wild brawl that ended up going back to the dressing room for a double-countout. Mankind won the rematch at *Summerslam* in a cage, morphing into alter ego Dude Love long enough to drop a big elbow and get the win. Chyna almost ruined the finish by interfering too early at one point, but they covered up for it well enough to make it a non-issue.

Finally, at the MSG *RAW* in September, Mankind made one final transformation for a match against HHH: Cactus Jack. They had a falls-count-anywhere match all over MSG, ending when Jack piledrove HHH through a table and got the pin. Both men were elevated by the awesome match, and now it was time

to take the next step with HHH.

Behind the scenes, Shawn was openly campaigning to be associated on-screen with his best friend HHH, so having nothing else to do with him, they decided to try that idea. One night on *RAW*, a tag match was set up by "Commissioner Slaughter" (the figurehead role played by Sgt. Slaughter) that put Undertaker and Shawn in a tag match together. In this case, it was Undertaker & Mankind v. Shawn & HHH. The heels immediately protested, as HHH felt it was beneath him as a blueblood to team with a degenerate like Michaels. They were forced to team up anyway, and ended up working surprisingly well together.

Well, not surprising when a week later they revealed that they were friends all along and had suckered Undertaker into a tag match with them by fooling everyone. HHH shed his blueblood image entirely with no real explanation, allowing his real-life personality to come through, and D-Generation X was born: Shawn Michaels, HHH, Chyna, and "insurance policy" Rick Rude. Rude was quickly signed away by WCW, and became the first person ever to appear on both *RAW* and *Nitro* on the same night, due to *RAW* being taped a week in advance the night he debuted for WCW.

In November, that whole Montreal thing happened, but HHH had little or nothing to do with it—even though some people would suggest otherwise.

DX's formative weeks were spent harassing Sgt. Slaughter, and a match was signed for the *D-Generation X* PPV between HHH and Slaughter, under "boot camp" rules. HHH won that one to get the rub, and the less said of the actual match the better. Later that month, Shawn was forced to either defend the European title or vacate it, so he laid down in a joke match against HHH, giving his friend the title. Owen Hart attacked HHH immediately after, setting off a feud between them.

Owen challenged HHH for the title at *Wrestemania XIV* and lost (thanks to Chyna, of course), but HHH was now starting to draw serious amounts of heat due to his involvement with DX, and with Shawn Michaels retiring following that show, the WWF decided an experiment was in order.

fans started to cheer. Loudly.

The next night on *RAW*, HHH fired Shawn from DX, claiming that he had "dropped the ball" against Steve Austin, and it was time for a change in leadership. HHH then re-introduced the world to his new partner—X-Pac, formerly the 1-2-3 Kid and Syxx in WCW. Later that night, the New Age Outlaws regained their tag titles from Cactus Jack and Terry Funk and joined the group as well, giving us the DX lineup that became so familiar for years to come.

This version of DX took the "degenerate" portion of the name to new heights (or depths, depending on how you look at it), with swearing, mooning the crowd, and convincing the female members of the crowd to flash them. They filmed skits in New York where they annoyed passers-by and visited strip clubs, and then did a notable skit where they went down to Atlanta to "invade" WCW offices. Then something wholly unexpected happened: The

HHH, for the first time in his career, was a top-level babyface with an over catchphrase (his ring intro consisted of him imitating ring announcer Michael Buffer and telling the fans "Let's get ready to suck it!"), so the WWF moved him up a notch. He was put into a feud with the hottest heel in the WWF, The Rock (after losing his European title to D-Lo Brown to get it off him) and they had a 2-of-3 falls match at *Fully Loaded '98*. It ended in a draw, setting up a ladder match at *Summerslam*. HHH was once again Intercontinental champion, but his good fortune was not to last long.

Many people watching that match commented on what a great job he did of selling his knee injury. That turned out to be because he really did suffer a bad knee injury, and he was forced to undergo surgery and vacate his newly won title without ever having defended it. He was out of action for six months, during which time he bulked up significantly (and not just from vitamin supplements) before returning at

*Royal Rumble '99* and starting a feud with Mr. McMahon's Corporation.

The Rock had won the WWF title for a second time from Mankind at the *Rumble* in an "I Quit" match, so HHH challenged the Rock to his own "I Quit" match for the title the next night on *RAW*. However, as HHH prepared to Pedigree Rock through a table for the win, the Corporation attacked Chyna, and forced him to voluntarily say "I Quit." And then, to add to the humiliation, Chyna suddenly turned on him, revealing that she too had joined McMahon's team. Chyna was now paired up with Kane, and a feud with HHH ensued.

HHH met Kane one-on-one at *Wrestlemania XV*, and there Chyna turned on Kane, rejoining HHH to the delight of the fans. But that delight didn't last long, as both HHH and Chyna interfered against partner X-Pac, costing him the match against Shane McMahon. HHH revealed that he, too, had been bought out by Mr. McMahon. The push was now on to get HHH into the main event by any and all means necessary on the WWF's part.

He was given new tights, new music, and tons of airtime on *RAW*. He beat X-Pac at *Unforgiven* in April, and was put back into a feud with the Rock. That feud saw him debut another signature: His trusty sledgehammer, with which he "broke" Rock's arm. They went to a DQ finish at the *Over the Edge '99* PPV, but their hearts weren't in it due to the death of Owen Hart earlier in the

evening. HHH interfered in Rock's WWF title match at *King of the Ring*, costing him the win against Undertaker, and that set up yet another Rock-HHH match, this one at *Fully Loaded '99*, with the winner getting a title shot at *Summerslam* against Steve Austin. HHH prevailed with the help of Billy Gunn, but still wasn't over enough to justify his insane push to the top.

With *Summerslam* approaching, the WWF decided to tweak his personality a little bit again. This time, he gave a speech on *RAW* where he called himself "The Game" and established himself as a master manipulator. That didn't work, either, but they were getting there. The *Summerslam* main event ended up being HHH v. Steve Austin v. Mick Foley in a three-way dance, won by Foley for his third WWF title. An enraged HHH demanded a shot at Foley the next night on *RAW*, and

HHH went over Steve Austin at *No Mercy* when Rock interfered and cost Austin the match by accident. This set up a three-way match at *Survivor Series '99* for the title between those three, but Austin was put out of the WWF for neck surgery, and Big Show took his place, winning the match by chokeslamming and pinning HHH to take the title. Things looked bad for HHH's career as a main eventer, but then something happened that changed his career for good.

See, way back in the early part of 1999, Mr. McMahon's corporate stooges had been opposed by a group calling themselves the "Union" (an inside joke for smart fans, noting Vince's hatred of unions and refusal to allow wrestlers to unionize), of which rookie Test was a member. Specifically to piss Vince off, Commissioner Shawn Michaels made a series of matches one night on *RAW* where the Union could pick any McMahon cohort they wanted for any match they wanted. Test picked Vince's daughter Stephanie—for a date. An enraged Vince forbade it, but it happened anyway. Sure enough, after what was supposed to be a one-off thing, Test and Stephanie began showing up together on a regular basis. Shane McMahon stepped in and challenged Test to a match at *Summerslam* for "custody" of his sister, but lost, then admitted Test was the better man and gave him his blessing. Test proposed to Stephanie in September, and the wedding was set for October. Stephanie got hit in

with the help of Shane McMahon he finally won his first WWF title there. He still wasn't over, however.

HHH went over the Rock on a few occasions to help build him as champion, then lost that title to a face-turned Vince McMahon on one of the first episodes of *Smackdown*, with help from Steve Austin. Austin refereed the "six-pack" match at *Unforgiven '99*, where HHH regained the title, then a singles match between the two was signed for *No Mercy '99* in October. HHH still couldn't draw the necessary heel heat, and around this time WWF head writer Vince Russo left for WCW, and now the WWF had a plan.

the head by a trash can courtesy of the British Bulldog and lost her memory, delaying the wedding for a bit. In reality, Vince Russo was out of the WWF and they had to rebook the wedding with a new story line.

The wedding finally came about in late November, and they were just about say "I Do"—when HHH came out to object to the marriage—on the grounds that he was already married to Stephanie! It seems that the night before he had bribed a bartender at Steph's bachelorette party to drug her; then HHH took her to a drive-through chapel in Vegas and faked her part of the wedding vows well enough to get an actual marriage certificate out of it. Vince McMahon, vengeful father that he was, wanted a match with HHH to settle things once and for all, and if HHH lost he would agree to annul the marriage.

In the end, Vince had HHH beat—but Stephanie turned on her father, revealing her love for HHH and shocking the crowd. And now, after a year of trying, HHH was truly the Game and the Main Event, finally getting over that last hurdle and becoming the most over heel in the business. Vince and Shane left the WWF to recuperate, leaving HHH and Stephanie in charge of the promotion. HHH played his "evil owner" role to the hilt, screwing over the babyfaces at every opportunity and becoming the biggest heel in the WWF's recent history. The WWF quickly put the title back on him, and set up a match with Cactus Jack at *Royal Rumble 2000*. That one ended up as a classic, so they had a rematch at *No Way Out 2000*, with the "Hell in a Cell" rules in effect. This time, if Jack didn't win, he had to retire. And that's exactly what happened, as he put HHH over huge and bowed out of the business.

There was at the same time another story line developing, as HHH's new wife Stephanie seemingly had a crush on WWF newcomer (and Olympic hero) Kurt Angle. HHH didn't seem thrilled with this and worked to screw Angle over whenever possible, but nothing came of it for the longest time. More on that in a bit.

At *Wrestlemania 2000*, HHH was set to defend the title against the Big Show, who had won the title shot from the Rock at *No Way Out 2000*. Rock won that shot back, making it a three-way. Finally, Linda McMahon added Mick Foley to make it a four-way main event,

with a McMahon in every corner. Vince McMahon was seemingly the pissed-off father-in-law who didn't approve of HHH's marriage to his daughter, and he was in Rock's corner to oppose HHH. However, as the match came down to Rock and HHH, Vince turned on Rocky and gave HHH the win to retain the title, shocking the fans.

Rocky won the title back at *Backlash* with help from Steve Austin, but HHH regained it the next month at *Judgment Day* in a memorable 60-minute Iron Man match. Kurt Angle was now reinserted into the story, slowly but surely hitting on Stephanie at every opportunity and annoying HHH, whose marriage had slowly but surely caused him to grow as a person from a cynical fake husband into an actual loving and mature partner in an equal relationship. For the record, this kind of character depth was completely unknown to wrestling before Vince Russo started writing it in 1997, and it was borrowed heavily from the soap opera formula.

HHH looked to have lost the WWF title to Chris Jericho on an episode of *RAW*, but the decision was later overturned due to a fast count from a biased referee. In June, HHH lost the title for real to the Rock at *King of the Ring 2000* in a six-man match, when partner Vince McMahon was pinned by Rocky. The stipulation dictated that the title was on the line and could be lost by whoever was pinned. HHH finished the issue with Chris Jericho at *Fully Loaded* in July, defeating him in a "Last Man Standing" match to avenge weeks of verbal abuse heaped by Jericho on HHH's wife Stephanie. He was growing increasingly paranoid of Kurt Angle's advances on his wife, however, and the situation finally exploded leading up to *Summerslam* as both men were named #1 contender to the Rock's title and given a title shot in a three-way match.

As of this writing, HHH seems destined to be a top babyface thanks to the Angle feud. As with anything in wrestling, however, that could change at any minute. One thing is for certain: HHH managed to prove everyone wrong, and he did it in style.

# "STONE COLD" STEVE AUSTIN

Steve Austin was left for dead by WCW in 1995 and recycled into the biggest thing ever in wrestling by the WWF: Bigger than Hogan, bigger than the nWo, and certainly bigger than the gimmick originally given to him by the WWF.

Born Steve Anderson in December 1964, he quickly changed his name to his stepfather's name of "Williams" because he had never known his biological father. After a successful football career in high school, he ended up working on a loading dock, barely missing a degree in physical education. A conversation with a wrestler convinced him to enroll in a nearby wrestling school and try his hand there.

While training for his debut, he learned of the existence of "Dr. Death" Steve Williams, so another name was clearly needed to avoid confusion. He went with the more Texas-sounding Steve Austin (ignoring the obvious *Six Million Dollar Man* confusion) and made his pro debut in 1989, getting introduced as a big blond babyface by mentor "Gentleman" Chris Adams in the USWA (the territory formerly known as World

Class). As was the plan all along, Austin quickly turned on his teacher and became a heel, then went one further and stole Adams's ex-wife Jeannie Clark from him. Austin and Jeannie were in fact an item in real life, and she figures into the story later on.

Despite not winning any major titles during that period, it was blindingly obvious that Austin was the hottest thing in the entire promotion, combining solid skills with a "major league" look and physique that drew the attention of WCW after only a year in the business. Austin debuted in WCW on a *Clash of the Champions* special, with valet Lady Blossom (Jeannie Clark) and a new nickname: "Stunning." "Stunning" Steve Austin was such an immense hit that he was given the TV title only two weeks into his run, a title that he proceeded to hold onto for an astounding 10 months. During that period, he joined Paul E. Dangerously's "Dangerous Alliance" and defended his title against nearly every midcarder in the entire promotion.

He lost the TV title to Barry Windham in April of '92, and won it back three weeks later to begin his second reign. Six months later, he lost for the last time, to Ricky Steamboat. As 1992 ended, Austin was without a doubt one of the biggest stars in the entire

## SUPERSTAR STATS:

**Steve Austin**

*Real name:* Steve Williams

*Height:* 6'2"

*Weight:* 241 lbs.

*Trademark move:* Stone Cold Stunner

*Aliases:* Stunning Steve Austin, Stone Cold Steve Austin, The Extreme Superstar, Ringmaster

promotion, but constant management shuffles were wreaking havoc on his ability to get over. The switch from K. Allen Frey to Bill Watts left Austin out in the cold somewhat, because Watts didn't feel Austin was a marketable singles wrestler (he preferred less "pretty boy" type wrestlers, which is ironic considering that Austin today is exactly the opposite of that image), and for lack of something better to do with him, he stuck him in the tag title match at *Halloween Havoc '92* with partner Steve Williams against the champs, Dustin Rhodes and Barry Windham. The match proved to be very good despite the short notice for Austin, so Watts decided to keep him as a tag wrestler and make him Barry Windham's partner when Windham turned on Rhodes.

At *Starrcade '92*, Austin and Windham made their debut, challenging new champions Ricky Steamboat and Shane Douglas for the titles, and losing in a hard-fought match. Windham, however, was promised a push to the NWA World title at that point, once again leaving Austin without a partner. Austin was given the recently turned Brian Pillman as a partner and essentially told to do whatever they wanted to create their own characters, because WCW had bigger and better things to worry about. Pillman and Austin proceeded to create the Hollywood Blonds, a pair of arrogant jerks who so blatantly lied, cheated, and stole every victory (complete with "movie camera" motions to mock the opponents and fake knee injuries at every chance)

that they suddenly became the biggest thing going in WCW. They even had a catchphrase: "Your brush with greatness is over."

This clearly disturbed new WCW head Eric Bischoff, who wanted to take credit for any successes, and the Blonds were buried doing match after match with Steamboat & Douglas on WCW's syndicated shows instead of being showcased on *WCW Saturday Night*, their main one. However, nearly all of those matches were over ****, and after a month or so of that, there didn't seem to be any way to avoid putting the tag titles on them, so WCW did just that. They even gave them a bit of a push, sort of.

Austin and Pillman's defining moment as heels came when they mocked Ric Flair's interview segment, renaming it "A Flair for the Old" and using a statue to portray Arn Anderson. Instantly, the Blonds were the biggest heels in the promotion, but it was to be short-lived because WCW didn't want them getting over. They were put into a program with Arn Anderson & Paul Roma for the tag titles, and it was there that WCW did their first Internet swerve.

You may recall the Disney tapings of 1993, where WCW gave away all the title switches for the three month period in one taping. Well, one of those changes had Anderson and Roma winning the tag titles from the Blonds. And they just happened to have a match coming up at *Beach Blast '93*, so everyone assumed that it would be the title change. And in fact it was supposed to be, but just to swerve the Internet fans, WCW changed it to the Blonds going over instead.

They were only able to

pat themselves on the back for cleverness long enough to find out that Brian Pillman was now injured and they had two weeks to change the titles before shows with the Horsemen as champions started airing. Oops. The elegant solution: Substitute Steven Regal for Pillman on a *Clash of the Champions* show and job the makeshift team to Anderson & Roma. And that was that for the Hollywood Blonds, as Austin was informed that he would be getting a singles push and Pillman would be turning face.

Given the team's unlimited potential and the fact that this had been the most he had ever been over as a heel, Austin was a bit upset at the sudden split. He was also upset at being given comedy manager Col. Robert Parker as his new manager, when he had never needed one before. Austin, less over than as a tag wrestler, was put over U.S. champion Dustin Rhodes at *Starrcade '93*, but didn't seem very inspired to hold that title. To make up for the treatment with the Blonds, WCW bookers

## WRESTLER SPOTLIGHT

# STEVE AUSTIN

**BIGGEST CONTRIBUTION**
It's Stone Cold Steve Austin, what else do you want?

**BEST MATCH**
Against Dude Love at *Over the Edge '98*, a wild and entertaining overbooked brawl (****3/4).

**BIGGEST MATCH**
Defeating Shawn Michaels at *Wrestlemania XIV* to win the WWF World title for the first time, and kicking the Attitude era into overdrive.

**BIGGEST RIVALS**
The Rock and HHH

**QUOTE**
"And that's the bottom line, because Stone Cold said so!"

promised him shots at the World title, and Ric Flair himself was eager to "make" Austin by putting him over as his big challenger for 1994.

1994 came around, and so did Hulk Hogan. Suddenly, Austin was left without a window into the main event, and was demoted into a feud with Ricky Steamboat where he lost the U.S. title. At *Fall Brawl '94*, he was given a rematch, but Steamboat had been forced into retirement by an injury two weeks prior and couldn't compete. Austin was given the title back, but was then made to defend against Hogan crony "Hacksaw" Jim Duggan, who proceeded to beat him in 30 seconds to win the title. Austin lost two rematches by DQ later in the year, and was sent to Japan to avoid listening to him complain about his treatment anymore.

While over there, Austin suffered a serious tricep tear, but failed to tell WCW about it or send proper medical documentation, and they fired him for no-shows early in 1995. Even more humiliating for Austin, he had fallen so far down WCW's ranks by this point that Bischoff's secretary did the deed by leaving a message on his answering machine. Bischoff did a series of interviews running down Austin's contributions to WCW, attitude, and potential stardom, just to completely bury him.

Austin rehabbed his arm injury and went to ECW to rehab it fully, calling himself "Superstar" Steve Austin and mocking WCW at every possible opportunity. While there, he predicted that one day soon he would be the biggest star in the sport thanks to WCW's treatment of him, and soon after the WWF called him.

Always eager for a chance to show up Ted Turner by signing an ex-WCW star, the WWF brought Austin in late 1995 with a new crewcut look and gave him Ted Dibiase as a manager, not knowing how well he could interview. Even worse, he was dubbed "The Ringmaster" and used as Dibiase's "Million Dollar Champion," given the honor of carrying Dibiase's "Million Dollar Belt." That went nowhere so fast that many people were predicting Austin would never escape the undercard in the WWF at this rate.

Rightly feeling that "Ringmaster" was quite possibly the dumbest name ever, Austin asked for a new gimmick, and the WWF, with no ideas for him, told him to think of whatever he wanted. Austin brainstormed some "serial killer" sounding names having to do with ice, and after some less-than-thrilling suggestions from the WWF marketing department, he went home to think it over. While there, his British wife Jeannie commented that a cup of tea was going to get "stone cold" if he didn't drink it, and "Stone Cold" Steve Austin was born that moment.

Even though he had a name change, a

Austin, in a stroke of genius, then cut a promo following that loss where he insinuated that he intentionally lost the match to get rid of Dibiase, making him out to be a cold-hearted jerk. To complete the transition, a new finisher was needed. He had been using Dibiase's "Million Dollar Dream" sleeperhold, but sleepers were passe and didn't fit the character, so instead the WWF gave him a jawbreaker, taken as a variation of a Japanese move called the Ace Crusher, and dubbed it the Stone Cold Stunner. He shaved his head and grew a goatee to complete his new "serial killer" look.

Fate then intervened again. Hunter Hearst Helmsley was set to win *King of the Ring '96*, but due to the "MSG Hugging Incident" with the Clique, he was removed from that position and the WWF took a chance with Steve Austin, not intending it to go anywhere. Austin beat Marc Mero in the semi-finals, splitting his lip open in the process. He rushed to the hospital to get stitched up and returned in time to beat Jake "The Snake" Roberts in the finals with his Stone Cold Stunner.

Then fate intervened yet again. Roberts was in his "born-again Christian" phase (which lasted all of a year) and gave interviews leading up to the show where he

bigger problem still remained: Austin wasn't any more over or higher in the card—he just had a cool name now. He was feuding with Savio Vega, and he beat Vega at *Wrestlemania XII* in a very good match that had no heat. Finally, with Ted Dibiase about to leave for WCW, Austin got his chance. Austin faced Vega in a strap match where Dibiase had to leave the WWF if Austin lost, and indeed both of those things happened.

frequently quoted the Bible. Playing off that, Austin gave a post-match victory interview where he told Roberts: "Talk about your psalms, talk about your John 3:16—but Austin 3:16 says I just whooped your ass!"

Suddenly, Austin was a very cool guy as far as wrestling fans were concerned. He still wasn't over to any great degree, but now he had the name, the look, the finisher, the catchphrase ("Austin 3:16"), and the attitude. And once those were in place, the WWF knew what to do with him. Austin had been associating with best friend Brian Pillman in order to torment the absent Bret Hart (who was in contract negotiations with WWF at the time), but to establish Austin's heartless persona he turned on Pillman and broke his ankle. Then, to combat WCW's total dominance in the Monday Night Wars, the

WWF did a segment where Austin broke into Pillman's house and threatened him with bodily harm, only to be met with a gun-toting Pillman and a gunshot as the lights went out.

The USA Network wasn't terribly thrilled with that one.

Bret Hart made his return to the WWF in October of 1996, and accepted the grandstand challenges Austin had been making for months. The match was hyped heavily and set for *Survivor Series '96*.

It ended up being a 30-minute classic, won by Bret Hart after reversing a sleeper, and should have reestablished Bret as the top babyface. It didn't, however. In fact, the cynical New York crowd booed Bret and cheered the ultra-cool Austin, showing their "Austin 3:16" signs in support. Those signs were starting to show up at legitimate sporting events, too, showing the underground appeal Austin was developing.

Austin drew #5 in the 1997 *Royal Rumble*, and plowed through all the competition until Bret Hart emerged at #21 for the inevitable showdown. The match ended up with Austin getting eliminated, but referee distraction meant that no one saw it. Austin came back to dump Vader, Undertaker, and Bret to win the match and earn a WWF title shot at *Wrestlemania*, much to the delight of the crowd.

Bret used this to launch his whiny heel persona, complaining on *RAW* the following night and "quitting" over the incident. To placate Bret, it was decided that there would be a "Final Four" match at the next PPV (luckily it had already been named *Final Four*, in case of such an emergency) featuring Austin v. Bret v. Vader v. Undertaker, with the winner getting the title shot at *Wrestlemania*. Then Michaels pulled his "losing my smile" act and vacated the title, meaning the winner of the match would be WWF champion.

Austin was booked to win, but injured his knee early in the match and needed medical attention, so he exited early and the match was rebooked on the fly, making Bret the four-time WWF champion when it was over. Austin clearly wasn't going to stand for that, and interfered in Bret's title defense against Sid the next night on *RAW*, costing Bret the title. Had Austin won the title, the same scenario would have occurred in reverse to keep the feud going.

Either way, it was now war. Austin and Bret signed for a submission match at *Wrestlemania 13*, and Bret got a rematch with Sid in a cage match on *RAW* the week before that. Undertaker was to challenge Sid at *Wrestlemania*, so a bizarre situation occurred with Austin and Undertaker both trying to help their *Wrestlemania* opponents win in an effort to get the title shot there. In the end, Undertaker's help proved the most helpful, as he slammed the cage door in Bret's face and gave Sid the win. Bret was to be interviewed by Vince McMahon, but launched into a swearing-filled rant and shoved Vince down on live TV, further turning him heel as Austin's no-BS personality got him over as a face.

At *Wrestlemania*, Bret and Austin engaged in a war of attrition, battling all over the arena for the better part of 30 minutes, as Austin opened a huge cut on his forehead and bled all over the ring, quite literally. Hart locked him in the Sharpshooter for the better part of five minutes, until Austin finally passed out from the pain. Hart continued the assault and left to boos, while Austin left to cheers and the crowd chanting "Austin" all the way back to the dressing room. Bret Hart went to the next level two weeks later on *RAW*, interrupting a match between brothers-in-law Owen Hart & British Bulldog to stop the match and tearfully reunite his family. Jim Neidhart and Brian Pillman soon joined the "family," and the Hart Foundation was reborn.

Steve Austin, of course, was determined to stop that bit of happiness at any cost. He continued attacking Bret relentlessly, including one notable *RAW* where he ambushed Bret in a street fight, injured Bret's knee, and then hijacked the ambulance to continue the assault! They fought nearly every week, non-stop, including a Bret-Austin rematch at the *Revenge of the Taker* PPV in April. In May, Austin got his first shot at WWF champion Undertaker, and Bret cost him the title there. At the end of the month, Austin got a bit of revenge, teaming with Shawn Michaels to win the WWF tag titles from Owen Hart & British Bulldog. Austin and Michaels were not the ideal tag partners, however, and ended up having a match at *King of the Ring '97* to settle their fighting. It went to a double-DQ, settling nothing, but Shawn was suspended for a fight with Bret shortly after and vacated the tag title as a result.

A tournament was set up with the top teams competing for a chance to meet Steve Austin and a partner of his choice in the finals for the titles—Owen Hart & British Bulldog won the tourney, while Mankind spent the entire show wearing a sign saying "Pick Me, Steve" to entice him to do just that. Finally, Austin refused Mankind's advances and went into the final match against the Hart Foundation alone. However, as Austin was getting beat on, Mankind emerged from the dressing room with a new identity—Dude Love. He assisted Austin in winning the match, and Austin gave him half of the tag titles as a reward, although he never really associated with him otherwise.

Meanwhile, Austin accepted a challenge to face the entire Hart Foundation at the *Canadian Stampede* PPV in Calgary, and reluctantly accepted Goldust, Ken Shamrock, and the Legion of Doom as his partners. In that match, the fans' allegiances were dramatically reversed, as the Canadians were treated as heroes and Austin was literally booed out of the building. Intercontinental champion Owen Hart pinned Steve Austin to win that match, setting up a title match between the two of them at *Summerslam '97*.

The finish of the match was supposed to see Owen deliver three piledrivers, only to have Austin hit a Stunner out of nowhere and get the pin. However, on the first piledriver, Austin's neck was accidentally compressed and he suffered a serious neck injury, temporary paralyzing him. Somehow, Austin managed to make it to his feet long enough to roll up Owen for the pin and the title, but he could barely walk back to the dressing room following that. The WWF's plans for the future were rapidly going up in smoke as doctor after doctor told Austin that his career was over, or at the very least on hold for six months. Austin recouped and returned in two.

He made his first appearance on PPV at *Ground Zero* in September, beginning a story line that would allow the WWF to reclaim the ratings lead from WCW. WWF Commissioner Sgt. Slaughter had informed Austin that he would have to vacate his half of the tag titles at that show, and Austin didn't take too well to hearing that. In fact, he delivered a Stunner to announcer Jim Ross to take out his frustration, and the crowd actually cheered the abuse of a beloved personality. The WWF saw money at that moment. Austin delivered Stunners to other prominent figureheads in the WWF in the weeks to come, including Jerry Lawler, Slaughter, and various head office types, until really there was only one target left unmolested by the Rattlesnake: WWF owner Vince McMahon.

Everyone kind of knew that McMahon was the owner and not just some schmuck announcer before that point, but they didn't really say so because that was part of the rules of the game. The WWF pretended Vince was just a guy, and the fans pretended to buy it. But this was simply too sweet an opportunity for character development to pass up, so Vince came out one week on *RAW* and informed Steve Austin that if he wanted to come back from his neck injury, he had to sign a waiver absolving the WWF of any responsibility for his actions. Vince added that the WWF loved him. But that was the last straw for Austin, and he delievered the first (of many) Stone Cold Stunners on Vince McMahon. The crowd ate it up.

Austin was forced to vacate the Intercontinental title for non-defense of it, and Austin interjected himself into the tournament for that title, helping Owen Hart beat Faarooq in the finals. This set up an Owen-Austin

Montreal) told him he would either defend that title against Rocky, or give it to him by forfeit. Austin chose the latter, and beat up McMahon again.

Austin won the 1998 *Royal Rumble*, elminating Maivia to win, and thus earned a shot at the WWF champion at *Wrestlemania XIV*. Vince was becoming noticeably agitated with Austin's actions as of late, and the biggest was yet to come. Vince introduced Mike Tyson to act as special referee for *Wrestlemania XIV*, on an episode of *RAW*, and Austin was there, too. He wasn't about to let Tyson upstage him, and got in his face, thus ruining the big moment for McMahon.

Soon after, McMahon was being interviewed on the situation, and when asked what the problem with

rematch for the title at *Survivor Series '97*, which Austin won despite being at maybe 10% of his total capacity. The neck injury had taken a serious toll on him, and now Austin was forced into completely readjusting his style and becoming a brawler instead of a technical wrestler.

The fact that he pulled it off so well speaks volumes of his natural talents. Austin moved onto a feud with Rocky Maivia, defeating him at *D-Generation X* to retain the title. The next night on *RAW*, however, Vince McMahon (now the evil owner following the events of

Austin was, he admitted that the WWF didn't want him as their champion, and in fact wanted someone more corporate and willing to change how the company wanted them to. Just to piss McMahon off, Austin won the WWF World title from Shawn Michaels at *Wrestlemania*.

The next night on *RAW*, Vince presented Austin with a new title belt to replace the aging one, and let him know that they could do things the easy way or the hard way. The easy way was to become a WWF puppet and conform, and the hard way was left open to interpretation. Austin chose the hard way, delivered a Stunner, and the war was on. The next week, Austin seemed to conform by wearing a suit out for an interview, but soon revealed his deception and tore it off, then hit McMahon with a lowblow to humiliate him. The fans were eating all of this up, but more important, so were the viewers. In fact, that week proved to be the final one in WCW's 82-week winning streak in the ratings, as the stale nWo angle couldn't hope to compete with Everyman Steve Austin assaulting his obnoxious boss on a weekly basis.

The deciding week in the ratings war came one week later, as a fed-up Vince McMahon challenged Austin outright to a match for the WWF title later in the evening. He even tricked Austin into asking for a stipulation where Austin's hands would be tied behind his back. Before they could lock up, however, Dude Love stopped the match and attacked Austin, setting up a title match for *Unforgiven '98*. The ratings damage was done, however, as the WWF won the night and never looked back again.

The *Unforgiven* match ended indecisively, so a rematch for *Over The Edge '98* was signed, but this time with a twist: Vince himself would referee, McMahon stooge Pat Patterson would be ring announcer, and Gerald Brisco, another McMahon stooge, would be timekeeper. To counter, Austin brought out the Undertaker to watch his back. The match was a wild brawl, Austin's best since returning from the neck injury, and it saw Vince get knocked unconscious by an errant chairshot from Dude Love and Austin count the pin with Vince's unconscious hand to win.

Vince next tried his luck sending Kane after Austin, signing a first blood match between the two at *King of the Ring '98*. Undertaker again tried to assist, but this time accidentally smashed a chair over Austin's head and drew blood, giving Kane the WWF title. That lasted all of 24 hours before Austin won the title back in a rematch. The tensions between Austin and Undertaker mounted as a title match for *Summerslam* between them was announced. Leading up to that, a tag match where they challenged Kane & Mankind for the tag titles was set for *Fully Loaded '98* in July, and the unlikely

Austin/Undertaker team won the belts. However, they lost it back to Kane & Mankind two weeks later under dubious circumstances, as Undertaker seemed to lose too easily to a Kane tombstone.

Austin questioned whether the estranged brothers were actually working together with Vince McMahon, but Undertaker denied it. Austin retained the title at *Summerslam*, but now Vince signed a match with Austin against Undertaker and Kane for *Breakdown*. And that proved to be too much, as both challengers simultaneously chokeslammed and pinned him. Neither man was champion, but Vince had the belt off Austin and that was good enough for him. Austin, on the other hand, had other ideas.

Vince celebrated on *RAW* the next night with Kane & Undertaker, only to see Austin drive out on a Zamboni and attack. Kane & Undertaker did nothing to help, so Vince dumped them as associates and set a match between them for *Judgment Day '98* with the title on the line. They responded by breaking Vince's leg, putting him in a wheelchair for the next three months. Vince was consoled by Mankind, but that didn't make him feel much better. Mankind tried again while Vince was in the hospital, attempting to cheer him up with a sock puppet dubbed "Mr. Socko," but any cheer that might have caused was gone when Steve Austin, dressed as a doctor, attacked him in his bed, zapped him with defribulation paddles, and gave him a forced enema.

Vince responded by forcing Austin to ref the title match between Kane & Undertaker, and telling him that he had to make a three count for someone, or be fired. Austin took the news fairly well, dumping a load of cement in Vince's new Corvette with a cement mixer that he had borrowed. That car now sits on display at Titan Towers, for those who might wish to visit.

At *Judgment Day*, Austin of course ignored McMahon's wishes and didn't make a count for anyone, and Vince fired him on the spot. The next night, Austin returned and kidnapped Vince, having receieved a new contract from Vince's son Shane. The kidnapping culminated with Austin firing a fake pistol at Vince in the ring (complete with a "Bang 3:16" sign coming from the barrel), which caused Vince to wet his pants in fear.

Austin took a spot in the *Survivor Series* title tournament, but bowed out in the semi-finals to Mankind when Shane McMahon turned on him and revealed that he had been with his father all along.

Austin got a shot at new champion The Rock the next night on *RAW*, and won by DQ. He was put into a feud with the now-evil Undertaker, however, and a match was set for *Rock Bottom* in December where the winner had to bury the loser in a grave. That one proved to be a huge mess as Austin got the win despite problems with a backhoe and timing. Austin was forced into drawing #1 for the *Royal Rumble*, to prevent him from winning by any means necessary. Vince himself drew #2 to personally be there to keep him from winning. Vince and Austin ended up being the last two men remaining, and the Rock distracted Austin long enough to give Vince the win.

However, the next night on *RAW*, Vince gave up the shot at the title voluntarily, thinking that he could give it to one of his men. Commissioner Shawn Michaels corrected that error, and noted that Steve Austin would get the shot because he was the runner-up. A match for the PPV before *Wrestlemania*, *St. Valentine's Day Massacre*, was set between Austin and

McMahon for ultimate ownership of that title shot, and it was a cage match just for fun. Austin beat McMahon within an inch of his life, and barely escaped the entrance of the Big Show into McMahon's Corporation, as he broke through the ring and tossed Austin out of the cage like a plaything. But that gave Austin the win, and he was bound for *Wrestlemania XV* and a shot at the Rock.

Austin won that match, and the rematch at *Backlash '99*, and now Vince had gone to the babyface side of things once Shane had decided he could no longer get the job done. At *Over the Edge '99*, Vince refereed a title match between Austin and the Undertaker (who was rapidly degenerating into a parody of himself with the "Ministry of Darkness" angle), and Shane's interference forced Vince to count a pin and give Undertaker the WWF title. Undertaker had been threatening Austin with a "Greater Power" who was above even Undertaker himself, and was set to reveal that identity soon after *Over the Edge*.

Unfortunately, in real life the WWF had no idea who to use in the role, despite all the hype for the secret, and after Mick Foley turned them down they were left with no choice but to go with another Vince McMahon heel turn and have him be the evil genius behind everything, despite how little sense that made. To distract from the goofiness of the story line and move things along as quickly as possible, Austin was made CEO of the WWF (in story line, of course) by Vince's wife Linda, and a match at *King of the Ring '99* was made with Austin v. Vince & Shane McMahon in a ladder match for full control of the company.

The McMahons won when the briefcase containing the WWF shares was mysteriously raised out of Austin's reach (the person who did it was never revealed, but Big Bossman is the logical choice) and the McMahons were allowed to grab it. To make up for the job, Austin was given the WWF title the next night on *RAW*, and set a ratings record in the process for his win over Undertaker.

One last Austin-Undertaker match was set for *Fully Loaded '99*, a first blood match where an Austin win

would take Vince McMahon off WWF TV forever, and an Undertaker win would mean no more title shots for Austin, forever. No one expected either stip to last more than a month, but the show did a good buyrate regardless. Backstage, the WWF wanted to use Austin to start elevating some midcarders, but Austin was reluctant to work with some of them. Specifically, Austin didn't want to do a program with Jeff

Jarrett because he felt Jarrett to be unworthy of his rub, a move that drove Jarrett to WCW when his contract expired two months later.

Austin was set to defend the WWF title against HHH at *Summerslam '99*, but the WWF didn't want a heel to go over with Jesse Ventura acting as guest referee. So they put Mankind into the match and put him over Austin clean, then HHH over Mankind the next night on RAW. This led to rumors of Austin not wanting to put HHH over, but those were only rumors. Austin was in desperate need of time off to heal his neck three years after the original injury, so he was slowly written out of the story lines for the time being.

He refereed a special "six-pack" match at *Unforgiven '99* for the WWF title, counting the pin that made HHH the WWF champion for the second time, and then challenged HHH himself at *No Mercy* in October. HHH scored a shocking upset over Austin to retain the title, with the

unintentional help of the Rock, and that set up a three-way match at *Survivor Series* with HHH against Rock and Austin. But Austin received some bad news from his doctors: His neck required surgery, and fast. Even worse, it would put him out for at least a year, if not for good. The WWF's plans for doing Rock v. Austin at *Wrestlemania 2000* were scrapped and Austin went under the knife, after running an angle where Austin was removed from *Survivor Series* thanks to a hit-and-run car accident and a "mystery driver." The surgery was sucessful and Austin spent the next few months recovering from the surgery at home in Texas. After a year's worth of hoopla, Rikishi was revealed as the driver of the automobile.

Austin made a brief return at *Backlash 2000* in April of last year, helping Rock defeat HHH to win the WWF title, and returned again in September 2000 to find out who actually hit him at that *Survivor Series*. The assailant was revealed to be Rikishi, and as of this writing current plans are to work Austin back into the story line for a showdown with the Rock at *Wrestlemania 2001* in Houston, Texas.

Whether or not Austin is fully able to recover from his neck surgery is immaterial—during his run at the top from '97-'99, he sold tens of millions of dollars of merchandise and established himself as the biggest star in the history of pro wrestling, outdrawing Hulk Hogan by quite a lot and setting ratings records in the process. His Everyman persona connected with a new generation of wrestling fans and brought wrestling back into the mainstream, as people weren't ashamed to wear "Austin 3:16" T-shirts in public.

Austin's influence on the business remains untouched, although challenged by the Rock. So, is there still more money to be made from Austin in the future? Oh, hell yeah.

# BILL GOLDBERG

WCW's downfall probably would have happened a year sooner than it did without the enormous jolt provided by Goldberg, the last real phenomenon to sweep wrestling and truly change the promotion around him. Sadly, the magic that created him would prove to threaten too many people and cause not only his own downfall, but that of everyone around him.

Born December 1966, Goldberg had a somewhat successful professional football career with the Atlanta Falcons before a serious knee injury ended his football days for good. Thanks to connections in WCW, Goldberg was recruited by the Power Plant training school and turned into a potential "shootfighting" character, in an attempt for WCW head Eric Bischoff to show the WWF the proper way to promote someone like Ken Shamrock, a real shootfighter turned professional wrestler. However, the initial reaction to Goldberg was quite different: Clad in simple black trunks and boots, and with a shaved head and goatee, many people wrote him off as a "Steve Austin clone" upon seeing him for the first time. He wrestled a few dark matches in late 1997 before making his debut on *Nitro* against Hugh Morrus. The unproven rookie shocked everyone by being booked to beat Morrus cleanly in his first televised match. It was obvious that WCW had huge confidence in Goldberg.

Goldberg was initially booked as a heel, and acted as a flunky for Debra McMichael, which led to a feud with Debra's then-husband Steve. Goldberg struggled to beat him at *Starrcade '97*, but was stuck in the lower card with no signs of escaping. So a makeover was quickly done to the still-fresh Goldberg. He was moved completely down

## SUPERSTAR STATS:

**Bill Goldberg**

*Real name:*
William Scott Goldberg

*Height:* 6'4"

*Weight:* 285 lbs.

*Trademark move:*
Jackhammer and Spear

*Aliases:* Goldberg

to the bottom of the card and given only jobbers to fight, and all mentions of heel/face distinctions were dropped. He was simply what he was and nothing more.

A winning streak was invented (with a fake "loss" retroactively given to him in a "dark match" with Hector Guerrero months before in order to make it sound more real), and a simple formula for his matches was established: Pound on jobber, show off a new move, spear, jackhammer, pinfall. The spear made the whole thing work, because Goldberg absolutely plowed into the poor guy like a train and made it seem more authentic. Goldberg's unique experimental power moves and submission wrestling won the fans over quickly, as his 2-minute squashes of lower-end talent suddenly started building him a fanbase. The short matches also disguised his weaknesses as a wrestler, making him seem all the more invulnerable.

His popularity grew by leaps and bounds, as a security force was added to his entrance, and elaborate pyro was set off as he entered the ring area. He won his first major title in April, ending Raven's U.S. title reign at 24 hours by annhiliating him on *Nitro* to win it. He started feuding with lower-end members of the New World Order, including Konnan and Curt Hennig. Soon his popularity was unmatched, and there only seemed to be one option left for him. In July of 1998, a main event of WCW World champion Hulk Hogan v. U.S. champion Goldberg was promoted, and at the last minute it was made into a title match. WCW was soundly criticized for giving away a potential PPV main event, but the rating was a monster, as Goldberg got an unheard-of clean win over Hogan in front of 40,000 people in the Georgia Dome to win the World title.

Two weeks later, he crushed Curt Hennig at *Bash at the Beach* to retain it for the first time. He was put into a feud with the Giant, and stunned fans by actually jackhammering the 400 pound monster. Goldberg's legend was growing by the second, and backstage Hogan and Kevin Nash were arguing like a bunch of petty high schoolers as to who would be the one to end the winning streak.

Diamond Dallas Page won WarGames at *Fall Brawl '98* to earn a title shot, and he and Goldberg stole the show at *Halloween Havoc '98* as a result, putting on Goldberg's best match of his career as Goldberg retained the title in a hardfought victory. Due to broadcast problems, the match was replayed the next night on *Nitro* and scored an 8.2 rating, making it the highest-rated wrestling match in cable history. However, Kevin Nash was given the head booker position, and he

immediately booked himself to win the *World War III* battle royale and thus earn a shot at Goldberg at *Starrcade '98*. In the story line world, Bam Bam Bigelow debuted and attacked Goldberg in an angle that never really went anywhere. Nash then defeated Goldberg for the title at *Starrcade '98* to end his winning streak at 172 and begin the permanent downfall of WCW.

The win had come with the help of Nash's friend/enemy Scott Hall, and a cattle prod. This led to a ladder match at *Souled Out '99* between the men, which Goldberg won. Hulk Hogan was once again WCW champion at the time, and while he had made the mistake of jobbing to Goldberg once, that wasn't about to happen again. Hogan feuded with Ric Flair while Goldberg was banished to the midcard to "pay his dues." Most outside the business thought Goldberg winning the title again was a mere formality after beating Kevin Nash at *Spring Stampede*, but it never happened.

In fact, by no small coincidence, booker Nash considered himself to be the fans' overwhelming choice for champion, and made it so at the next PPV, defeating Diamond Dallas Page. Goldberg fought Sting to a blasé double-DQ at *Slamboree*, and had a memorable run-in with Bret Hart in Toronto on *Nitro*. Goldberg tried to spear Hart, but he was wearing an iron plate under his jersey and Goldberg was knocked out as a result. That feud never went anywhere, either, because of backstage fear that it might eclipse the "name" players in terms of money drawn. By this point the WWF was handing WCW its butt every week in the ratings with no signs of stopping.

Goldberg suffered a knee injury at the hands of Hart that put him on the shelf while the Nash-booked

WCW continued to self-destruct without Goldberg. Goldberg returned in August to face Rick Steiner in a nothing feud and disposed of him easily, and from there moved into a rehash of the DDP feud from '98, but with a less-inspired DDP and an injured Goldberg. The results weren't pretty.

Vince Russo was given the creative reigns of WCW in October of 1999, and immediately wanted Goldberg to become the top babyface again. He pushed him into a feud with U.S. champion Sid Vicious, and had Goldberg win that title at *Halloween Havoc '99*. Later in that show, World champion Sting threw out an open challenge that was answered by Goldberg, resulting in a quick World title win. However, it was reversed the next night on *Nitro* and a tournament was held for the belt. Goldberg lost in the first round to Bret Hart, thanks to interference from the reunited Outsiders, and somehow lost the U.S. title to Hart in the process.

A rematch with Vicious at *Mayhem* in Toronto served to frustrate him further, as Canadian fans were clearly behind Vicious and booed Goldberg mercilessly. Goldberg won that one and was set to face Hart at *Starrcade '99* for the title, but Russo had other plans there, too. He wanted to recreate the famous Montreal finish, and have Bret "screw" Goldberg out of the title. During that match, however, Goldberg kicked Bret in the head too hard and caused him a serious concussion.

Poetic justice then struck Goldberg, as he was shooting a skit with him chasing down Vince Russo's limousine. He was supposed to smash in the windows with a lead pipe in his fist, but he dropped it after the second window. The third one he did with his own fist, and as a result he nearly severed his own hand on the broken glass, and suffered damage that kept him out of the ring for nearly six months.

While Goldberg is still the biggest star WCW has left, the times have passed him by already and the ratings are no longer there for him, and neither is the fan support. An ill-advised heel turn in June killed his remaining fanbase and now he struggles for main event legitimacy again after years of bookers working against him. Such is life in wrestling. Fortunately for Goldberg,

he still has the intensity and charisma to take things to the next level—if he is ever given the chance.

# GOLDBERG

**BIGGEST CONTRIBUTION**
Kept WCW on life-support in 1998 by providing a fresh face in the main event and someone the fans could rally behind.

**BEST MATCH**
Against DDP at *Halloween Havoc '98*, a hard-fought power match laid out in detail beforehand by Page.

**BIGGEST MATCH**
Defeating Hulk Hogan for the World title on *Nitro* in July of 1998 in front of 40,000 people in his hometown.

**BIGGEST RIVALS**
Rivalries with both Sid Vicious and Scott Steiner are notable.

**QUOTE**
"Who's next?"

# EPILOGUE

S o what's the big appeal behind pro wrestling? The violence? The drama? The soap-opera story lines? Some combination of all of the above?

If promoters knew that, they'd simply do it all the time and draw buckets of money. But they don't, and so wrestling remains a cyclical business, getting hot for short periods of time, cashing in on that success, and then dying off again as the fad wears off and people find something new to spend their money on. Some companies like WCW have only ever had one run at the top, others like the WWF have only ever had one anywhere but the top. Most come and then go again after five years or so.

Wrestling is essentially an acquired taste, and an addictive one at that. Generally, once a casual fan starts watching, he will either decide very quickly that something else is more worthwhile, or be hooked for life. Much like wrestling itself, being a fan is a very all-or-nothing proposition.

The easiest answer to the question "Why do you watch pro wrestling?" is the one people have been using for decades: "Because I like it." Other arguments are just impossible to deal with.

BILL GOLDBERG

# ROPE OPERA!

"Don't you know it's fake?" is a popular burn on wrestling fans. The implication here is that the watcher must be stupid if he doesn't realize what he's watching isn't "real." But hey, sitcoms aren't "real." Generally speaking the people watching it are aware of the fact that the actors are actors and just reading from a script. Unfortunately, wrestling is built on a weird foundation of lies and half-truths, where wrestlers maintain their characters outside of the ring if at all possible and sometimes even start believing their own character. If they can't even draw the line between fact and fiction, how can the fans?

That's why wrestling has always been, and always will be, it's own worst enemy. It desires mainstream respect but when it gets there, it insists on playing the same old game of carny tricks and inside jokes to make sure that no one is let into the inner circle.

It's a complicated business, and many fans come to realize after years of this treatment that there will never be any great payoff at the end—it's always one more sneak attack by the heel leading to one more big match on PPV that doesn't have a finish. But there's always that other promotion, and this one says they would NEVER do something like that as long as you give them your money—

HULK
HOGAN

and the cycle repeats itself again.

That is wrestling. A world of dirty politics and money-grubbing with fake-looking punches and moves that defy the laws of physics executed by heavily muscled freaks with make believe social problems that would get any normal human being locked away in Sing Sing for life. Violence solves everything, talking only prolongs the fight until the next PPV. Men are real men, women are objects of desire, and punches directly to the head don't do serious damage unless augmented by a roll of quarters.

In the end, wrestling is defined only by what makes money. In the '80s, Hulk Hogan vanquishing the evil foreigner made money, so the WWF served up lots of that and made millions. In the '90s, they spent five years trying to figure out what to do next and stopped making money. By the end of the decade, wrestling fans wanted to know what was happening "behind the scenes," so the WWF lifted the magic curtain and gave them a peek, when in fact they were only showing them what they wanted to show them. That's always been the rule: We only know what they want us to know.

Remember, no matter how much you learned from this book, there's always one more layer of the onion to be peeled back, one more bit of inside info that they have and you don't, one more PPV that promises that this time it's the absolute last time this person will face that person, guaranteed. Just give us your money and we'll tell you whatever you want to hear.

We are all marks in the end. And we wouldn't have it any other way.

# A

Aberg, Alex, 11
Acton, Joe, 10
Adonis, Adrian, 48
American Wrestling Association (AWA),
    9, 151-156
Anderson, Gene, 13
Anderson, Ole, 13, 51
Asian mist, 28
Austin, Steve "Stone Cold," 16, 193-205

# B

Baba, Shohei "Giant," 12-13
Backlund, Bob, 6, 9, 11, 13, 42
Barbwire match, 30
Bass, "Outlaw" Ron, 62
*Battle of the Belts III*, 74
Battle Royal, 30
Bauer, Thebaud, 10
Beefcake, Brutus, 50, 61
Billington, Tom "Dynamite Kid," 54
Bischoff, Eric, 158
Blassie, Classy Freddie, 50
blood, 27
Bockwinkel, Nick, 13-14, 40
*Body Slam*, 48
Bollea, Terry, 40
bomb, 20
Bombers, Blond, 59
Booty Man, The, 50
Boy, Davey, 57
Brainbuster, 21
*Braveheart*, 4

Brazil, Bobo, 12
Brisco, Jack, 13
British Bulldogs, the, 49, 54-58
Brown, Orville, 8
Bruti, Brother, 50
Bundy, King Kong, 44
*Bunkhouse Show*, 76
Burns, Martin "Farmer," 10
Butcher, Abdullah the, 12
Butcher, The, 50

# C

# D

# E

# F

 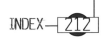

# G

Gagne, Verne, 9, 13, 40

Geigel, Bob, 71

George, Gorgeous, 49

Giant, Andre the, 12-14, 39-40, 45

gimmicks, 18-19

Goldberg, Bill, 206-208

Gorilla Monsoon, 9

Gotch, Frank, 11

Gourdbuster, 21

Graham, "Superstar" Billy, 6, 13

*Great American Bash '88*, 76

*Great American Bash '89*, 80

*Great American Bash '91*, 69, 74

# H

Hackenschmidt, George, 4, 7, 10-11

Hall, Scott, 16, 132-136

*Halloween Havoc '89*, 80

Hansen, Stan, 13

Hardcore match, 30

Hart, "Colonel" Jimmy, 59

Hart, Brett "The Hitman," 54, 137-145

Hart, Bruce, 54

Hart, Owen, 16

Haynes, Billy Jack, 52

HBK, 16

Hebner, Dave, 66

Heenan, Bobby, 14, 40, 44, 65

*Hell Comes to Frogtown*, 49

Hewlett, Elizabeth, 51

HHH, 16, 184-192

Hogan, Hulk, 5, 9, 13-16, 39-46, 49, 98-107

Honky Tonk Man, the, 59-63

Hulkamania, 14

hurricanrana, 24

# I

Inoki, Antonio, 6, 12-13

Iron man match, 30

# J

Jenkins, Tom, 10-11

Johnathan, Don Leo, 12

# K

Kane, 16

Karbo, Wally, 8

kayfabe, 31

Kid, Dynamite, 56, 58

Kid, The, 55

Kido, Osamu, 12

*King of the Ring*, 16

Kiniski, Gene, 71

Koloff, Ivan, 6, 11, 74